Trends in Biogeography

(Eastern Himalaya and North Bengal)

Editors :

Dr. Kishore Kumar Thapa
Assistant Professor, Department of Botany,
Dinhata College, Cooch Behar, W.B.

Dr. Bappa Sarkar
Assistant Professor, Department of Geography,
Dinhata College, Cooch Behar, W.B.

Mr. Manjil Gupta
Assistant Professor, Department of Zoology,
Dinhata College, Cooch Behar, W.B.

RAJESH PUBLICATIONS
NEW DELHI - 110 002

Trends in Biogeography

(Eastern Himalaya and North Bengal)

Published by :
Sanjay Gupta
RAJESH PUBLICATIONS
1, Ansari Road, Darya Ganj
New Delhi - 110002
Ph.: 011-23274550, 43084725
Email : rajeshpublications@gmail.com
Website : www.rajeshpublications.com

First Published in India : 2022

ISBN: 978-93-91139-40-7

Printed in India by :
Aryan Digital press
Delhi-110002

COOCH BEHAR PANCHANAN BARMA UNIVERSITY
Vivekananda Street, Cooch Behar - 736101, West Bengal, India
Ph. : (03582) 229030, Tele-Fax : (03582) 224011
E-mail : vc@cbpbu.ac.in, debkumarmukherjee1@gmail.com
debkumart@yahoo.com, Website : www.cbpbu.ac.in

Dr. Debkumar Mukhopadhyay
Vice-Chancellor

Foreword

To understand Biogeography we need to understand a lot of things - for example evolution, geology, ecology, climatology and so on. Thus a book such as this plays a vital role in depicting the essence of biogeography of the Eastern himalayas. The most striking and important fact about the book is that, it encapsulates the work of authors from relevant disciplines with a unified aim towards understanding the distribution of floral and faunal diversity, agro-diversity, ethonomedicine, wildlife conservation, population dynamics and land use in context to the North Bengal region. A holistic approach towards current trends in research of biogeography has been adopted for the readers to get aquainted with the outstanding biogeographical features of the Eastern Himalayas and adjoining areas.

I extend my good wishes to everyone involved with the publication of the book and earnestly hope that it would be a good read.

(Debkumar Mukhopadhyay)

Preface

The eastern Himalaya and North Bengal is endowed with density and diversity of biodiversity, physiography and ethnicity. It is a part of one of a global "Biodiversity Hotspot". Its physiographic feature extends from hot subtropical plains to the snow clad mountains in Sikkim, where lies mount Kanchenjunga, the third highest mountain peak of the world. The ethnic communities include Austro-Mongoloids to Mongoloids and Indo- Aryans to Dravidians.

There are a good number of texts in books journals with expertise in the respective fields perhaps no such reference is available in a single book to explain bio-geography of the region. Thus this edited volume is an attempt to familiarize the readers the mentioned subject in a single book.

The first article explains on Saxifragaceae and Crrassulaceaae, two important plants families having a good number of representatives in the sub- alpine and alpine areas of Sikkim for needs of their conservation and sustainable medicinal utility.

In the second article Dr. Durga Pradhan and his co-authors have put insights on some vanishing clans of the Lepcha communities in Sikkim. Lepchas are the indigenous tribes of the region with the status of primitive tribal group.

On the theme "rural economy and women empowerment" Dr. Shibu Barman and Dr. B.N. Chakraborty have highlighted on the scope of Mushroom cultivation in North Bengal. They worked out on the economy of its cultivation and role as plant protein supply to supplement nutrition among the common mass.

The review article of Dr. Aninda Mandal and Debarun Chakraborty mentions on the importance of ethnomedicine among the local communities of Cooch Behar and they have specially focused on the skin diseases in relation to use of different medicinal plant families.

In her article Dr. Sanjita Allay reviewed on the role of Asbiculas as a biofertilizer for the three principal crops of the region i.e. tea, mandarin orange and ginger.

Dr. Jyotshna Das opined on the scope and need of preservation of herbal medicinal knowledge among different communities is North Bengal as this local treasure is being erodaded rapidly due to various reasons.

In his article Somnath Kundu reviewed on major eco-friendly local plant based protective North East Indian approach against Mosquitoes.

Dr. Gobinda Chanda Ray has put his candid concerns on protected areas in the North Bengal for its biodiversity and sustainable tourism.

Large cardamom is the most valuable and indigenous spice having potential market value that is being cultivated in Sikkim and Darjeeling-Kalimpong hills but its productions is declining due to various reasons. Dr. Pushpanjali Ray in her article mentions a concise accounts on its botany, cultural practices, economy and has substantiated the matted with SWOT analysis.

The editors, are very much honoured in having the Foreword for the book by Dr. Debkumar Mukhopadhyay, the Honourable Vice Chancellor of Cooch Behar Panchanan Barma University.

The editors would like to express their thankful acknowledgements to all the contributors for the valuable articles and time.

They also would like to thank Rajesh Publications, New Delhi for accepting our request to publish the book.

To the readers, this hand book in with you and the editors eventually wait for your comments and suggestions so that further publications be updated and enriched.

Acknowledgements

We express our heartfelt gratitude to Dr. Debkumar Mukhopadhyay, Honourable Vice Chancellor, Cooch Behar Panchanan Barma University, Cooch Behar for providing us with his prized foreword for this book. We thank him for his constant support.

We extend our thanks to Dr. Abdul Awal, Principal, Dinhata College for his constant encouragement. His motivating demeanor always inspires us.

We also thank all our colleagues at Dinhata College for supporting us directly or indirectly in this endeavour.

We are extremely grateful to all the authors who contributed their valuable research work for this edited volume. Without their contributions, the whole idea of this book would not have materialized in the first place.

Thanks are due for all our family members for always being with us in our thick and thin.

Lastly, this acknowledgement will be incomplete without thanking our publisher Mr. Sanjay Gupta, Rajesh Publications, New Delhi for making our humble attempt a successful one.

Dr. Kishore Kumar Thapa,
Dr. Bappa Sarkar
& Mr. Manjil Gupta

Contents

C. Agrodiversity

D. Environment and Land Use Pattern

Biodiversity

1

Phytogeography of Saxifragaceae and Crassulaceae in the Sub-Alpine and Alpine Sikkim Himalaya

D.K. Pradhan

ABSTRACT

The uniqueness of the sub-alpine and alpine vegetations of Sikkim is known across many explorers and researchers. Several explorers identified and reported new species from the regions mentioning the holotypes from the Sikkim Himalaya.

The representative plant specimens of Saxifragaceae and Crrassulaceaae are recorded species from the Sikkim Himalaya which are unique to the flora of India.

The article attempted to mention the distribution matrix of these representative species in Sikkim covering their nomenclatures as some are endangered and threatened species which need to be conserved. Additionally, these plants are used for the medicinal purposes for treating aliments by the several communities in the hills.

Key Words : Alpine vegetation, Crassulaceae, Endemic, Saxifragaceae, Sikkim Himalaya.

Quality Control Laboratory-HARC
Sikkim State Forest Herbarium (SSFH)
Forest and Environment Department Govt. of Sikkim, Deorali-777102, Gangtok, Sikkim, India.
Email: pradhansikkim@gmail.com

The Sikkim Himalaya bestowed with the rich biodiversity representing many species having ecological significance. These species were studied by the several researchers from time to time. Nonetheless the distribution matrix of the species is important for the understanding of resources of which some of the species are the type specimens. The distribution of the resources across the regions and their availabilities are certainly holding a merit whether the species populations were increasing.

Most of the plants are the representative species of the high altitude where by these are difficult to access accordingly it is focused on the distribution matrix and their protologues for the correct identification. Though all species cannot be covered but it indicates the distribution matrix of the plant species in the sub-alpine and alpine regions of the Sikkim Himalaya.

The given representative specimens are used for the traditional medicine in the hills of Sikkim thus the synonyms and uses included referring to the previous reports. Although there are many species from the different families representing in the sub-alpine and alpine regions but it covers Crassulaceae and Saxifragaceae reflecting medicinal uses of specimens.

The representative specimens of the sub-alpine and alpine vegetation are as under :-

(Abbreviations: A: Altitude; D: Distribution in Sikkim Himalaya; F: Family; Syn: Synonyms ; U: Use; V: Venacular name ; Lep: Lepcha; Nep: Nepali)

1. *Rhodiola bupleuroides* (Wallich ex J. D. Hooker & Thomson) S. H. Fu, Acta Phytotax. Sin., Addit. 1: 124. 1965; F: Crassulaceae; *Syn. Sedum bupleuroides* Wallich ex J. D. Hooker & Thomson; *Rhodiola bhutanica* (Praeger) S. H. Fu; R. *hookeri* S. H. Fu; *Sedum bhutanense* Praeger; S. *bhutanicum* Praeger; S. *cooperi* Praeger (1919), not Clemenceau (1868); S. *gorisii* Raymond-Hamet.; D: Changu, Yumthang, Kussong, V: Baklareep

(Lep); U: Young rhizome's decoction use to control inflammation and abscus, anti-aging (Zhuang et al, 2019).

2. *Rhodiola wallichiana* (Hooker) S. H. Fu, Acta Phytotax. Sin., Addit. 1: 125. 1965; F: Crassulaceae; D: Thangu; V: Sargo reep (Lep.); U: Traditional Medicine.
3. *Rhodiola fastigiata* (J. D. Hooker & Thomson) S. H. Fu, Acta Phytotax. Sin., Addit. 1: 122. 1965; F: Crassulaceae; Syn. *Sedum fastigiatum* J. D. Hooker & Thomson; *Chamaerhodiola fastigiata* (J. D. Hooker & Thomson) Nakai; *S. quadrifidum* Pallas var. *fastigiatum* (J. D. Hooker & Thomson) Fröderström; *Triplostegia pinifolia* H. Léveillé; U: Traditional Medicine (Kapoor et al, 2018).
4. *Rhodiola humilis* (J. D. Hooker & Thomson) S. H. Fu, Acta Phytotax. Sin., Addit. 1: 119. 1965 ; F: Crassulaceae; Syn. *Sedum humile* J. D. Hooker & Thomson; *Chamaerhodiola humilis* (J. D. Hooker & Thomson) Nakai; *Rhodiola karpelesae* (Raymond-Hamet) S. H. Fu; *Sedum barnesianum* Praeger; *S. karpelesae* Raymond-Hamet; S. levii Raymond-Hamet; D:Gochung; U: Traditional Medicine (Kapoor et al, 2018).
5. *Rhodiola himalensis* subsp. *himalensis* FOC 8 : 260; F: Crassulaceae; Syn. *Sedum himalense* D. Don, *Chamaerhodiola himalensis* (D. Don) Nakai; *S. quadrifidum* Pallas var. *himalense* (D. Don) Fröderström; D:Surrounding lake Thangu to Goichand to Sipbla, Kupup U: Traditional Medicine (Kapoor et al, 2018).
6. *Rhodiola coccinea* (Royle) Borissova in Komarov, Fl. URSS. 9: 41. 1939; D:Lasha chu, Dzongri-Tshoka; U: Traditional Medicine (Tao et al 2019).
7. *Rhodiola amabilis* (H.Ohba) H.Ohba ; F: Crassulaceae; D:Chungthang U: Traditional Medicine.
8. *Rhodiola cretinii* (Raymond-Hamet) H. Ohba, J. Jap. Bot. 51: 386. 1976; F: Crassulaceae; D: Thangsing to Gochela U: Traditional Medicine.
9. *Rhodiola atsaensis* (Fröderström) H. Ohba, J. Jap. Bot. 51: 386. 1976; F: Crassulaceae; D: Dzongri-Tsoka; U: anti-fatigue.
10. *Rhodiola chrysanthemifolia* (H. Léveillé) S. H. Fu, Acta

Phytotax. Sin., Addit. 1: 127. 1965 ; F: Crassulaceae; D:Chholhamu- Donkiala; U: Herbal remedy (Tao et al., 2007)

11. *Rhodiola fastigiata* (J. D. Hooker & Thomson) S. H. Fu, Acta Phytotax. Sin., Addit. 1: 122. 1965; F: Crassulaceae; D:Llonak la; A: 16500 ft U: Blood circulation and cough (Liu et al., 2006)
12. *Rhodiola quadrifida* (Pallas) Schrenk in Fischer & C. A. Meyer, Enum. Pl. Nov. 1: 69. 1841; F: Crassulaceae; Syn. *Sedum quadrifidum* Pallas, Reise Russ. Reich. 3: 730. 1776; *Chamaerhodiola quadrifida* (Pallas) Nakai; U: adaptogenic, antifatigue, antidepressant, antioxidant, anti-inflammatory, antinoception, and anticancer activities, and the modulation of immune (Hsiu et al, 2015).
13. *Philadelphus tomentosa* Wall ex G.Don in Gen. Hist. 2: 807 (1832); F: Crassulaceae; D:Lachen (Glacial Valley); U: Traditional Medicine.
14. *Astilbe rivularis* Buchanan-Hamilton ex D. Don, Prodr. Fl. Nepal. 211. 1825 ; F: Saxifragaceae; D: above Lachung U: Herbal medicine (Timalsena and Lamicchhane, 2019).
15. *Saxifraga mucronulata* Royle, Ill. Bot. Himal. Mts. 1: 227. 1835 ; F: Saxifragaceae; Syn. *Saxifraga flagellarioides* Engler; S. *flagellaris* Willdenow ex Sternberg subsp. *megistantha* Handel-Mazzetti; S. *flagellaris var. mucronulata* (Royle) C. B. Clarke; *S. flagellaris subsp mucronulata* (Royle) Engler & Irmscher; *S. spinulosa* Royle (1835); U: Kidney stone (Koul et al 2020).
16. Saxifraga indica (Clarke) Wadhwa in GBIF Secretariat (2019). GBIF Backbone Taxonomy. Checklist dataset; F: Saxifragaceae; D: Gaigong to Riuulet / Thangu, Gurudongma; U: Traditional Medicine.
17. *Saxifraga mucronulata* subsp. *sikkimensis* Royle, ; in H. Hara & Williams, Enum. Flow. Pl. Nep. 2: 153 (1979); F: Saxifragaceae; U: Kidney stone (Koul et al 2020).
18. *Saxifraga andersonii* Engler & Irmscher, Bot. Jahrb. Syst. 48: 609. 1912; F: Saxifragaceae; D: Lohnak Valley; U: Traditional Medicine.

19. *Saxifraga serrula* H. Smith serrula, Bull. Br. Mus. (Nat. Hist.) B. 2: 252, f. 13 f-h, t. 21A (1960). East: Dobremez 253.
20. F: Saxifragaceae; D: Kishong; U: Traditional Medicine.
21. *Saxifraga punctulata* Engler, Bot. Jahrb. Syst. 48: 601. 1912; F: Saxifragaceae; D: Lasha chhu from Thangu; U: Traditional Medicine.
22. *Saxifraga cordigera* J. D. Hooker & Thomson, J. Proc. Linn. Soc., Bot. 2: 68. 1858; F: Saxifragaceae; D: Jalepa, Dzongri; U: Traditional Medicine.
23. *Saxifraga brachypoda* D. Don, Trans. Linn. Soc. London, Bot. 13: 378. 1822 ; F: Saxifragaceae;
Syn. *Hirculus brachypodus* (D. Don) Losinskaja; Saxifraga *glandulosa* Wallich ex Seringe; D: Tamzey; U: Traditional Medicine.
24. *Saxifraga aristulata* J. D. Hooker & Thomson, J. Proc. Linn. Soc., Bot. 2: 68. 1858; F: Saxifragaceae; U: Traditional Medicine.
25. *Saxifraga strigosa* Wallich ex Seringe in de Candolle, Prodr. 4: 41. 1830; F: Saxifragaceae; Syn. *Hirculus strigosus* (Wallich ex Seringe) Losinskaja; *Saxifraga echinophora* H. Léveillé; S. *strigosa* f. ramosa Engler & Irmscher; S. strigosa f. simplex Engler & Irmscher; *S. strigosa* f. subasexualis Engler & Irmscher; D: Lachen & Thangu; U: Traditional Medicine.
26. *Saxifraga moorcroftiana* (Seringe) Wallich ex Sternberg, Revis. Saxifrag. Suppl. 2: 28. 1831; F: Saxifragaceae; Syn. *Saxifraga diversifolia* Wallich ex Seringe var. *moorcroftiana* Seringe; *Hirculus moorcroftianus* (Seringe) Losinskaja; *S. kuana* Zhmylev; *S. lysimachioides* Klotzsch; *S. nyanangensis* J. T. Pan; *S. reflexa* T. C. Ku (1989); D: Donkiala; A: 4000m U: Stomach ache and diarrhea and Traditional Medicine (Kumari et al., 2018).
27. *Saxifraga brunonis* Wallich ex Seringe in de Candolle, Prodr. 4: 45. 1830; F: Saxifragaceae; Syn. *Hirculus brunonianus* Losinskaja; *Saxifraga brunoniana* Sternberg, nom. illeg. (included S. brunonis); *S. brunoniana* var. majuscula Engler & Irmscher; *S. brunoniana* var. *majuscula* subvar. *exunguiculata* Engler & Irmscher; *S.*

brunoniana var *majuscula* subvar. *unguiculata* Engler & Irmscher; D: Gaigong to Gurudongma Lake U: Traditional Medicine.

28. *Saxifraga assamensis* Wadhwa in Bull. Bot. Surv. India 50:205,2009; F: Saxifragaceae; D: Gaigong to Gurudongma Lake; U: Traditional Medicine.
29. *Saxifraga lepida* H. Smith in Döring M (2017). GBIF Type Specimen Names. GBIF Secretariat. Checklist dataset; F: Saxifragaceae; D: Gaigong to Gurudongma Lake; U: Traditional Medicine.
30. *Saxifraga jacquemontiana* Decne. in Jacq.,Voy.Bot. 68,t.78.f.2. 1844; F: Saxifragaceae; D: Sebu la; A: 4960 m; U: Traditional Medicine (Kumari et al., 2018).
31. *Saxifraga lychnitis* J. D. Hooker & Thomson, J. Proc. Linn. Soc., Bot. 2: 68. 1858; F: Saxifragaceae; D: Phim la, Lashar U: Traditional Medicine.
32. *Saxifraga pallida* Wallich ex Seringe in de Candolle, Prodr. 4: 38. 1830 ; F: Saxifragaceae; D: Thangshing, Khola near bridge; U: Traditional Medicine.
33. *Saxifraga melanocentra* Franchet, J. Bot. (Morot). 10: 263. 1896; F: Saxifragaceae; D: Phalung, Lashar, Sebula, Lohnak Valley; U: antiviral (Zuo et al 2005).
34. *Saxifraga saginoides* J. D. Hooker & Thomson, J. Proc. Linn. Soc., Bot. 2: 68. 1858; F: Saxifragaceae; Syn. *Hirculus saginoides* (J. D. Hooker & Thomson) Losinskaja. D: Lasha Chu, Sebu la, Donkiya La, Memsamdung U: Traditional Medicine.
35. *Bergenia purpures* Linn., Sp. Pl. 1:375.1753; F: Saxifragaceae; D: Lasha chu, Sebu la; U: Curing diabetes, cancers, gastrointestinal disorders, cardiovascular and urological disorders (Koul et al 2020).
36. *Bergenia ciliata* (Haw.) Sternb., Rev. Saxif. Suppl. 2:2.1831; F: Saxifragaceae; D: Bakhim U: cancers, gastrointestinal disorders (Koul et al 2020).
37. *Chrysosplenium griffithii* J. D. Hooker & Thomson, J. Proc. Linn. Soc., Bot. 2: 74. 1858; F: Saxifragaceae; D: Memyochu, Kupup; U: Liver disease (Li et al 2018).
38. *Chrysosplenium nudicaule* Bunge in Ledebour, Fl. Altaic. 2:114.1830; F: Saxifragaceae; D: Memyochu, Kupup; U:

Stomach Cancer (Luo et al 2016).

39. *Chrysosplenium serreanum* Handel-Mazzetti, Oesterr. Bot. 2:80: 342: 1931; F: Saxifragaceae; Syn. *Chrysosplenium alternifolium* L; *Chrysosplenium sibiricum* (Seringe) Kharkevich; D: Kisoong U: Skin disease (Gudej and Czapski, 2009).
40. Chrysosplenium nepalense D. Don, Prodr. Fl. Nepal. 210. 1825; F: Saxifragaceae; Syn. *Chrysosplenium guebriantianum* Handel-Mazzetti; *C. nepalense* var. *yunnanense* (Franchet) Franchet; C. *sulcatum* Maximowicz; *C. yunnanense* Franchet; D: Tendong; U: Liver disease (Li et al 2018).
41. *Parnassia chinensis* Franchet, Bull. Soc. Bot. France. 44: 252. 1897; F: Saxifragaceae; D: Lashar U: Traditonal Medicine.
42. *Parnassia cabulica* Planch. ex Clarke in Hook.f., Fl.Brit.Ind. 2:403. 1878; F: Saxifragaceae; F: Saxifragaceae; D: Thangu- Muguthang; U: Novel drug (Singh et al 2020).
43. *Parnassia nubicola* Wallich ex Royle, Ill. Bot. Himal. Mts. 1: 227. 1835; F: Saxifragaceae; 2700-3900 m; U: Snake bite (Upasni et al, 2018).
44. *Parnassia wightiana* Wallich ex Wight & Arnott, Prodr. Fl. Ind. Orient. 35. 1834;F: Saxifragaceae; U : Gastric, anticancer activity (Gao et al , 2015).
45. *P. wightiana* Wallich ex Wight & Arnott, Prodr. Fl. In. Orient. 35. 1834 ;F: Saxifragaceae; Syn. *Parnassia ornata* Wallich ex Arnott; D: Tholung to Kishong U : Herbal treatment (Gao et al, 2015).

CONCLUSION

The sub-alpine and alpine vegetation matrix of Sikkim possess numerous plant specimens however the chapter includes the representative plant specimens having unique sustainable uses in the Sikkim Himalaya. Although there are many species which are endangered and threatened that need to be taken care for the ecological balance.

Likewise, several species are yet to be analysed and scientifically validated for the efficacies nonetheless the ethnic tribes of the regions are using the plant specimens for treating diseases. The methods of the preparation of their ethnomedicines by the alpine inhabitants are yet to validate the usefulness and harmfulness which require subsequent researches.

Nevertheless, the distribution matrix of the representative specimens of the sub-alpine and alpine vegetations of the Sikkim Himalaya is the valuable input mentioning the synonyms whereby the included areas hold the merit as the type specimens of Wallich, King, Hooker's collections belonged to these regions.

REFERENCES

1. Gao, Z.F., Zhou, B.H., Zhao, J.Y., Cao, F.J., Zhou, L., & Geng, H.L. (2015). Further Study on Chemical Constituents of *Parnassia wightiana* Wall: Four New Dihydro-?-agarofuran Sesquiterpene Polyesters. *Int J Mol Sci.*, 16(5): 9119-9133.
2. Gudej, J. & Czapski, P. (2009). Components of the petroleum ether and chloroform extracts of Chrysosplenium alternifolium. *Chemistry of Natural Compounds*. 45, 717-719.
3. Hsiu-M.C., Chen, H.C., Wu, C.S, Wu, P.Y., Wen, K.C. (2015). *Rhodiola plants: Chemistry and biological activity.* Journal of Food and Drug Analysis, 23(3), 359-369.
4. Kapoor, S., Bhardwaj, A., Naryal, A., & Kumar, K. (2018). *Ethnobotanical, phytochemical and pharmacological properties of genus Rhodiola (l.) In india: a high-altitude plant with potential medicinal applications.* Defence Institute of High Altitude Research (DIHAR), Ministry of Defence - Govt. of India.
5. Kumari, P., Samant, S.S., & Puri, S. (2018). *Diversity, distribution, indigenous uses and conservation of medicinal plants in central Himachal Pradesh, North Western Himalaya JMPS*, 6(5), 45-68.
6. Koul B., Kumar, A., Yadav, D., Jin, J.O. (2020). *Bergenia*

Genus: Traditional Uses, Phytochemistry and Pharmacology 25 (5555), 1-19.

7. Li, Q., Li, H.J., Xu, T., Du, H., Gang, C.L.H., Fan, G., & Zhang, Y. (2018). Natural Medicines Used in the Traditional Tibetan Medical System for the Treatment of Liver Diseases. *Front. Pharmacol.*, 30.
8. Liu, H.J., Xu, Y., Liu, Y.J., & Liu, C.Z. (2006). *Plant Regeneration from Leaf Explants of Rhodiola fastigiata In Vitro Cellular & Developmental Biology. Plant,* 42(4).
9. Luo, Y., , Yu, H., Yang, Y., Tian, W., Dong, K., Shan, J., Ma, X. (2016). A flavonoid compound from Chrysosplenium nudicaule inhibits growth and induces apoptosis of the human stomach cancer cell line SGC-7901 *Pharm Biol* 54(7):1133-9.
10. Singh, B., Singh, S., Singh, B., & Nazir, M. (2020). *Plants For Novel Drug Molecules Ethnobotany To Ethnopharmacology*. Bikarma Singh Yash Pal Sharma, New India Pub. Agency, New Delhi.
11. Tao, X., Chen, S., Chen, S., Zhang, D., Zhang, D., Gao, Q., & Ge, X.J. (2007). *ISSR analysis of genetic diversity of the Qinghai-Tibet Plateau endemic Rhodiola chrysanthemifolia (Crassulaceae). Biochemical Systematics and Ecology,* 35. 209-214. 10.1016/j.bse.2006.09.016.
12. Tao, H., Wu, X., Cao, J., & Peng, Y., & Wang, A., Pei, J., Xiao, J., Shengpeng, W., & Wang, Y. (2019). *Rhodiola species: A comprehensive review of traditional use, phytochemistry, pharmacology, toxicity, and clinical study. Medicinal Research Reviews.* 39. 10.1002/med.21564.
13. Timalsena, S., & Lamichhane, P.P. (2019). Astible Rivularis: Bioactive Compounds and Pharmacological Functions Chinese. *Journal of Integrative Medicine Chin J Integr Med,* 25(10), 795-799.
14. Upasani, M.S., Upasani, S.V., GokulBeldar V., Gokul Beldar C., Gujarathi, P.P. (2018). eInfrequent use of

medicinal plants from India in snakebite treatment. *Integrative Medicine Research,* 7(1), 9-26.

15. Zhuang, W., Yue, L., Dang, X., Chen, F., Gong, Y., Lin, X., & Luo, Y. (2019). *Aging Dis. (Rhodiola): Potential Applications in Aging-related Diseases,* 10(1), 134-146.
16. Zuo, G.Y., , Li, Z.Q., Chen, L.R., & Xu, X.J. (2005). In vitro anti-HCV activities of Saxifraga melanocentra and its related polyphenolic compounds *Antivir Chem Chemother,* 16(6), 393-8.

2

Human-Wildlife Conflicts in Buxa Tiger Reserve, West Bengal

Pinku Das[1] & Dr. Nazrul Islam[2]

ABSTRACT

HWC is a common scenario in every protected area. Somewhere no. of incidence is less and somewhere is more. BTR is located in Alipurduar district of West Bengal. It has two divisions East and West. Total area of BTR is 761.01 sq. km. including R.F, P.F, U.S.F, W.L.S and N.P. This article is mainly prepared on the basis of secondary data which collected from Office of the Deputy Field Director BTR East and West Division, Alipurduar, West Bengal and various journals. Main causes of HWC in the study area are scarcity of natural food sources of wild herbivores and availability of nutritious food in agricultural field especially in paddy season. Apart from this grazing, increase in human population growth, increasing no. of wildlife due to conservation strategies, forest land encroachment, natural habitat degradation also matter of concern. Conflict with Elephant, Leopard and Bison are mainly observed in BTR. Human

[1]Research Scholar, Department of Geography, Cooch Behar, Panchanan Barma University, Cooch Behar, West Bengal.
Email: geopinku100@gmail.com
[2]Associate Professor, Department of Geography, Cooch Behar, Panchanan Barma University, Cooch Behar, West Bengal,
Email: islamnazrul975@gmail.com

death because of HWC is more in BTR West than East division and in case of injury it is more in East division than West division. No. of cattle lifted by leopard is more in East than West division. Crop raiding cases is more in East than West division but incidence of hut damage is more in West than East division. Some recommendation to prevent or reduce HWC also incorporated.

Key Words : HWC, BTR, Herbivore, Grazing, Cattle, Crop raiding.

1. Introduction:

Human-Wildlife Conflict (HWC) is defined as "any interaction between humans and wildlife that results in negative impacts on human social, economic or cultural life, on the conservation of wildlife populations, or on the environment." (Human Wildlife Conflict Manual). According to the World Conservation Union, HWC occurs when wildlife's requirements overlap with those of human populations, creating costs to residents and wild animals. Direct contact with wildlife occurs in both urban and rural areas, but it is generally more common inside and around protected areas, where wildlife population density is higher and animals often stray into adjacent cultivated fields or grazing areas (Distefano, 2005).

Man-animal conflict has been in existence for as long as human existence and wild animals and people have shared the same landscapes and resources (Lamarque, 2008). With increasing population and pressure on forest areas, human-wildlife interaction and resultant conflict is also increasing (Zubri & Switzer, 2001).

Encroachment of forests, loss of habitats, habitat degradation and developmental activities like construction of roads and railway lines and increasing number of both human beings and wild animals, especially wild herbivores, are bringing human and wildlife in close proximity resulting in many human-wildlife conflicts in the state (Bhattacharyya and Padhy, 2013).

Although in most of the cases the conflicts and casualties are projected in an animo-centric orientation, emphasizing the deaths and depletions of wildlife, however, in recent years, there have been a huge life and property loss in part of human beings as well (Chakraborty, 2015).

2. Objectives:

Main aim of this study is to assess the status of HWC in BTR and suggest some measures to reduce HWC.

3. Study Area:

BTR is located in Alipurduar District of West Bengal. It shares northern boundary with Bhutan, eastern boundary with Assam, western boundary with Madarihat-Birpara Block and southern boundary with Alipurduar-I and II Block. It lies between 23°30'N to 23°50'N latitudes and 89°25'E to 89°55'E longitudes. Total area of the BTR is 761.01 sq. km. out of which 330.93 sq. km. is R.F, 7.08 sq. km. is P.F, 32.42 sq. km. is U.S.F, 273.48 sq. km. is W.L.S and 117.10 sq. km. is N.P. Temperature varies from 15°C to 39°C and rainfall varies from 3570 mm to 5600 mm. The lowest point is 125 m above M.S.L and the highest point is 1750 m above M.S.L. Most of the rainfall is received during June to September and Pre-monsoon showers occur during May. Weather is sultry almost throughout the year (Annual Report, 2014-15).

Table 1
Different Types of Forest, BTR

Type of Forest		Area in Square Km.		
		BTR East Division	**BTR West Division**	**BTR Circle/ Total**
I.	As per Indian Forest Act' 1927			
1)	Reserve Forest (R.F)	97.44	233.49	330.93
2)	Protected Forest (P.F)	6.96	0.12	7.08
3)	Un-Classed State Forest (U.S.F)	13.32	19.10	32.42
	Total	**117.72**	**252.71**	**370.43**

II. As per Wildlife Protection Act' 1972			
1) Wildlife Sanctuary (W.L.S)	204.20	69.28	273.48
2) National Park (N.P)	72.51	44.59	117.10
Total	**276.71**	**113.87**	**390.58**
Grand Total	**394.43**	**366.58**	**761.01**

Source: Annual Report (2014-15), Directorate of Forests BTR East and West Division, Alipurduar

4. Database and Methodology:

This study is fully based on secondary data and all secondary data are collected from Annual Report (2014-2015),

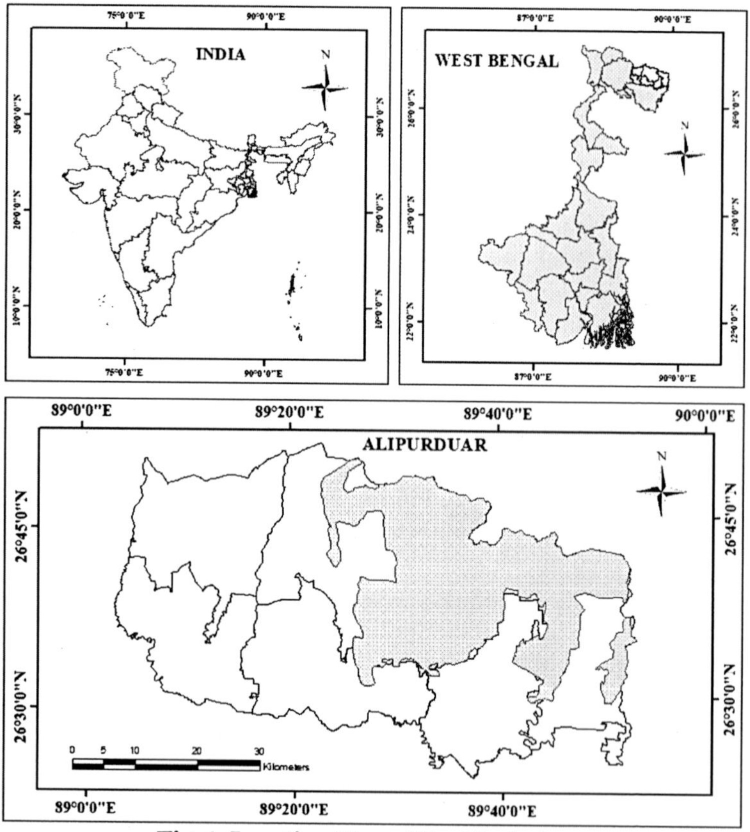

Fig. 1: Location Map of the Study Area

Directorate of Forests BTR East and West Division, Alipurduar; Annual Administrative Report (2016-2017), Department of Forests, Government of West Bengal; Tiger Conservation Plan of BTR andvarious journals, books etc. All collected data are classified and tabulated systematically and then these tabulated data have been analysed and interpreted. Location Map is prepared on the basis of collected data by using Arc GIS.

5. Result and Discussion:

5.1. Background of HWC:

HWC arises from a range of direct and indirect negative interactions between humans and wildlife. These can culminate in potential harm to all involved, and lead to negative human attitudes, with a decrease in human appreciation of wildlife and potentially severe detrimental effects for conservation (De Boer & Baquete, 1998; Nyhus et al., 2000). Conflict generally arises from economic losses to agriculture, including loss of cattle through predation and destruction of crops. Conflict situations can arise anywhere, but they are frequently concentrated at the fringes of reserves where wildlife enjoys protection and land is often fertile, leading to a wealth of agriculture (Nelson et al., 2003). There are other socio-economic costs associated with HWC which can outweigh the direct costs of agricultural damage and be a major component of the conflict as perceived by local people (WWF, 1997).

5.2. Causes of HWC:

HWC is very common in forest villages and forest fringe villages of BTR and main causes of HWC are given below-

i) Increase in human population growth
ii) Forest land encroachment by villagers
iii) Natural habitat degradation and fragmentation
iv) Developmental activities like construction of roads and railways
v) Increase in no. of livestock population

vi) Increase in no. of wildlife population as a result of conservation strategy
vii) Decrease in availability of natural prey and food sources
viii) Forest fire

5.3. Human Casualties due to HWC:

5.3.1. Human-Elephant Conflict:

Elephants are moving together as a team to gather food from forest as well as agricultural field of nearby villages. Due to increase in human population demand of agricultural land also increase which leads to natural habitat fragmentation and fragmented habitat suitable to elephant for crop raiding. Elephants have wide home ranges, typically between 100 and 1000 km^2, a fragmented habitat or obstruction to traditional migration path is bound to bring many human-elephant conflicts resulting in damage to agricultural crops, property, household, injury and mortality to both humans and elephants. Furthermore, on an average, they annually affect crops over an area of 0.8 to 1 million hectares which is turn affect the livelihoods of at least 5,00,000 cultivators (Sukumar and Murali, 2010).

Major elephant movements take place through the tea gardens. Almost 90% tea gardens of Jalpaiguri and Alipurduar are within the zone of conflict (Mukherjee, 2016). Haphazard labour line distribution and their activities for crop cultivation and brewing rice alcohol are the major problems for Man-Elephant Conflict in North Bengal (Das, 2013).

Most of the deaths of elephants have taken place in the Alipurduar Junction-Siliguri Junction railway section. The section is also known as killer track which claims on an average at least five elephants every year. In the past 13 years, 51 elephants have died on railway tracks in this section (The Telegraph, Calcutta (Kolkata), 4th February, 2013).

In January, 2013 three elephants were killed and two injured between Alipurduar Junction and Rajabhatkhawa under the Buxa Tiger Reserve (The Telegraph, Calcutta

(Kolkata), 7th January, 2013).

No. of people killed and injured by elephant in BTR East and West division and compensation paid by forest department during 2014-15 and 2016-17 are given in Table-2 and no. of elephant killed in BTR East and West division during 2014-15 are given in Table-3 & Table-4.

Table 2
Human Being Killed/Injured by Elephant

	2014-15			2016-17		
	BTR East	BTR West	BTR Circle (Total)	BTR East East	BTR West	BTR Circle (Total)
No. of Human Being Killed	4	3	7	6	1	7
Compensation Paid (in Rs.)	200000	300000	500000	1000000	0	1000000
No. of Human Being Injured	12	6	18	11	2	13
Expenditure on Treatment (in Rs.)	Not Paid	50000	50000	125000	0	125000

Source: Annual Report (2014-15 & 2016-17), Directorate of Forests BTR East and West Division, Alipurduar

Table 3
Elephant Killed in BTR East Division during (2014-2015)

Year	Range	Compartment/ Location	No. of Elephant Killed
21.11.2014	South Rydak	SRD-5	1
21.11.2014	South Rydak	SRD-2	1
18.12.2014	South Rydak	MKT-1	1
19.02.2015	Hatipota	SK-2	1
		Total	**4**

Source: Annual Report (2014-15), Directorate of Forests BTR East Division, Alipurduar

Table 4
Elephant Killed in BTR West Division during (2014-2015)

Year	Range	Compartment/ Location	No. of Elephant Killed
01.07.2014	HTG	Rly. Track Point 137/8 to 137/9	1
01.07.2014	HTG	Rly. Track Point 137/8 to 137/9	1
26.08.2014	Pana	Bhatpara T.E	1
07.10.2014	HTG	BHT-5	1
21.12.2014	HTG	Bhutri-2	1
20.02.2015	ERVK	PAN-5	1
20.03.2015	Nimati	NMT-6	1
23.03.2015	EDPO	Checko-6	1
Total			**8**

Source: Annual Report (2014-15), Directorate of Forests BTR West Division, Alipurduar

5.3.2. Human-Leopard Conflict:

Changing trend of land use pattern due to encroachment of forest land leads to human-leopard conflict. Forest land of Northern West Bengal including BTR mainly encroached for tea plantation which is harmful for both human beings and leopards. Tea gardens act as hotspots for conflicts as leopards can prey upon cattle kept by tea garden workers (The Times of India, Kolkata, 17th January, 2013).

A recent analysis of human-leopard conflict scenario in western duars also reveal keeping domestic animals like cattle, goats and dogs among others can attract leopards to human settlement as these are easy prey in comparison to wild herbivores (Bhattacharjee and Parthasarathy, 2013).

On an average 6 leopards and 2 human beings are reported to get killed in conflicts every year in Northern West Bengal (The Times of India, Kolkata, 17th January, 2013).

Moreover, 90% of the cases of human depredation by leopards have been recorded from tea garden and only 10% of the cases are from villages located at the periphery of the forested tracts (Bhattacharjee and Parthasarathy, 2013).

5.3.2.1. Cattle Lifting by Leopards in BTR East and West Division:

Incidence of cattle lifting by leopard frequently happens in both division of BTR but comparatively east division was much more affected in terms of no. of cattle. In BTR east division maximum cattle lifted from Hatipota Range (39) followed by South Rydak Range (38), North Rydak Range (29) and 4 cattle lifted from each range of Bholka, Kumargram, Buxaduar. Out of 118 cattle's 79 were Cow, 36 Goat, 2 Pig and 1 Buffalo. (Table-5)

On the other hand in BTR west division highest no. of cattle lifted from East Rajabhatkhawa Range (25) followed by West Rajabhatkhawa Range (13), Pana and West Damanpur Range (12), Hamiltonganj Range (10), Nimati Range (6) and East Damanpur Range (2). Out of 80 cattle's 66 were Cow, 13 Goat and 1 Buffalo. (Table-6)

Table 5
Cattle Lifting by Leopards in BTR East Division (2004-2012)

S.No.	Year	Range	Compartment/ Location	No.	Species
1	2004	North Rydak	BHT-1, NR-3	2	Cow
2		North Rydak	Rahimabad USF	4	Cow
3		North Rydak	Turturi Khand	1	Buffalo Calf
4		North Rydak	CR-4	1	Cow Calf
5	2005	North Rydak	Rahimabad T.G	2	Cow
6		North Rydak	NR-2	2	Cow
7		North Rydak	KT P.F	1	Pig
8		North Rydak	KT P.F	1	Cow Calf
9		North Rydak	NR-2	1	Cow Calf
10		Hatipota	Rahimabad T.G	2	Goat

11	2006	North Rydak	NR-1	1	Cow
12		North Rydak	NR-3	1	Cow
13		North Rydak	BHT-1	2	Cow
14		North Rydak	Kartik T.G	1	Cow
15		Hatipota	Rahimabad T.G	1	Cow
16		Hatipota	Nurpur	1	Cow
17	2007	South Rydak	Forest Village	35	Cow & Goat
18		North Rydak	Forest Village	9	Cow
19		Bholka	Revenue Village	1	Cow
20		Hatipota	-	24	Cow & Goat
21	2008	Bholka	Forest Village	2	Cow
22		Buxaduar	STB-4	2	Cow
23		Buxaduar	NRVK-1	1	Pig
24		Buxaduar	STB-3	1	Goat
25	2009	Hatipota	PHK-3	1	Goat
26		Bholka	NBH-4	1	Cow
27		Hatipota	PHK-3	1	Cow
28		Kumargram	KG-1	1	Cow
29	2010	Hatipota	USF-1	1	Cow
30		Hatipota	JNT-2b	1	Goat
31		Kumargram	SK-1	1	Cow
32		Hatipota	JNT-2b	1	Goat
33		Hatipota	JNT-6b	1	Cow
34		Hatipota	JNT-2b	1	Goat
35		Kumargram	SK-2	1	Cow
36	2011	Kumargram	NLS-2	1	Cow
37	2012	South Rydak	DH-1	1	Goat
38		Hatipota	JH-1	1	Cow
39		Hatipota	HP-2a	1	Goat
40		South Rydak	Uttar Rampur	1	Cow
41		South Rydak	SRD-2	1	Cow
42		Hatipota	Rahimabad T.G	1	Cow
43		Hatipota	HP-2b	1	Cow

Source: Tiger Conservation Plan of BTR, Alipurduar

Table 6
Cattle Lifting by Leopards in BTR West Division (2005-2012)

S.No.	Year	Range	Compartment/ Location	No.	Species
1	2005	ERVK	Panbari	2	Cow
2	2006	ERVK	Panbari	5	Cow
3		ERVK	-	2	Cow
4		Pana	-	2	Cow
5		WRVK	-	3	Cow
6	2007	WRVK	-	2	Cow
7		WDPO	-	2	Goat
8		HTG	-	2	Cow
9		ERVK	-	6	Cow
10		Pana	-	1	Cow
11	2008	ERVK	Panbari	4	Goat
12		ERVK	Checko	3	Cow
13		WRVK	Dima	2	Cow
14		WDPO	East Garam	1	Cow
15		Pana	Raimatang	3	Cow
16		Nimati	Nimati	1	Cow
17	2009	Pana	RTG-4	1	Cow
18		Nimati	NMT-4	1	Cow
19		WRVK	SRVK-5	1	Cow
20		WDPO	DPO-7	1	Goat
21		WRVK	24th Mile	1	Buffalo
22		ERVK	Panbari	1	Goat
23		ERVK	Panbari	1	Cow
24		Nimati	NMT-3	1	Cow
25		WRVK	Dima-3	1	Cow
26		WRVK	Dima-3	1	Cow
27		Pana	Bhutri	1	Cow
28		WRVK	SRVK-9	1	Cow
29		HTG	RTG-4	1	Cow
30	2010	Nimati	NMT-3	1	Cow
31		Pana	Pana-1	1	Cow
32		Pana	RTG-10	1	Cow
33		ERVK	Gadadhar-3	1	Cow

34		Pana	Pana-1	1	Cow
35		Nimati	NMT-2	1	Cow
36		Nimati	NMT-1,2	1	Cow
37		HTG	BHT-1	1	Cow
38		HTG	BNB-4	1	Cow
39		WRVK	SRVK-16	1	Cow
40	2011	WDPO	Poro-3	1	Cow
41		HTG	RMT-2	1	Goat
42		EDPO	Checko	1	Cow
43		Pana	RTG-9	1	Cow
44		EDPO	Checko	1	Cow
45		WDPO	-	1	Cow
46		HTG	BNB-3,4	1	Cow
47	2012	HTG	RMT-2	1	Cow
48		WDPO	Poro-7	1	Goat
49		WDPO	Poro-7	2	Goat
50		WDPO	Poro-7	1	Goat
51		HTG	RMT-1	1	Cow
52		HTG	RMT-2	1	Goat
53		WDPO	Poro-10	1	Cow
54		WDPO	Poro-10	1	Cow

Source: Tiger Conservation Plan of BTR, Alipurduar

5.3.2.2. Leopards Killed in BTR East and West Division:

In BTR east division four leopards were killed out of which one from South Rydak Range, one from Bholka Range and two from Hatipota Range. (Table-7)

In case of BTR west division six leopards were killed out of which each one from Hamiltonganj and Pana Range and two from Nimati and West Damanpur Range. (Table-8)

Table 7
Leopards Killed in BTR East Division during (2014-15)

Date	Range	Compartment/ Location	No. of Leopard Killed
22.04.2014	South Rydak	Sec. 11, Rydak T.G	1

25.11.2014	Hatipota	Sec. 26 of Chuniajhora T.E	1
18.12.2014	Bholka	SB-3a Comptt. of Ghoramara Beat	1
12.01.2015	Hatipota	Sec. 28 of Chuniajhora T.E	1
		Total	**4**

Source: Annual Report (2014-15), Directorate of Forests BTR East Division, Alipurduar

Table 8
Leopards Killed in BTR West Division during (2014-15)

Date	Range	Compartment/ Location	No. of Leopard Killed
18.04.2014	Nimati	Bhatkhawa T.E	1
21.04.2014	HTG	Chuapara T.G	1
18.11.2014	WDPO	NH 31C, Culvert No. 211/2	1
17.12.2014	WDPO	West Garam Beat	1
22.12.2014	Pana	RTG-9	1
23.01.2015	Nimati	Nimatijhora T.E	1
		Total	**6**

Source: Annual Report (2014-15), Directorate of Forests BTR West Division, Alipurduar

5.3.3. Human-Bison Conflict:

In BTR no. of Indian Bison was 782 in 2013-14 (SFR, 2013-14). No. of Bison was around 2000 in the year 2010 which increase to around 4000 in 2012 in all the protected areas of Northern West Bengal (The Telegraph, Calcutta (Kolkata), 9th January, 2013). So in the protected areas of Northern West Bengal including BTR, Gorumara National Park and Chapramari Wildlife Sanctuary there has been a firm increase in Indian Bison population where Tiger not present in Gorumara National Park and Chapramari Wildlife Sanctuary and the no. of Tiger decrease day by day in BTR which is the main predator of Bison. This situation create food chain imbalance and leads to Human-Bison conflict in forest as well as fringe area.

The fodder available in forest is not sufficient to sustain the increased no. of Bison hence forcing them to forage in to the human habitat increasing the chances of Human-Bison conflict (Nelson et al., 2003). The fallouts between villagers and Bison have led to damages on both sides (The Times of India, Kolkata, 7th February, 2013).

Total five Bison was killed in BTR west division during 2014-15. Out of which one was from Pana Range, two from West Rajabhatkhawa and East Damanpur Range. Table-9

Table 9
Bison Killed in BTR West Division during (2014-15)

Date	Range	Compartment/ Location	No. of Bison Killed
02.08.2014	WRVK	SRVK-3	1
17.08.2014	Pana	RTG-3	1
10.10.2014	WRVK	Dima-2	1
16.11.2014	EDPO	DPO-8	1
06.03.2015	EDPO	DPO-7	1
	Total		**5**

Source: Annual Report (2014-15), Directorate of Forests BTR West Division, Alipurduar

5.4. Human Death and Injury due to HWC:

HWC not only kill or injured wildlife but also leads to human death and injury. Table-10. shows the no. of person killed and injured during 2005-2012 in BTR East and West division due to conflict with Elephant, Leopard and Bison.

Table 10
Human Death and Injury by Wildlife in BTR (2005-2012)

Year	BTR East		BTR West		Total	
	Person Killed	Person Injured	Person Killed	Person Injured	Person Killed	Person Injured
2005	4	10	13	8	17	18
2006	4	6	5	4	9	10

2007	2	7	5	9	7	16
2008	4	15	8	10	12	25
2009	6	0	4	8	10	8
2010	3	8	32	5	35	13
2011	4	16	3	17	7	33
2012	6	23	10	11	16	34

Source: Tiger Conservation Plan of BTR, Alipurduar

5.5. Economic Loss due to HWC:

HWC not only cause human life loss and injuries but it also the reason behind huge economic loss every year. Because of wildlife depredation Central and State Govt. has to pay huge amount of money as compensation to the affected family.

During 2005-12 in BTR east division highest no. of crop raiding cases was recorded in 2012 (2125) and highest amount of compensation also paid in the same year (Rs. 1074710). Lowest no. of crop raiding cases was recorded in the year 2010 (769) and lowest amount of compensation paid in the year 2009 (Rs. 71520). On the other hand highest no. of hut damage was recorded in the year 2007 (490) and lowest in 2009 (90). Compensation paid for hut damage was highest in the year 2012 (Rs. 707270) and lowest in 2006 (Rs. 51350). Table-11

In BTR west division during 2005-12 no. of crop raiding cases was highest in the year 2012 (1617) and lowest in 2011 (521). Compensation paid for crop damage was highest in the year 2012 (Rs. 1109750) and lowest in 2005 (Rs. 270000). In case of hut damage no. was highest in the year 2012 (699) and lowest in 2006 (82). Maximum amount of compensation for hut damage was paid in the year 2012 (Rs. 962750) and minimum amount was paid in 2006 (Rs. 80400). Table-11

Table 11

Crop and Human Properties Damage by Wildlife in BTR (2005-2012)

Year	BTR East				BTR West			
	Crop Damage		Hut Damage		Crop Damage		Hut Damage	
	No. of Cases	Compensation Paid (Rs.)	No. of Cases	Compensation Paid (Rs.)	No. of Cases	Compensation Paid (Rs.)	No. of Cases	Compensation Paid (Rs.)
2005	967	363173	93	54600	675	270000	86	97200
2006	897	390500	102	51350	708	318600	82	80400
2007	1283	389200	490	157400	723	289200	102	110800
2008	849	418400	107	52000	958	475350	108	122000
2009	1448	71520	90	106400	800	395750	140	147850
2010	769	425700	148	240500	1303	775200	167	221000
2011	805	329300	113	186500	521	303500	219	308999
2012	2125	1074710	421	707270	1617	1109750	699	962750

Source: Tiger Conservation Plan of BTR, Alipurduar

5.6. Strategies to Minimize HWC in the Study Area:

i) Electric fencing is not available in most of the forest villages of BTR. Electric fencing must be installed and maintain properly to reduce HWC.

ii) Increase fodder grass plantation inside the forest to fulfill demand of food of wild herbivores.

iii) Grazing must be stop inside the forest because itcreate scarcity of food for wild herbivores and also increase incidence of cattle lifting.

iv) Night patrolling by forest guard within the periphery of villages should be done.

v) In forest fringe area solar panel light should be installed to watch movement of wildlife into the villages as well as agricultural field.

vi) Domestic cattle must be kept inside the cage during night as most of the cattle lifting case happen in night.

vii) Watch tower should be built in the boundary of agricultural field to follow wildlife movement.

6. CONCLUSION

It is not possible to fully stop HWC but if forest villagers and forest department will take precautionary measures that should reduce the no. of incidence. Sustainable utilization of forest resource is necessary which maintain the flow of natural food source to wildlife. Some awareness campaign should be arranged by forest department to aware villagers about HWC. In this article causes of HWC in BTR, human casualties due to HWC, conflict between Human and Elephant, Human and Leopard, Human and Bison analysed. Data about cattle lifting by Leopard, no. of Leopard, Elephant, Bison killed also presented. Not only that human death and injury done by various wildlife, economic loss due to wildlife depredation and strategy to minimize HWC also discussed.

REFERENCES

1. Bhattacharyya, M.K. and Padhy, P.K. (2013). Forest and Wildlife Scenarios of Northern West Bengal, India: A Review, International Research Journal of Biological Sciences, 2(7): 70-79.
2. Bhattacharjee, A. and Parthasarathy, N. (2013). Coexisting with Large Carnivores: A Case Study from Western Duars, India, Hum. Dimens. Wildl., 18(1): 20-31.
3. Chakraborty, S. (2015). Human-Animal Conflicts in Northern West Bengal: Losses on both sides, International Journal of Pure and Applied Bioscience, 3(3): 35-44.
4. De Boer, W.F. & Baquete, D.S. (1998). Natural resource use, crop damage and attitudes of rural people in the vicinity of the Maputo Elephant Reserve, Mozambique, Environmental Conservation, 25:208-218.
5. Distefano, E. (2005). Human-Wildlife Conflict worldwide: Collection of case studies, analysis of management strategies and good practices, www.fao.org/3/a-au241e.pdf
6. Das, K. (2013). Man-Elephant Conflicts in North Bengal accessed from www.teriuniversity.ac.in/mct/pdf/assignment/Kalyan-Das.pdf on 7th April, 2021.

7. Depleting Green Cover a Threat to North Bengal Animals, The Times of India, Kolkata, India, Thursday, February 7 (2013).

8. Expert to Inspect Dooars Tracks, The Telegraph, Calcutta (Kolkata), India, Monday, February 4 (2013).

9. Food Chain Imbalance Swells Bison Count, The Telegraph, Calcutta (Kolkata), India, Wednesday, January 9 (2013).

10. Human Wildlife Conflict Manual: Wildlife Management Series, WWF-World Wide Fund for Nature (formerly World Wildlife Fund) Southern African Regional Programme Office (SARPO), http://wwf.panda.org/... Wildlife Management Series (2005).

11. Jumbo Hit by Train Pulled out of Ditch and Given Treatment, The Telegraph, Calcutta (Kolkata), India, Monday, January 7 (2013).

12. Lamarque, F. (2008). Human-Wildlife Conflict in Africa-An Overview of Causes, Consequences and Management Strategies, Working paper of IFCW and FAO, Rome.

13. Mukherjee, N. (2016). A Brief Appraisal of Human Wildlife Conflict in Jalpaiguri and Alipurduar District of West Bengal, International Journal of Scientific and Research Publications, 6(8): 131-136.

14. Nyhus, P.J., Tilson, R. & Sumianto. (2000). Crop raiding elephants and conservation implications at Way Kambas National Park, Sumatra, Indonesia, *Orxy*, 34: 262-274.

15. Nelson, A., Bidwell, P. & Sillero-Zubiri, C. (2003). A review of human-elephant conflict management strategies, *People and Wildlife Initiative, Wildlife Conservation Research Unit, Oxford University.*

16. Sukumar, R. and Murali, L. (2010). Elephants, People & the Battle for Peaceful Coexistence, Current Conservation, Special: Wildlife-Human Conflict, 4(4): 6-11.

17. Spotted Pride under Attack, The Times of India, Kolkata, India, Thursday, January 17 (2013).

18. State Forest Report (2013-14), West Bengal, Govt. of West Bengal, Directorate of Forests, Office of the Principal Chief Conservator of Forests and Head of Forests Force, Aranya Bhaban, Salt Lake, Kolkata, http://westbengal forest.gov.in/..../SFR-2013-14.pdf (2015).

19. World Wide Fund for Nature (1997). Conserving Africa's elephants: Current issues and priorities for action, In H.T. Dublin, T.O. McShane and J. Newby, WWF International Report, Gland, Switzerland.

20. Zubiri, C., Switzer, D. (2001). Crop raiding primates: searching for alternative human ways to resolve conflict with farmers in Africa, People and Wildlife Initiative Wildlife Conservation Research Unit, Oxford University, UK.

Abbreviation:

HWC - Human-Wildlife Conflict
BTR - Buxa Tiger Reserve
RF - Reserve Forest
PF - Protected Forest
USF - Un-classed State Forest
WLS - Wildlife Sanctuary
NP - National Park
MSL - Mean Sea Level

3

Constitutional Safeguards for Biodiversity Protection: Implementation Aspects, Prospects and Problems pertaining to sub-Himalayan Terai and Dooars of West Bengal

Dr. Gobinda Chandra Roy

Introduction

In an ever expanding civilization, natural forests and their habitats are becoming endangered every day. The forested areas of Northern West Bengal present a plethora of wildlife. Imagine a stretch of land 130 km. long by 48 km. wide where nature has lavished all her bounties and you know it Dooars. Here, an unending stretch of virgin forests is crisscrossed by the river Teesta and her innumerable tributaries. Beautiful motorable roads cut through deep forests, rich with wildlife. Mauve hills stand at the end of velvet green plains. The forests echo with the melody of birds. In between, there are fabulous National Parks, Wildlife Sanctuaries with picture-postcard, log cabin lodges and valleys carpeted with tea gardens. So Terai and Dooars, the hunting ground of Rajas probably derived its name from many duars like Alipurduar, Buxaduar etc. what are dotted by whispering pristine forest, exotic diversity of flora and fauna, torrential rivers and flushing tea gardens provides ample excitement, thrill and adventure. But unfortunately in the last 50 years, human actions have

M.Sc (Zoology), Ph.D., B.Ed, M.A. (Education)
Department of Zoology, Dinhata College, Cooch Behar-736135, West Bengal, India
Email: gobindar82@gmail.com

misrepresented the diversity of life on the planet more than any other time in history. At this time a number of questions of truth have been elevated pertaining to the policies for the better management.

Important places of Terai and Dooars at a glance

Out of 92 National Parks and 421 Wildlife Sanctuaries in India, the sub-Himalayan Terai and Dooars encompasses with four (4) National Parks and two (2) Wildlife Sanctuaries, many reserve forest, protected areas and more than 300 tea gardens which are acting as buffer region between forest and human settlement. 500-600 elephant roam about 2200 sq km area of Dooars and Eastern India every year. So in 2002 these areas were declared as "Eastern Dooars Elephant Reserve."

Climatic situation of the study area

Area: 9000 km^2 (3400 sq miles).

Temperature varies in different seasons: Nov-Feb 6-20°c / March-April 21-26°c / May -Oct 27-35°c

Rainfall: 5000 mm/year.

Relative humidity: 80-90%

Monsoon: June -September.

Vegetation: Tree, timber, shrubs and herbs etc.

Soil: Sandy loam.

Best season: October to May, chiefly March and April, when new grasses grow.

Best time to visit: Between September and March, especially in winter to grasp a view of the migratory birds.

Off season: 15th June to 14th September (National Parks and Sanctuaries closed).

Clothing: Summer-Cottons, Winter- Woolens.

Language spoken: Bengali, Hindi, Nepali and English.

Mahananda Wild life Sanctuary

The place was declared as a Sanctuary in the year 1959 to protect the extremely endangered species of Royal Bengal Tiger, gaur, Himalayan black bear and clouded leopard. The Mahananda Wildlife Sanctuary constitutes the forests of the lower catchment area of the Mahananda River, and spreads a total area of 159.86 sq km in Jalpaiguri and Darjeeling district. Situated at the western end of the elephant migration route, more than 150 elephants, shelter here during the monsoon and winter seasons. Migratory water birds are frequent in winter. The other animals found are the rare mountain goat (Serow), some tigers and herds of gaur, leopard, wild pig, varieties of deer and monkeys, jungle cats, porcupines, civets, monitor lizards and snakes. The Sanctuary offers some stunning trekking routes from Sukna. Golaghat, Deorali and the Latpancher-Mana track are the favorites for trekking and bird watching. Sukna, about 7 km from Siliguri, is the main entry point, and has a Nature Interpretation Centre.

Chapramari Wildlife Sanctuary

Chapramari Wildlife Sanctuary located in the bio-geographic zone of Lower Gangetic plain as recognized by Rodgers and Panwar, 1988 (W.I.I. Dehradun). It is located in the Nagrakata block of Jalpaiguri district just at the foothills of Kalimpong district and on the banks of Murti River. It was declared as a Game Sanctuary in 1939. In view of its great diversity of flora and fauna it was declared as Wildlife Sanctuary in 1998 comprising a total area of 9.6031 sq km. This Wildlife Sanctuary is a home of a number of animals of scheduled-I (Wildlife Protection Act, 1972). It includes, Indian pangolin - *Manis crassicaudata,* Indian elephant - *Elephas maximus,* gaur (Indian bison)-*Bos gaurus*, leopard - *Panthera pardus,* rock python - *Python molurus,* Malayan giant squirrel - *Ratufa bicolor* etc.

Neora Valley National Park

It covers a total area of 88 km^2 and is a compact patch of virgin forest, rich in biodiversity located in the Eastern Himalaya. It was notified as a National park in the year 1992. The southern boundaries of the park are adjoining to the forest of Jalpaiguri district which has connectivity with the Chapramari Wildlife Sanctuary and the Gorumara National Park. 308 bird species and numerous butterflies and moths of this park are indicators of a healthy environment and ecosystem. The Royal Bengal Tiger can be found here recently with other numbers of the cat family.

Gorumara National Park

It is located in the flood plains of Murti and Jaldhaka rivers of Dooars regions of Jalpaiguri district in West Bengal. It was declared as National Park (1994) comprising 79.99 sq km of diverse forests and further inclusion of 6 sq km in under consideration. The flora and fauna breaks all records of bio-diversity. Though this park is gaur (Indian bison) stronghold, near extinct species like hispid hare and pygmy hog have reported here. This is the migratory route of the Asiatic elephant. After reaching an all-time low in the mid-seventies, the population of rhino has now bounced back (52) and the rhinos are kept under constant surveillance. A large number of rivers and streams, gushing and gurgling down the hills congregate here.

Jaldapara National Park

It is the youngest National Park in the country perhaps (11th May, 2012). It was established in 1941 as Wildlife Sanctuary for the safeguard of One horned rhino (recently 204 in number-2021), elephant, gaur, hog deer, etc. 216 sq km of it covers a mosaic of wood, perennial streams, sandy river banks and extensive belts of tall savanna grass. This forest of Alipurduar district is a home to numerous rare and endangered species of mammals and birds. Bengal Florican, an endangered bird had been photographed in Jaldapara National Park. It holds the largest expanse of Terai grasslands in North Bengal intersected with riverine forests, dry-mixed forests and wet-forests. Tall riparian grasslands lined with bamboo clumps are the favorite homes of the rhino and the Asiatic elephant. A host of other species like the python, monitor lizard, kraits, cobra and a variety of frogs can be seen here. Hog deer, a typical animal of short grasslands quite often shoots out of cover in small groups on approach. The cheetal is confined to the edge areas between tree lands and grasslands. The sambar hides in good shrubby undergrowth. Gaurs roam over grasslands and forest. A tiger or leopard may be surprised on the sandy banks of a stream. Apart from this species like cheetah, wild boar and barking deer are also found here. Forest safari in stealthily moving elephants is a most wonderful experience in Jaldapara. Settlements of small tribes like Mech, Rava, Oraon, Munda, Kora etc. and yet the smallest surviving tribe, the Toto is also bringing into being.

Buxa Tiger Reserve (BTR)

The BTR in the Alipurduar district was set up as the 15th Tiger Reserve in 1983 vide Government of India's notification No J-M025/18/B/FRY (PT) dated 16.02.1983 at the North-Eastern corner of West Bengal bordering Bhutan and Assam. The area of the reserve encompasses 760.87 sq km having a sanctuary of 269 sq km and a National Park of 117.10 sq km of pristine forest in January 1992. Jayanti region (117 sq km) of it was declared National Park vide notification No 3403-for/11B-6795 dated 05.02.1997. The Buxa Fort is located at an altitude of about 2600 ft A.S.L (Above mean Sea Level) at a two-hour trekking distance from Santrabari. The trek is a very pleasant one with some beautiful panorama along the route. Originally established as a cantonment by the British East India Company in 1873, it was used by the British as a deportation camp (next to Andaman cellular jail) for political prisoners during India's struggle for freedom. The area's general in accessibility, as well as dense forests, made it ideal for this. Some illustrious freedom fighters who were imprisoned here were - Triloki Sen, Arun Guha, Surendra Mohan Ghosh, Hemendra Ghosh, Anil Roy, Maj. Satya Gupta, Amalendu Dasgupta, Jagannath Das Gupta, Khitish Chandra Mullick, Bhupati Majumdar and many others. Post-independence, it lost its significance and until today remains rather neglected. In the sixties, Buxa Fort was used as a relief camp for Tibetan refugees. The Tibetan Buddhist monks, who also sheltered here, attracted quite a few national and international tourists. During 1970-71, it was again used as a relief camp for Bangladeshi refugees for about six months. The trekking route to the fort both from Mahakal and Santrabari, is set amidst breathtaking scenery and provides trekkers with an opportunity to sample nature in a form unspoiled by modern influences. Satellite view reveals that the Buxa Tiger Reserve (BTR) is the largest dense forest in the West Bengal. It is fringed by 34 tea gardens and has 300 tree species, 250 shrub species, 400 herb species,9 cane species,10 bamboo species,150 orchid species,100 grass species,130 aquatic flora,70 sedges, and a variety of tiger species. It is also called as Birds' Paradise. Recently a vulture project has been taken to bring back its population at Rajabhatkhawa (100 sq ft) where its six (6) species out of 9 species in India are kept but 97% reduction has already occurred in North Bengal in last 15 years.

After getting a glimpse of all these spectacular places, don't think that the wildlife region of Terai and Dooars has an unexplored potentiality for research? So visit these regions not only for pleasure but also for educational purposes and take back exotic memories to cherish all through life.

Constitutional safeguards to defend biodiversity

India has the glory to enact a wild life protection act almost certainly first in the world which dates back to 1887. Though it was started simply with the wild birds and animals protection and passed in 1887, came in existence when repealed in 1927. Later for giving protection to the wild life in the country, the forest act 1926 was enacted in 1927. In the later consequences, Indian Board for Wildlife was established in 1952 followed by setting up of wildlife boards in different states. Though it is 48 years old the Wildlife Protection Act of 1972 is till the latest one having no any major amendment keeping pace with the present scenario of faunal and floral status of the country.

This act covers the issues of possession, trapping, shooting of wild animals alive or dead, serving their meat in eating, their transport and export in any form and all are controlled and watched by special staff. This was no doubt an extra ordinary but perhaps no longer enough to protect the wildlife in all perspectives of today's context where breach of rules are being done slowly, indirectly, lawfully and institutionally.

Then subsequent environmental legislations were taken afterwards.

1. The Insecticide Act, 1968.
2. The Wild life (Protection) Act, 1972 (Last amended in 2006).
3. The Water (Prevention & Control) Act, 1974.
4. The Forest (Conservation) Act, 1980.
5. The Air (Protection & Control) Act, 1981.
6. The Environmental (Protection) Act, 1986.
7. The National Environment Tribunal Act, 1995.
8. National Forest Policy, 1998.
9. Biological Diversity Act, 2002.
10. Scheduled Tribe & Forest dwellers Act, 2006.
11. National Green Tribunal Act, 2010.
12. National Wildlife Action Plan, 2002-2016.

With all regards to these acts, policy and plan, some questions of facts have been raised concerning the policies for the improved management of germplasm of the threatened, endangered, extinct species in the recent context of new era of ecotourism industry, professional shifting in the forest life, problem of rehabilitation, infiltration of plastic pouches and forest resorts in the dense forest of the well-known National Parks and Sanctuaries of Sub Himalayan Terai and Dooars of West Bengal in particular.

Wildlife conservation ethics

1. Take entry permit before entering the National park/ Sanctuary/Reserve forest.
2. Choose khaki, olive green, dark or natural toned cloths that blend with the forest and stay away from bright color

clothes.

3. Remain aware from wild animals like elephant, tiger, leopard and snakes. They have the right of way so treat them with respect.
4. Park your dependable vehicles at the parking area. Try to use CNG (compressed natural gas) driven vehicle as it is less polluting and noisy. Slow down your cars at turns and bends consciously.
5. Keep silence (can talk in whisper). Watch and observe nature in all its glory and let it speak for you. Get pleasure from the sound of silence/wilderness. Please do not shout, play music or blow horns while in the National Park/ Sanctuary/Reserve forest.
6. Keep pets at home but bring water bottle, a field note book, binoculars, camera and field guide book on birds and animals to record attention-grabbing findings.
7. Always take a guide to trail the specific road/path merely.
8. Don't tease the wild animals. Watch and observe nature noiselessly.
9. Keep the forest dirt free. Do not litter with plastic (soft and hard), paper, cellophane etc.
10. Keep fire away. This is the most destructive of all forces. Please do not kindle fires, throw lighted matches, cigarettes, biddies etc.
11. Do not hold firearms, explosive, etc. These are banned as per law.
12. Drive unhurriedly (permissible speed is 20-25 km/hr.).
13. Driving inside the National Park after sunset and before sunrise (6.00 pm-6.00 am) is firmly illegal.
14. Keep sober. Do not consume alcoholic drinks within the National Park/Sanctuary/Reserve forest.
15. Picnics are not allowable within the National Park/ Sanctuary/Reserve forest.
16. No person shall hunt, destroy, remove or collect any forest produce or wildlife. Fishing is rigorously forbidden.
17. Ignore inconveniences and follow park rules stringently.

Violation of these and any act and rules shall be punishable under Wildlife (Protection) act, 1972 and Indian

Forest Act, 1927.

Contemporary eminences:

The Board functions towards ensuring proper implementation of the Biological Diversity Act, 2002 and the West Bengal Biodiversity Rules, 2005.

1. To make people aware of the biodiversity and its significance in human well being.
2. Constitution of Biodiversity Management Committees (BMC) in the panchayet samity and municipal level.
3. Documenting biodiversity, their uses, traditional knowledge's, practices associated with those in the form of Peoples Biodiversity Register (PBR) involving local people through the concern BMC's.
4. Identification of heritage sites and sacred groves of the state and set up the management plan of those areas in consultation with the concern BMC's.
5. Conducting studies on biodiversity related issues of the state.
6. Regulating commercial activities related to bio-resources of the state as per the Biological Diversity Act, 2002.

Why constitutional safeguards are so important?

1. Habitat loss and alteration.
2. Illicit grazing.
3. Deterioration and breakup of forest area.
4. Unlawful hunting and poaching (over-exploitation) of wild animals (banned in 1970).
5. Monoculture practices.
6. Soil erosion through trampling.
7. Shifting of agricultural and non-agricultural areas by tea garden.
8. Environmental pollution by infiltration of plastic pouches, construction of rail way lines and bridges, dolomite mining, metallic path and electric connections, e-wastes, and microwaves of mobile phone towers etc.
9. Unprofessional conduct of tourism, infiltration of forest resorts, lodges, hotels and random jungle safari.

10 Lack of suitable treatment of wild animal diseases.
11. Constrained range.
12. Particular habitation.

Supplementary prospects

a) Development of eco-tourism.
b) Mounting a number of new-fangled of tourism like tea-tourism, nature-tourism, and adventure-tourism etc.
c) Local participation of the people in the maintenance of forestry to prevent poaching wildlife animals i.e. employment of local people.
d) Foreign exchange generation and recreational amenities by infrastructure development.
e) Rigorous protection mechanism against degradation and disaster management tools should be ensured by the government for conservation of forest and wildlife.

Problems of implementation

a) Except a few who will drive slow?
b) Is it a solution to drive slowly through the National Parks and Wildlife Sanctuaries?
c) Is it an urgent to construct national high way through National Park/Sanctuary?
d) Why not a long fly over or diversion?

The meter gauge rail line build by British Government (1900-1910) has been transformed into broad gauge rail line (2004). Heavy speedy trains running over number of elephants, bison's, pythons regularly (only tremendous ones are reported).

1) Was this transformation from meter gauge to broad gauge compulsory throughout Terai and Dooars?
2) If necessary why not long fly over and adequate diversion?
3) Will the driver stop the train to avoid an accident seeing the herd of animal?
4) Is there any advanced novel technology to stop the train abruptly after seeing the object?
5) Is it possible to change the route of different trains

permanently?

Professional shifting and its impacts on forest life

A. Suppose, 50 farmers ploughed, after coming one tractor who manufacture plough and who ploughed, 40 of them become firstly workless then homeless.
B. Massive lock out in the tea gardens makes thousands of people workless.

All these driving forces compelled forest people to unethical felling and snatching inside the forest recurrently.

CONCLUSION

There are 3 kinds of people, those who let it happen, those who make it happen and those who speculate what happened? In the past actions and programmers that promoted conservation and the sustainable use of biological diversity restricted biodiversity loss. Sustainable human development remains the primary goal and we need to strengthen the range and power of our ability to respond to biodiversity loss. To reduce and stop biodiversity loss a whole host of new and stronger action and constitutional safe guards are obligatory. The size of the task ahead of us is so huge that the 2015 biodiversity target and its implication will only realistically be achieved in certain regions if we fit into place in substantial legally recognized efforts.

ACKNOWLEDGEMENT

We gratefully acknowledge Dr. Bappa Sarkar, Assistant Professor of Geography, Dinhata College for constructing the study area map and for sincere assistance, constructive criticism with necessary help as and when needed.

Conflict of interest

The authors speak out that there is no clash of interest.

Literature cited

1. Buxa Tiger Reserve - Wikipedia, the free encyclopedia IUCN category II (National Park). It is the eastern most

extension of extreme bio- diverse North-East India & represents highly endemic Indo-Malayan region. The fragile.... There are forest rest houses of West Bengal Forest Development Corporation at *...en.wikipedia.org/ wiki/Buxa Tiger Reserve.*

2. Gorumara National Park, Jalpaiguri - History The Gorumara National Park bears its significance in the International context for ... included in the Red Data Book (R.D.B.) of the IUCN and the appendices of *...www.jalpaiguriwildlife.org / ghistory.html.*
3. IUCN Red List - Wikipedia, the free encyclopedia.
4. IUCN Red List ... Calcutta 700 091, India. Managing Director, West Bengal Forest Development Corporation Ltd. Jurisdiction ... Chapramari WLS (Jalpaiguri District). Divisional ... *www.wildbengalcom /urls / contacts.htm.*
5. The IUCN Red List of Threatened Species (also known as the IUCN Red List or Red Data List), founded in 1963, is the world's most comprehensive inventory of *...en.wikipedia.org /wiki / IUCN Red List.*
6. Wikipedia, the free encyclopedia Again in the year 1869, Innumerable*...en.wikipedia.org / wiki / Dooars.*

4

Declining Vulture Population in India: Effect of 'Diclofenac' - A Non-Steroidal Anti-Inflammatory Drug

Suchandra Bhattacharya[1] & Satadal Adhikary[2]

ABSTRACT

Vultures play crucial roles in the ecosystem as they perform the role of the 'cleaning crew' of nature. Unfortunately, the population of vultures has declined very rapidly in the last few decades. Among many other contributing factors, the role of 'diclofenac' - a Non-Steroidal Anti-Inflammatory Drug (NSAID) has been conclusively established. Diclofenac is used as veterinary medicine and vultures become susceptible to it by consuming diclofenac treated animal carcasses. The present review is a brief account of the declining vulture population in India and emphasizes the role and mechanism of action of diclofenac in leading to its depletion.

Key Words : Diclofenac, Nephropathy, Population, Toxicity, Vulture

1. Introduction

The Indian vulture (*Gyps indicus*) is an Old World Vulture found in the Indian subcontinent which has been listed as

[1]Department of Chemistry, ABN Seal College, Cooch Behar, WB-736101, India.

[2]Department of Zoology, ABN Seal College, Cooch Behar, WB-736101, India.

Email: sadhikaryrnj@gmail.com

Critically Endangered on the IUCN Red List since 2002 (Hilton-Taylor, 2000). Vulture populations have declined across the Indian subcontinent since 1990 and several species, like the oriental white-backed vulture (*Gyps bengalensis*), long-billed vulture (*Gyps indicus*) and slender-billed vulture (*Gyps tenuirostris*) have been severely affected, leading to a more than 95% decline in their population within about a very short span of 10 years (Green et al., 2004). Population sizes of these three species as per the latest figures are 6,000, 12,000, and 1,000, respectively conforming to the decline of the population of vultures in the country from 40 million to 19,000 in a span of over three decades ('The Hindu', 2019).

The array of reasons responsible for the depletion of vultures in the wild are many, among which consumption of the flesh of dead livestock treated with diclofenac needs special mention (Oaks et al., 2004). Diclofenac, a NSAID was used to treat pain, fevers, and inflammation accompanying disease or wounds in cattle, pigs, etc.

2. Vultures & Their Importance in the Ecosystem & Society

There are 23 species of vultures in the world, classified into two categories, Old World Vultures and New World Vultures. 16 species belong to the Old World (family: Accipitridae), which are found in Africa, Asia, and Europe. The 7 species of New World vultures (family: Cathartidae) are found in America. Out of 23 species of vultures in the world, nine species are found in India and their IUCN status is tabulated in Table 1. (Wani et al., 2019).

Table 1
IUCN Status of Vulture Species Found in India

S.No.	Species (Common name)	Species (Scientific name)	IUCN Status
1	White rumped vulture	*Gyps bengalensis*	Critically endangered
2	Slender billed vulture	*Gyps tenuirostris*	Critically endangered

3	Long billed vulture	*Gyps indicus*	Critically endangered
4	Red headed vulture	*Sarcogyps calvus*	Critically endangered
5	Egyptian vulture	*Neophron percnopterus*	Endangered
6	Himalayan vulture	*Gyps himalayensis*	Near threatened
7	Cinereous vulture	*Aegypius monachus*	Near threatened
8	Bearded vulture	*Gypaetus barbatus*	Near threatened
9	Indian griffon	*Gyps fulvus*	Least concern

(Wani et al., 2019)

Vultures are the apex predator and are crucial to the ecosystem and perform the role of scavenging on animal carcasses, serving as the cleaning crew of nature (Ali & Ripley, 1968). They are found in open arid lands and live chiefly on the decaying flesh of dead animals where they tear meat from carcasses. Thus they prevent the spread of diseases originating from purifying flesh which could have affected other mammals, including humans. In absence of vultures, carcasses keep on decaying in the environment which not only creates an unpleasing smell but also invites pests such as rats which are transmitters of zoonotic diseases.

Apart from the roles played by the vultures as the scavengers, they are also responsible for some other indirect effects on the human community. With the rapid decline in the vulture population in India, the stray dog population has been increased in absence of competition for food, creating its own set of problems. Statistics have been recorded for 2.06 bites occurring annually for every 1000 people causing the elevated incidence of hydrophobia (Markandya et al., 2008).

Apart from that, in densely populated poverty-stricken parts of India, the collection of bones for further processing in fertilizer industries had been an important source of income for many people (Markandya et al., 2008). The decrease in the vulture population has limited the ability of these people to collect the bones from animal corpses - a problem that is very much underrated.

3. Diclofenac: A Non-Steroidal Anti-Inflammatory Drug (NSAID)

Diclofenac (figure 1) with a molecular formula C14H11Cl2NO2 (IUPAC name: 2-[2-(2,6-dichloroanilino) phenyl] acetic acid) is available with the different brand names around the world. Many of the above-mentioned medicines are present in the form of either sodium or potassium diclofenac. It is used as an anti-inflammatory and analgesic drug in livestock farming. This drug was widely used for domestic livestock which ultimately became the cause of renal failure and subsequent death of vultures as they were exposed to the diclofenac treated animal carcasses (Swan et al., 2006).

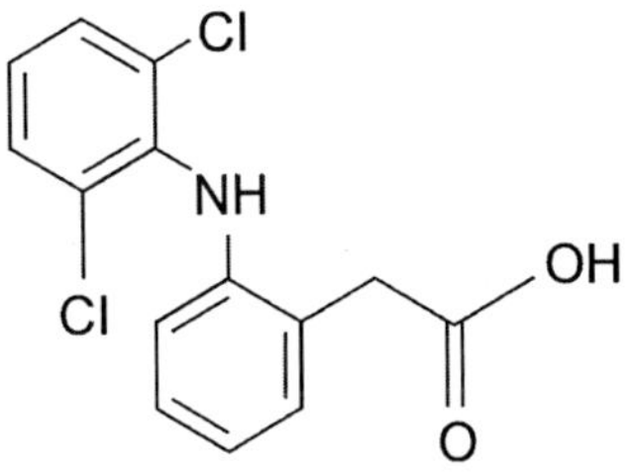

Fig. 1: Structure of Diclofenac

4. Diclofenac Toxicity in Vultures

The decline in the vulture population has been conclusively linked to the use of diclofenac as veterinary medicines. In Assam, among all vulture deaths, 99% of mortality of Oriental, White backed, slender billed and long billed vultures took place due to diclofenac (Hussain, 2015). Although the mechanism of toxicity among these birds is not yet fully deciphered. The postulated mechanisms are discussed in the following sections.

4.1. Ischemic Nephropathy

One of the views on the effect of diclofenac among vultures is the nephrotoxicity resulting from the inhibition of renal prostaglandins followed by ischemia (Meteyer et al., 2005). In the mammalian kidney, blood supply is derived from the efferent arterioles arising from the renal artery, whereas the avian kidney receives a secondary blood supply from the hindquarters via the external iliac vein. In birds, a unique structure - the renal portal valve plays an important role in regulating the blood supply to the kidneys under stress conditions. The valve is innervated by muscarinic and beta receptors, and acetylcholine induces valve closure during normal physiological conditions. On the other hand, stressed conditions characterized by the release of adrenaline lead to dilatation of valves (Burrows et al., 1983; Glahn et al., 1993).

In the 'open' state the valve allows blood from the external iliac vein to enter directly into the caudal vena cava by passing the kidney. In the 'closed' state blood from the external iliac enters into the kidney to support normal nephron functioning. Under the stressed condition, the body maximizes venous return by inducing vasoconstriction of peripheral vessels. The endogenous modulators involved with this action include adrenaline, vasopressin, and angiotensin II (Dunn & Hood, 1977). Complete vasoconstriction is detrimental for the body, thus prevented by the concomitant production of prostaglandin I2 by the vascular smooth muscle. Diclofenac is known to inhibit the formation of PGI2 and PGE2, through its cyclo-oxygenase (COX) inhibitory effect (Murray & Brater, 1993). Without this modulation, complete vasoconstriction is induced and renal ischemia occurs.

4.2. Organic Anion Transporter (OAT) Antagonism

Birds are uricotelic in that they don't conserve uric acid in their body (Dantzler & Braun, 1980). The precise pathways involved in the excretion of uric acid are unknown in vultures, while most of the literatures available are on chicken. Birds, contrary to humans are minimalist in terms of the reabsorption of uric acid, although, similar to mammals, glomerulus is effective in the process of filtration of uric acid. Birds also utilize organic anion transporters (OAT) OAT1 & OAT3 channel to actively transport uric acid from the blood into the cell (Dudas, Pelis, Braun, & Renfro, 2005). Intracellular uric acid is then excreted into the tubule by the multiple resistance protein (MRP) MRP2 & MRP4 channels. From this point onwards, unlike humans, birds do not conserve uric acid by reabsorption, owing to the absence of uric acid transporter (UAT) URAT1 channel (Dudas et al., 2005). However yet not established in birds, assuming the drug diclofenac is channel-specific, it has been proposed that diclofenac inhibits the OAT3 pump in the vulture renal tubular epithelial cells, resulting in an increase in uric acid in the blood, eventually leading to gout. Among the vultures, the half-life of diclofenac has also been found to be relatively higher (Naidoo, 2008).

4.3. Hepatotoxicity

Diclofenac works as hepatotoxin in human as it gets converted into 5-OH-diclofenac and N,5 (OH)2-diclofenac by CYP2C9 enzyme in the liver (Bort, Ponsoda, Jover, Gómez-Lechón, & Castell, 1999). This is followed by the continuous inter-conversion of the N,5 (OH)2-diclofenac, and 5-OH-diclofenac resulting in the oxidation of NADPH and production of reactive oxygen species (ROS). This in turn disrupts the integrity of the mitochondrial membrane and ultimate activation of apoptotic pathways by Caspase 2, 8 & 9 activations (Gómez-Lechón et al., 2003). Necrosis of hepatocytes following diclofenac toxicity has been documented in some avian species (Hussain et al., 2008). Vultures may also be susceptible in the same way.

4.4. Kidney Failure

Mitochondrial oxidative damage and NADPH depletion cause cellular death in the kidney (Hickey et al., 2001; Ng et al., 2006). Diclofenac brings about calcium-ion efflux from the mitochondria of the renal tubular epithelial (RTE) cells. Electron transport chain in the RTE cells with disrupted mitochondria functionally collapses, resulting in decreased NADPH formation. This eventually causes the cellular respiration to shut down, with no ATP generation, finally leading to the activation of the caspase pathways of apoptosis (Naidoo, 2008).

5. CONCLUSION

Apart from the role of diclofenac, many other factors have caused the gradual decline of vultures in India. These include habitat loss, habitat fragmentation, infectious diseases, lower availability of natural food due to scientific corpse disposal, environmental changes to name a few. Since vultures play a crucial role in the food chain, the decline of vultures should be seriously taken into account by the environmentalists, NGOs, and the government. Better monitoring of the population from regional to the national level and increased emphasis on the facts behind their depletion can be the key to serve this purpose. At the same time, the pharmacological uses of certain approved chemicals need to be reconsidered not only from the perspective of the target species but also from the point of view of its impact on the environment and biodiversity.

REFERENCES

1. Ali, S., & Ripley, S. D. (1968). Handbook of the birds of India and Pakistan: together with those of Nepal, Sikkim, Bhutan and Ceylon. Oxford University Press, New York.
2. Bort, R., Ponsoda, X., Jover, R., Gómez-Lechón, M. J., & Castell, J. V. (1999). Diclofenac toxicity to hepatocytes: a role for drug metabolism in cell toxicity. *The Journal of Pharmacology and Experimental Therapeutics*, 288(1), 65-72.
3. Burrows, M. E., Braun, E. J., & Duckles, S. P. (1983). Avian renal portal valve: a reexamination of its innervation. *The American Journal of Physiology, 245*(4), H628-34.
4. Dantzler, W. H., & Braun, E. J. (1980). Comparative nephron function in reptiles, birds, and mammals. *The American Journal of Physiology,* 239(3), R197-213. doi:10.1152/ajpregu.1980.239.3.R197
5. Dudas, P. L., Pelis, R. M., Braun, E. J., & Renfro, J. L. (2005). Transepithelial urate transport by avian renal proximal tubule epithelium in primary culture. *Journal of Experimental Biology, 208*(Pt 22), 4305-4315. doi:10.1242/jeb.01879
6. Dunn, M. J., & Hood, V. L. (1977). Prostaglandins and the kidney. *American Journal of Physiology, 233*(3), 169-184.
7. Glahn, R. P., Bottje, W. G., Maynard, P., & Wideman, R. F. (1993). Response of the avian kidney to acute changes in

arterial perfusion pressure and portal blood supply. *The American Journal of Physiology, 264*(2 Pt 2), R428-34.

8. Gómez-Lechón, M. J., Ponsoda, X., O'Connor, E., Donato, T., Castell, J. V., & Jover, R. (2003). Diclofenac induces apoptosis in hepatocytes by alteration of mitochondrial function and generation of ROS. *Biochemical Pharmacology, 66*(11), 2155-2167.
9. Green, R. E., Newton, I. A. N., Shultz, S., Cunningham, A. A., Gilbert, M., Pain, D. J., & Prakash, V. (2004). Diclofenac poisoning as a cause of vulture population declines across the Indian subcontinent. *Journal of Applied Ecology, 41*(5), 793-800. doi:10.1111/j.0021-8901.2004.00954.x
10. Hickey, E. J., Raje, R. R., Reid, V. E., Gross, S. M., & Ray, S. D. (2001). Diclofenac induced in vivo nephrotoxicity may involve oxidative stress-mediated massive genomic DNA fragmentation and apoptotic cell death. *Free Radical Biology & Medicine, 31*(2), 139-152.
11. Hilton-Taylor, C. (2000). IUCN red list of threatened species. IUCN http://www. redlist. org. Retrived on May 15, 2021, from https://portals.iucn.org/library/sites/library/files/documents/RL-2000-001.pdf
12. Hussain, I., Khan, M. Z., Khan, A., Javed, I., & Saleemi, M. K. (2008). Toxicological effects of diclofenac in four avian species. *Avian Pathology, 37*(3), 315-321. doi:10.1080/03079450802056439
13. Hussain, S. (2015). A study on vulture decline in Assam, India. *Environmentalism,* 1, 8-14.
14. Markandya, A., Taylor, T., Longo, A., Murty, M. N., Murty, S., & Dhavala, K. (2008). Counting the cost of vulture decline-An appraisal of the human health and other benefits of vultures in India. *Ecological Economics,* 67(2), 194-204. doi:10.1016/j.ecolecon.2008.04.020
15. Meteyer, C. U., Rideout, B. A., Gilbert, M., Shivaprasad, H. L., & Oaks, J. L. (2005). Pathology and proposed pathophysiology of diclofenac poisoning in free-living and

experimentally exposed oriental white-backed vultures (Gyps bengalensis). *Journal of Wildlife Diseases, 41*(4), 707-716. doi:10.7589/0090-3558-41.4.707

16. Murray, M. D., & Brater, D. C. (1993). Renal toxicity of the nonsteroidal anti-inflammatory drugs. *Annual Review of Pharmacology and Toxicology, 33,* 435-465. doi:10.1146/annurev.pa.33.040193.002251
17. Naidoo, V. (2008). Diclofenac in Gyps vultures?: a molecular mechanism of toxicity. Retrieved on May 14, 2014 from https://repository.up.ac.za/bitstream/handle/2263/26027/Complete.pdf?sequence=7
18. Ng, L. E., Vincent, A. S., Halliwell, B., & Wong, K. P. (2006). Action of diclofenac on kidney mitochondria and cells. *Biochemical and Biophysical Research Communications,* 348(2), 494-500. doi:10.1016/j.bbrc.2006.07.089
19. Oaks, J. L., Donahoe, S. L., Rurangirwa, F. R., Rideout, B. A., Gilbert, M., & Virani, M. Z. (2004). Identification of a novel mycoplasma species from an Oriental white-backed vulture (Gyps bengalensis). *Journal of Clinical Microbiology,* 42(12), 5909-5912. doi:10.1128/JCM.42.12.5909-5912.2004
20. Swan, G. E., Cuthbert, R., Quevedo, M., Green, R. E., Pain, D. J., Bartels, P. et al. (2006). Toxicity of diclofenac to Gyps vultures. *Biology Letters, 2*(2), 279-282. doi:10.1098/rsbl.2005.0425

21 'The Hindu' (2019) Sharp decline in vulture population, from 40 million to 19,000: Prakash Javadekar - Retrieved May 14, 2021, from https://www.thehindu.com/sci-tech/energy-and-environment/sharp-decline-in-vulture-population-from-40-million-to-19000-prakash-javadekar/article28586530.ece

22 Wani, H. M., Bhat, B. A., Fazil, M. F., & Shansaz, U. H. (2019). Status of vultures in India: A review. *International Journal of Advanced Scientific Research and Management, 3*(12), 181-187.

5

Relooking on Totos, a primitive tribe of West Bengal from contemporary eyes

Avishek Saha[1], Ranjan Barman[2] & Kishore Thapa[3]

If people can't acknowledge the wisdom of indigenous cultures, then that's their loss.
– *Jay Griffiths*

ABSTRACT

The Toto people are one of the seventy five primitive tribes in India. Though their population is increasing as per the Census reports attention from all corners is needed to preserve their vanishing language and culture. The present study contended incremental growth of population but the living standard, literacy rate and cultural preservation need much attention. More focused programmes and intervention form the all corners are imperative to protect and preserve their rich culture and indigenous knowledge. Intensive scientific research is needed to explore this particularly vulnerable tribal group of the globe.

Introduction :

Tribes are the vehicle of original and natural human

[1]Department of English,
[2]Department of Mathematics,
[3]Department of Botany
Dinhata College, Dinhata-736135, District Cooch Behar, West Bengal

culture. It is very fascinating to consider them to be savage and machine dependent people as advanced. They carry roots of development like medicine, indigenous technology and so on.

If we are to make a common definition of tribe, it may be agreed that they are a group of people that all have common ancestry, or a common ancestor, a common culture, and live in their own enclosed society. Actually all so called advanced communalities too have originated from such primitive tribe. A parallel term for such tribe, not literarily, is an indigenous people. According to the United Nations indigenous people are inheritors and practitioners of unique culture and ways of relating to people and the environment. Different countries and organisations have different ways to define tribe. In India, there are many communities which dovetailed with definition of tribe but some are included in the scheduled list under the Article 342 of the Constitution of India.

There are many more schemes implemented by the government and other agencies for upliftment of the tribes of India, however, there are some tribal groups still in very backward stage in respect to their socio-economic condition (Dash Sharma, 2006).

About Primitive Tribes:

In India, as tribal people are enlisted under various socio-political reasons and the government policy is to uplift them in all angles especially with regards to their literacy, economy and other social status. Some of the tribes have started getting the benefits but some are still at level of nothingness as per development index due to their primitive traits, geographical isolation, shyness to admix with other communities, low literacy, pastoral agroforestry nature of livelihood which lead them to be vulnerable from the history of mankind and hence, the government initiated to identify such tribes giving them status of Primitive Tribal Groups for their all round development. In Sikkim Lepchas were also recommended to be include in this group (Thapa and Allay, 2021). The government put following criteria in identifying the Primitive Tribal Groups:

a) A stagnant and diminishing population
b) Pre-agricultural level of technology
c) Very low level of literacy

In 2006 the government of India renamed Primitive Tribal Group as Particularly Vulnerable Tribal Group ant till 2011 census they are 75 in number. (Table 1).

Table 1
State/Union territories wise lit of PVTGs in India

S.No.	State/Union Territory	PVTG(PTG)
1.	Andhra Pradesh including Telangana	1. Bodo Gadaba
		2. Bondo Poroja
		3. Chenchu
		4. Dongria Khond
		5. Gustob Gadaba
		6. Khond Puroja
		7. Kolam
		8. Kondareddis
		9. Konda Savaras
		10. Kutia Khond
		11. Parengi Poroja
		12. Thoti
2.	Bihar including Jharkhand	13. Asurs
		14. Birhor
		15. Birjia
		16. Hill Kharia
		17. Korwas
		18. Mal Paharia
		19. Parhaiya
		20. Saurina Paharia
		21. Savar
3.	Gujrat	22. Kathodi
		23. Kotwalia
		24. Padhar

		25. Siddi 26. Kolgha
4.	Karnataka	27. Jenu Kuruba 28. Koraga
5.	Kerela	29. Cholanaikayan 30. Kadar 31. Kattunayakan 32. Kurumbas 33. Korang
6.	Madhya Pradesh (including Chattisgarh)	34. Abhuj Marias 35. Baigas 36. Bharias 37. Hill Kobras 38. Kumars 39. Saharias 40. Birhors
7.	Maharashtra	41. Katkaria (Kathodia) 42. Kolam 43. Maria Gond
8.	Manipur	44. Marram Nagas
9.	Orissa	45. Birhor 46. Bondo 47. Didayi 48. Dongria-Khod 49. Jaungs 50. Kharia 51. Kutia Kondh 52. Lanjia Sauras 53. Lodhas 54. Mankidias 55. Paudi Bhunyans 56. Saura 57. Chuktia Bhunja
10.	Rajasthan	58. Seharia
11.	Tamil Nadu	59. Kattu Nayakans 60. Kotas

		61. Kurumbas 62. Irulas 63. Paniyans 64. Todas
12.	Tripura	65. Reangs
13.	Uttar Pradesh (including Uttrakhand)	66. Buxas 67. Rajis
14.	West Bengal	68. Birhor 69. Lodhas 70. Totos
15.	Andamans & Nikobar Islands	71. Great Andamanese 72. Jarawas 73. Onges 74. Sentinelese 75. Sohm Pens

The above Table 1 indicates that there are only three PVTGs in West Bengal and more precisely only one in North Bengal. The present communication tries to put some insights on the only PVTG in North Bengal i.e. Toto.

Totos, really a unique tribe:

A unique enclave dweller surrounded by Bhutanese, Nepalese, Bengali, Koch, Mech and Adivasies, the Totos with small area to live and scanty population have separate means of socio-anthropological identity in North Bengal. They are exogamous, have their language of their own, rituals, houses, livelihood options, way of worship and in totality, a unique culture. These features have attracted many anthropologists, ethnobiologists, linguists and other researchers to for their comprehensive study.

Totopara, where they are living time immemorial:

The area is a small village named as Totpara (Fig. 1) in the Madarihat Community Development Block of Alipurduar District located between 89°20'E and 26°50'N and, this place in addition to have natural picturesque rather attracts researchers and tourist for the local inhabitants the Totos, the only primitive tribe in the North Bengal. The village with an area of 8.0814 Km^2 is only 22 km away from Madarihat. There exits six segments in Totopara namely Panchyatgaon, Mandalgaon, Subbagaon, Mitranggaon, Pujagaon and Dumchigaon.

Their history, which needs more focus research:

The region was under the Bhutanese administration until the British Government ceded it to India the Bhutan was in 1865, (Chowdhuri, 2005). According to Sanyal (1955) the first settlement survey of this area was conducted by Sunder, a settlement officer of Jalpaiguri) from 1889 to 1894. Later B.K. Barman made comprehensive ethnographic study on Tottos and published the works in various social science journals (Chowdhuri, 2005). Owing to the unique features of the local inhabitant, the Totos, he declared Totopara mouza as reserved and restricted to Totos (Dutta, 2014).

Population in year 2041, $=1387+109.64*3+\{3*(3+1)/2\}*12.8$
$=1792$

Population in year 2051, $=1387+109.64*4+\{4*(4+1)/2\}*12.8$
$=1953$

How they look like?

Totos physical appearance (Fig. 6) is recognised by their flat nose, small eyes with black iris, broad and square checks, and somewhat thick lips and for this they are supposed to have mongoloid origin (Sinha and Pal, 1983). In regards to their skin colour as it appears black they are placed nearness to equator (Debnath, Das and Saha, 2019).

Their food habit:

Their staple food is rice, cheera (flattend rice), pulses, vegetables (home grown or wild edibles and market purchased), eggs, fish and meat. As they rear cattle, milk is also a prominent item of their diet though now they sell milk outside as a source of income for their livelihood. They are non-vegetarian, so they normally keep pigs, goats, fowls as diet supplement and also as additional income source. From nearby jungles they bring various types of non timber forest products (NTFP) like mushrooms, edible ferns, roots, fruits, honey, medicinal herbs etc. and they collect fish from nearby rivers like Torsha and other small streams.

Their shelter:

Two naturally available plant resources bamboo and trees are the materials that Toto people use to construct their houses. (Fig. 2) Their houses are generally about 5-6 ft above the ground as the lower portion is used a shed for their animals like pigs, goats, fowls etc. But nowadays some use wooden planks and mud to construct their (Fig. 4) and animals are kept elsewhere like fowls are kept in chicken coop (Fig. 3). Paddy thatch or areca nut leaves were used as roofing materials but now corrugated roof is used by some effluent families. There are generally three sections in the house the centre one is room for their deities and other two are meant for them and the guests. They normally do not construct toilets and defecation is either open air or inside the house as the animals would feed and clean the faeces. Being originally forest dweller and also practice agro-forestry system panting areca nut, beetle nut in their home gardens are inevitable.

Clothing:

The modern generation Toto youths are influenced by the cotemporary cultures and so they use shirts and trousers but traditionally they use a prototype of Bhutia dress. A piece of cloth is tied at the neck which covers upper part of the body till the knees. A cotton belt is used to tight it at the waist and have a big pocket at the upper part used to keep small usable items like beetle nut, knife etc. On the contrary women folk use four piece of clothes one at the waist (Bijang) and the other at the front and back portion (Tumba), another one piece hanged from the waist upto knee (Mera) and the last one used to cover the head (Pari). Modern generation women, use blouses and lungies (a wrapper to cover the lower portion).

Toto language at the crossroad:

Toto people speak Toto language which is considered to be a branch of Sino-Tibetan language. The UNESCO has classified four level of languages endangerment between "safe" and "extinct" and Toto language is enlisted as a Critically Endangered (the youngest speakers are grandparents and older, and they speak the language partially and infrequently) in the 191 languages of India that are classified as Vulnerable or Endangered. Dr. P. Perumal Samy has rigorously described Toto language's phonetics and other aspects of linguistics in his paper "A linguistic Description of Toto language spoken in West Bengal. However, Toto language too as in case of other languages, well influences by other languages like Nepali and Bengali normally spoken by surrounding people. Consequently, Shiv Sahay Singh in the 'Hindu' daily reports that Toto language is more endangered than the tribe itself.

Their populations:

Low population reflects primitive characters of Toto people. Being exogamous and matrimonial relations among themselves is also a feature for their population intensity. However, the decadal grown rate (Table 2) reveals normal growth of population except in 1931-1941 where their increase is shown as -3.89.

Table 2
Decadal Male-Female population as recorded through Census Report, Das and Kanchan

S.No.	Year	No. of Male	No. of Female	Total	DGR
1.	1901	72	99	171	-
2.	1911	125	110	235	37.42
3.	1921	140	131	271	15.31
4.	1931	130	204	334	23.25
5.	1941	159	162	321	-3.89
6.	1951	161	160	321	
7.	1961	206	189	395	91.90
8.	1971	352	318	650	
9.	1981	362	352	712	23.05

10.	1991	471	457	928	30.06
11.	2001	620	575	1195	67.84
12.	2021	737	650	1387	16.07

Population increase analysis:

By applying incremental increase method with following formula

Pn=P+nx+[n(n+1)/2]y

Where Pn= Population after nth decade, x=Average increase, y=Incremental increase

following figures could be derived

Year	Population	Increase (x)	Incremental increase (y)
1901	171	-	-
1911	235	64	-
1921	271	36	-28
1931	334	63	27
1941	321	-13	-76
1951	321	00	13
1961	395	74	74
1971	450	45	-29
1981	712	262	217
1991	928	216	-46
2001	1195	267	51
2011	1387	192	-75
	Total	**1206**	**128**
	Average	**109.64**	**12.8**

Hence the trend of population in the following decades can be forecasted as under,

Population in year 2021, = 1387+109.64*1+{1*(1+1)/2}*12.8
= 1509

Population in year 2031, =1387+109.64*2+{2*(2+1)/2}*12.8
=1644

Similarly their education status can also be quantified and forecasted.

Education was supposed to be a matter of taboo for Totos till last generation. But nowadays due to various government schemes they are getting benefit to have formal education. Currently most of them go to school and some also have become graduate.

Photo Plate 1: Figures 1-6 showing photographic outlook of Toto people and Totopara.

Fig. 1: View from Totopara

Fig. 2: A Toto house

Fig. 3: A chicken coop

Fig. 4: A house with wooden plank partition

Fig. 5: A modernized house of Toto

Fig. 6: A Toto Family

Toto Healthcare:

Sardar et al (2021) reported that more than 68% of Toto family believe in ethnomedicine whereas about 32% depend on modern medicine. Healthcare facility in the region is poor as in other rural parts of the country. Even the nearest Primary Healthcare Centre is located at Dalgaon, which is 40 Km away. (Singh, 2021). He reports that while interviewing a medical officer there it was realized that Totos primarily suffer from Tuberculosis, diarrhea and hypertension

A discussion:

Toto is one of the smallest indigenous groups of the world. Their exact lineage and reason of scarce population is a matter of intensive research. Their identity regarding ethnicity, culture, region and on the top their language is to be conserved and preserved. Language is most likely to be influenced by other culture. If a generation neglects it the intensity of its decline is exponential. Various developmental schemes need to be percolated with a mind to consider their identity. Healthcare facility, education, sanitation and other livelihood options are to be improvised. A sign of good hope is there a new school is constructed in Totopara and government policy of right to education must be appreciated. Their birth rate, postnatal mortality rate is to be reduced. The decadal population rate is positive (Table 2) but needs to be observed minutely among this endogamous community as there is trend to be endogamous which may effect this positive rate. A simple calculation done applying incremental increase method also gives a positive trend. Their meager developmental look is of great concern in the 21st century.

CONCLUSION

The field studies and literature review indicate that even passing two decades of the 21st century Toto, particularly vulnerable tribal group of India still in the cross road on any developmental activities. No intensive programmes particularly relating to their all round development or on themselves have been noticed. They get benefit from the government as a paradigm shift. Researches too have published papers and books regarding their findings only without any focused solution of their socioeconomic issued. Their language and ethnobiological knowledge are eroding at a rapid pace and at alarming situation. An interface between technical inputs and indigenous technical knowhow is the matter to be seriously thought of from all corner of the society to conserve this indigenous vanishing tribe.

ACKNOWLEDGEMENT

The authors are thankful to Sri Tanamoy Saha, Department of Geography, Dinhata College for some of the photographs.

REFERENCES

1. Annonymous. 2011. A linguistic description of Toto language spoken in West Bengal. *Linguistic Survey of India, West Bengal. Census of India*, 2011.Vol.1. Part I.
2. Bhattacharya, K.K. , Hoque., M. and Biswas, T.K.. 2006. Nuritional Status of Two Primitive tribes of Eastern India. *Anthropology of Primitrive Tribes in India* (Ed. Dash Sharma, P). Serials Publications. New Delhi. India.
3. Choudhury, M.K. 2005. The Totos. In Primitive tribes of contemporary India. Vol.I. (Eds. Chaudhari S.K. and Choudhari S.S.). Mittal Publications. New Delhi. India.
4. Das, Jayanta. 2011. Factors influencing the socio-economic status of Toto tribe in Madarihat Block of Jalpaifuri district, West Bengal. *Geo-Analyst.* 1(2):66-71.
5. Dawn, Anandita. 2014. A peep into the lifestyle of the endangered Toto tribe of Jalpaiguri district of West Bengal. *Int. J. Modn. Res. Revs.* 2(4): 161-164.
6. De, Subhasis and Datta, Kanchan. 2014. Multidimentional poverty index of Toto: The smallest and primitive tribe in Jalpaiguri district of West Bengal. *Economic Affairs.* 59(4): 605-611.

7. Ghosh, Debashis and Saha, Snehasis. 2017. Transformation of traditional livelihood and economic Composition of Population: A case study of Totopara village, West Bengal. JOSR-JHSS. 21(7):1-7.

8. Hoque, Md Ziaul and Ansor, Md Kowsar. 2015. Socio-cultural and economic distinctiveness and transformation of the Toto tribe. *International Journal of Innovative Research and Advanced Studies.* 2(5): 30-34.

9. http://wbnorthbengaldev.gov.in/HtmlPage/toto.aspx

10. Sardar, Akrom, Paul, Mondal, Priyobatra and paul Suvankar. 2021. Ethnomedicinal practices among the Toto tribe in Alipurduar, West Bengal. Int. j. Community Med. Public. Health. 8(6):2069-2073.

11. Singh Shiv Sahay. 2014. Toto language is more endangered than tribe. The Hindu, Kolkata, August 01,2014.

12. Thapa K.K. and Allay, S. 2021. Lepcha agriculture on primitive agro-system perspective. *Science of Eastern Himalaya Journal. 1*(1): 77-82.

6

Checklist of Lepcha Clans and their Extinct Clans Shuzamyoung Pucho and Chunglem Pucho

Durga Kumar Prashan[1], *Norden Lepcha*[2]
& Kishore Kumar Thapa[3]

ABSTRACT

The Dzongu is the place of Lepcha which is dedicated for the preservation of genetic race of Lepcha.

This paper is an account of the vanishing clans of Lepcha in Dzongu. In the recent study, the three clans of tribes found extinct inter alias Shuzamyoung Pucho from Tingvong, Chunglem Pucho from Lingko and the Snake eater Lepcha clan from Sakyoung-Pentong. Thus, the paper attempted to enumerate the clans of Lepcha in the different panchayat wards of Dzongu, Sikkim for the documentation and future reference.

Key words : Dzongu, Lepcha, Sikkim, vanishing tribe.

[1]Quality Control Laboratory-HARC
Sikkim State Forest Herbarium (SSFH)
Forest and Environment Department Govt. of Sikkim, Deorali-777102, Gangtok, Sikkim, India.
Corresponding author: pradhansikkim@gmail.com
[2]Tungvong Dzongu, North Sikkim
[3]Department of Botany, Dinhata College, Dinhata-736135, Cooch Behar.
Corresponding author: pradhansikkim@gmail.com

Introduction

Many literatures are available mentioning the Lepcha as the vanishing tribe (Foning, 1987, Gorer, 1984) but the list of clans of Lepcha of Dzongu and vanishing tribe clan were not reported till date.

The culture and coustoms and their traditions of Lepcha available in the lakes, peaks and jungle (Rustomgi, 1987), furthermore, about the knowledge of the Lepcha on the resources, it is established fact that the Lepcha community is having good knowledge in flora and fauna (Hooker, 1855; Cowan, 1929) and are aboriginal inhabitants of Sikkim (Gorer, 1984; Thakur, 1988).

Such a knowledgeable community is facing threat in survival, therefore, the paper attempted to enumerate the information for its documentation.

Materials and Methods

The study area of Dzongu located at 27°28' - 27°-38'N and 88°23' - 88°38'E having the altitudinal gradients of 700 to 6000 m. The geographical area of Dzongu is 78 square kilometers that includes the tropical to the alpine regions having the population of Lepcha community only.

Survey and Data collection

The field survey conducted and the data was evaluated using the method of Thomas et al (2007). The primary reliable data was obtained communicating in the Lepcha language taking consent of the respondents.

Results and Discussion

The Lepcha tribe of Sikkim possesses many clans depending on the place of origin of their ancestors. It is basically link to the name of lakes and peaks. In brief survey, it was noted that the communities was found originated from the different locations (Table 1). They often described these lakes and peaks during offering their deities. Such occasions of offerings are Sutap Rumfaat (Hailstone worship), Chureem Rumfaat (Nature worship), Muud Rumfaat (Hunters' Diety worship, twice in a year), Sukya Rumfat, Aajuk Rumfaat etc. Generally, the tribe offers to the deities in the beginning of year which are their social set up.

Table 1

Tabulated data of the clans of Lepcha of Tingbong GPU, Dzongu (Sikkim) depicting the lakes, peak and the land of their origins

(Abbreviation: NA: Not found during the survey and required investigation)

No	Panchayat		CLAN	LAKE (Dho)		PEAK (Chu)	(Cave) LEPP
1	Tingvong Ward	1.	Aramu Pucho	NA		NA	NA
		2.	Aram-panchyat Pucho	NA		NA	NA
		3.	Pakimoo Paucho	Nahol Dho	3.	Pakichu	NA
		4.	Simick Pucho	NA	4.	Sumick Sadam Chu	NA
		5.	Taryum Pucho	NA			Chuchen
		6.	Zam-youngmu pucho	NA		NA	Manku
2	Kussong Ward	1.	Kamyanmu Pucho	Yuksom Dho		Munom chu	NA
		2.	Pakimoo Pucho	Nahol Dho		Pakichu	NA
		3.	Zamyoung Pa pachen Pucho	NA		NA	NA
		4.	Shu Zam-youngmu Pucho	NA		NA	NA
3	Lingkoo Ward	1.	Pakimoo Pucho	Nahol Dho		Pakichu	NA

4	Namprick Ward	1.	Aramu Pucho	NA	NA	NA
		2.	Demikmo Pucho	NA	NA	NA
		3.	Zam-youngmo Pucho	NA	NA	NA
		4.	Pakimoo Pucho	Nahol Dho	Pakichu	NA
5	Nung Ward	1.	Aram-panchyat Pucho	NA	NA	NA
		2.	Zumchung Pa pachen Pucho	NA	NA	NA
		3.	Pakimoo Pucho	Nahol Dho	3 Pakichu	NA
		4.	Luksom Pucho	NA	NA	NA
		5.	Gharkam Pucho	NA	NA	NA

Further, the detail list of the clans of Lepcha of Dzongu enumerated including fifty five clans from the different gram panchayat units of Dzongu along with their present status in the hills of Dzongu (Table 2). The primary data of the survey reveals that some of the clans of Lepcha, Shuzamyoung Pucho from Tingvong, Chunglem Pucho from Lingko and the snake eater lepcha clan from Sakyoung-Pentong got extinct from 2019 onwards. No such clans were living in the Dzongu hills so it is assumed that the community vanished from the hills of Dzongu.

Table 2

Depicting the clans of Lepcha in the respective villages of Dzongu along with present status

(Abbreviations : Ex : Extinct; PE: Population exist; GPU: Gram Panchayat Unit)

S. No.	Lepcha Clan	Gram Panchayat Unit/ Village name	Remark
1	Kamyenkumzyet Pucho	Tingvong	PE

2	Arampanchyat Pucho	Hee-Gyathang, Tingvong	PE
3	Aramu Pucho	Hee-Gyathang, Tingvong, Lum Gor, Lingdong Burfok	PE
4	Demik Pucho	Tingvong	PE
5	Zamyoungmoo Pucho	Tingvong	PE
6	Teem Pucho	Sakyoung Pentong, Lingdong Burfok	PE
7	Solong Pucho	Sakyoung Pentong	PE
8	Simick Pucho	Tingvong	PE
9	Luksom Pucho	Tingvong, Lum Gor, Passingdong Saffo, Shipgyer Ramom	PE
10	Zumchungmo Pucho	Lindong Burfok, Shipgyer Ramom	PE
11	Hee-moo Pucho	Hee-Gyathang	PE
12	Hee youngming moo Pucho	Hee- Gyathang	PE
13	Sangdyangmoo Pucho	Lum Gor	PE
14	Turyum Pucho	Hee-Gyathang, Tingvong,	PE
15	Thingtembu Pucho	Shipgyer Ramom GPU	PE
16	Endongmoo Pucho	Sakyoung-Pentong	PE
17	Debongmoo Pucho	Hee-Gyathang	PE
18	Pakimoo Pucho	Tingvong, Lingthem Lingdem, Sakyoung-Pentong	PE
19	Zumchung Pa pachen Pucho.	Tingvong	PE
20	Chunglem Pucho	Lingko	Ex
21	Gharkam Pucho	Tingvong	PE
22	Sangvyal Pucho	Sakyoung-Pentong	PE
23	Sangenmoo Pucho	Hee-Gyathang	PE
24	Aafimoo Pucho	Hee- Gyathang, Passingdong Safoo	PE
25	Sangdupmoo Pucho	Hee-Gyathang	PE
26	Chakumoo Pucho	Hee-Gyathang	PE
27	Shuzamyoung Pucho	Tingvong	Ex

28	Zyer Sukdum Pucho	Sakyoung- Pentong	PE
29	Naka Choka Pucho	Sakyoung-Pentong	PE
30	Snake eater community of Lepcha (name could not trace)	Sakyoung-Pentong	Ex
31	Tukzokmu	Taryang Ward, Loom-Ghor Gram Panchayat Unit	PE
32	Tungdupmu	Taryang Ward, Loom	PE
33	Rayrepchungmu	Taryang Ward, Loom	PE
34	Chyakawmu	Taryang Ward, Loom	PE
35	Tunglemu	Taryang Ward, Loom	PE
36	Regimu	Taryang Ward, Loom	PE
37	Padtaribu	Taryang Ward, Loom	PE
38	Kumzam	Taryang Ward, Loom	PE
39	Abisukin	Lingdong Barfung	PE
40	Sangdyanmu	Lingdong Barfung	PE
41	Lanthendupmu	Lingdong Barfung	PE
42	Sambarmu	Lingdong Barfung	PE
43	Gorsungzammu	Lingdong Barfung	PE
44	Engrongmu	Lingdong Barfung	PE
45	Subsukney Pucha	Leek ward under Passingdang Saffo GPU	PE
46	Pacawlingay Pucho	Leek ward under Passingdang Saffo GPU	PE
47	Yougmingmu Pucho	Leek ward under Passingdang Saffo GPU	PE
48	Bhuktongdup Pucho	Shipgyer Ramom GPU	PE
49	Leepa arangmo Pucho	Shipgyer Ramom GPU	PE
50	Rehearehet Pucho	Shipgyer Ramom GPU	PE
51	Suburriknitmoo Pucho	Shipgyer Ramom GPU	PE
52	Sambomu Pucho	Shipgyer Ramom GPU	PE
53	Athing Linggamu Pucho	Shipgyer Ramom GPU	PE
54	Tareng Pucho	Shipgyer Ramom GPU	PE
55	Mon aphibo Pucho	Shipgyer Ramom GPU	PE

This paper intends to document the available information of Lepcha clans and its extinct races for the future investigation. Although the details of the Lepcha clans' origin could not trace completely due to unavailability of literatures and sources which warrants further research on the primitive tribe in future.

CONCLUSION

Nevertheless the State Government of Sikkim is taking many protecting initiatives for the Lepcha community even so the extinction of clans of Lepcha is alarming. Thus, it is proposed for the socio-economic protections of the community of far flung hills of Dzongu so that the other clans of the primitive tribe, the Lepcha, can be protected.

ACKNOWLEDGEMENTS

Authors are thankful to the Department of Forest and Environment, Government of Sikkim for the kind support as well as the people of the Dzongu who had participated in the survey during the study.

Authors thank to the staff for helping in the qualitative study to improve the content.

REFERENCES

1. Cowan, J.M . (1929). *Rec . Bot. Surv. Ind.* 12 (1): 1-74.
2. Foning, A.R. (1987). Lepcha My Vanishing Tribe, Oriental Univ Press, pp-2-152.
3. Geoffrey, G. (1984). The Lepchas of Sikkim, Cultural Publishing House, Delhi (rep), pp 188-208.
4. Hooker, J.D. (1855). Himalayan Journals , Vol I, Today and Tomorrow's Printers and Pub, New Delhi, pp 120-129.
5. Rustomji, N. (1987). Sikkim A Himalayan Tragedy, Allied Pub Pvt Ltd, New Delhi, p 9.
6. Thakur, R.N (1988). Himalayan Lepchas, Archives Pub , New Delhi, pp 46-47.
7. Thomas E, Vandebroek I, Damme P.V. (2007). What Works in the Field? A comparison of different interviewing methods in Ethnobotany with special reference to the use of photographs. *Econ Bot,* 61(200&): 376-384.

7

Population Dynamics of North Bengal: Evidence from Census, 2011

Moslem Hossain[1], Manoj Dakua[1], Mihir Adhikary[1], Tushar Dakua[1], Nazrul Islam[2]

ABSTRACT

The study traces the dynamic of the population in the northern part of West Bengal, which is called North Bengal. This current study reviews the size, growth, and structure of the North Bengal region. For the comparative population distribution analysis, the census data of 2011 has been used at the district level. The study reveals that the sex ratio is highest in Darjeeling, followed by Dakshin Dinajpur and Jalpaiguri, and lowest in Uttar Dinajpur. However, the child sex ratio is comparatively higher in Dakshin Dinajpur and Jalpaiguri than in other districts. The Child-woman ratio is an essential indicator of reproductive behaviour, determined by the ratio of children under the age of five to per thousand women of child-bearing age, usually as 15 - 44. One of the crucial findings is that Koch Bihar disclosed the worst position in child sex ratio in north Bengal. Work participation rate and age dependency ratios are the measures for understanding economic life. The preceding analyses have examed that there is no such massive difference among districts in the region.

[1]Research Scholar, International Institute for Population Sciences, Mumbai

[2]Associate Professor, Cooch Behar Panchanan Barma University, Cooch Behar.

The results suggest that Darjeeling has the highest literacy rate, followed by Koch Bihar, Jalpaiguri, and Dakshin Dinajpur. It is clear from this study that Uttar Dinajpur has the worst position in terms of literacy rate. In our study, the crude birth rate has been calculated to determine the region's fertility differences. The data depicts that the CBR is highest in Uttar Dinajpur and Maldah, and Darjeeling and Dakshin Dinajpur show an improved CBR. The mean age is also known as the average age, is just the average age of a group of people, which was more or less the same in all the districts of North Bengal. The average TFR of North Bengal near about replacement level which is 2.3, but there was much variation among inter-district. Uttar Dinajpur is the highest TFR which is 3.1, followed by Maldah and Dakshin Dinajpur, Darjeeling and Jalpaiguri were the below replacement level. This present study adds the significant demographic events of North Bengal district-wise variation.

Key Words : Population, Sex Ratio, Dependency Ratio, Mean Age, North Bengal.

1. Introduction

The dynamics of the population known as the study of the composition of the population of which embraces basic personal, social and economic characteristics or attributes of any population: age, sex, race, nationality, religion, composition, literacy and educational attainment, employment status etc. (Bhende and Kanitkar, 1991). Population dynamics refers to the phenomena of populations of a species change over time. Going by population geography definition, population dynamics refers to studying how and why people change in size and structure over time. Demographic event is most important and influenced by various factors. The influences are not constant over time and space, thus demographic rate consideration variation. Essential factors in population dynamics include rates of reproduction, death, and migration. Population dynamics depend on community complexity, varying across different communities like migration (McGrady et al. 2000 and Dey et al. 2013). The study by Ried, 1966 and Sengupta 2002, West Bengal has been a popular subject of academic study because of its importance in culture, religious reform, politics and education, the growth of trade union movements. In the past, India's population has increased and has imposed a substantial burden of youth dependency on the Indian economy. However, in recent years, India's demographic profile has evolved in a potentially more favourable economic growth. Today's large cohorts of working-age individuals will be large cohorts of elderly dependents in the future. The share of India's 50+ population today is relatively small, accounting for only 16% of India's population. As we advance, however, India will witness rapid 21 growth among this age group. The main force driving India's changing age structure is the maturing of past birth cohorts, upward trends in life expectancy due to increasing survival rates at older ages, and falling fertility (LASI report). This study examined the issues related to the north Bengal region population and intends to identify the characteristics of the population keeping in mind the districtwise pattern of the population of North Bengal.

2. Data & Methods

Our study based on secondary data collected from the Census of India. The present study focuses on the northern part of West Bengal, which namely called North Bengal. For the comparative population distribution analysis, the census data of 2011 has been used at the district level. There are six districts, Darjeeling, Jalpaiguri, Cooch Behar, Uttar Dinajpur, Dakshin Dinajpur and Maldah. The study illustrated the demographic information in that region. All the event were calculated for North Bengal using census data for individual district. The st udy includes some rates and ratios of population composition; these are Sex Ratio (SR), Child Sex Ratio, Child Women Ratio (CWR), Crude Birth Rate (CBR), Density, Decadal growth rate, Literacy Rate, Work Participation Rate (WPR), Mean Age, Dependency Ratio, Migration Rate. All the rates and ratios were calculated by using standard formulas of the census of India.

3. Results and Discussion

3.1 District wise percentage distribution of North Bengal population:

The total population of North Bengal as per the 2011 census is 17.2 million, of which Maldah district having the largest share of 23.2 percent, followed by Jalpaiguri, Uttar Dinajpur, Koch Bihar, Dakshin Dinajpur, and Darjeeling. It can be apparent from table 1 that the sex-wise distribution is almost the same in all the districts. It consists of more than 51 percent male and more than 48 percent female population in almost all the districts. Table 1 also reveals that Darjeeling district has the most significant urban population share, followed by Jalpaiguri district, 39.4%, and 27.4%, respectively. The most possible and well-accepted reason for most urban population share in Darjeeling and Jalpaiguri is Siliguri city, which rapidly expands its area through these districts. Other districts have only 10 to 14 percent of the urban population share; Koch Bihar district has the lowest urban population. Indian religions are sometimes known as a dharmic or Indic religion, and North Bengal is not far away. North Bengal religions are connected through the history of India. Hindu and Muslim communities dominate almost all the districts of North Bengal. Jalpaiguri is the first position in terms of the Hindu population, which is near 82%, followed by Koch Behar. Utter Dinajpur and Maldah were showing one of two Hindu and one of two Muslim population. Most of the minority communities are residing in the Darjeeling district of North Bengal. Caste-wise variation also has been shown in this table. It can be seen that Koch Bihar has the highest share of the SC population, which is more than 50 percent, followed by Jalpaiguri (37.65%), Dakshin Dinajpur (28.8%), Uttar Dinajpur (26.9%), Maldah (20.9%), and Darjeeling (17.2%). Koch Bihar also has the lowest share of ST population, which is only 0.64 percent. The highest share of the Scheduled tribe population can be seen in Darjeeling, followed by the Jalpaiguri district. Most of the hilly and forest areas of these two districts are home to many ST populations.

Table 1

District wise percentage distribution of population in North Bengal

Population Composition	Parameter	District					
		Koch Bihar	Jalpaiguri	Darjeeling	Uttar Dinajpur	Dakshin Dinajpur	Maldah
Population	Total	2819086	3872846	1846823	3007134	1676276	3988845
Resident	Rural	89.73	72.62	60.58	87.95	85.9	86.42
	Urban	10.27	27.38	39.42	12.05	14.1	13.58
Sex	Male	51.49	51.2	50.75	51.58	51.14	51.43
	Female	48.51	48.8	49.25	48.42	48.86	48.57
Religious community	Hindu	74.06	81.51	74	49.31	73.55	47.99
	Muslim	25.54	11.51	5.69	49.92	24.63	51.27
	Christian	0.15	4.81	7.68	0.56	1.48	0.33
	Sikh	0.02	0.08	0.11	0.02	0.02	0.02
	Buddhist	0.02	1.31	11.33	0.01	0.01	0.01
	Jain	0.07	0.04	0.10	0.04	0.02	0.02
	others	0.01	0.61	0.84	0.05	0.17	0.20
Caste	SC	50.17	37.65	17.18	26.87	28.8	20.94
	ST	0.64	18.89	21.52	5.41	16.43	7.87
	OBC	49.19	43.45	61.3	67.72	54.77	71.18

Source: Census of India, 2011

Diversified religiousity is the beauty of our nation; North Bengal also has this diversity in it.

3.2 Sex and reproductive behaviour

Sex ratio, Child sex ratio, and child women ratio can portray many socio-economic and demographic perspectives. In table 2, the sex ratio is shown as the total number of women per 1000 male population. The sex ratio is highest in Darjeeling, followed by Dakshin Dinajpur and Jalpaiguri, and lowest in Uttar Dinajpur. The child sex ratio, on the other hand, is comparatively higher in Dakshin Dinajpur and Jalpaiguri than in other districts. In terms of child sex ratio, Koch Bihar disclosed the worst position. Child women ratio is the ratio of children aged 0 to 6 and women aged 15 to 49. Table 2 reveals that in Uttar Dinajpur, there are 70 children per 100 women of reproductive age 15-49 years. The lowest child-women ratio can be found in the Darjeeling district. It suggests that the fertility rate in Darjeeling is probably lower than in other districts, and in Uttar Dinajpur, the burden of children on women is probably higher. The average TFR of North Bengal is 2.3, but there was much variation among inter-district. Uttar Dinajpur is the highest TFR which is 3.1, followed by Maldah and Dakshin Dinajpur, Darjeeling and Jalpaiguri were the below replacement level.

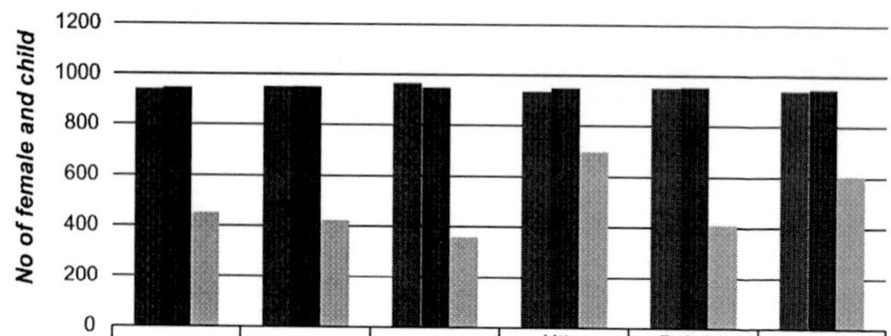

	Koch Bihar	Jalpaiguri	Darjiling	Uttar Dinajpur	Dakshin Dinajpur	Maldah
■ sex ratio	942	953	970	939	956	944
■ Child sex ratio	948	955	953	953	957	950
■ Child woman ratio	453	424	360	700	411	607

Fig. 1: Sex and Reproductive behaviour of North Bengal

Source: Census of India, 2011

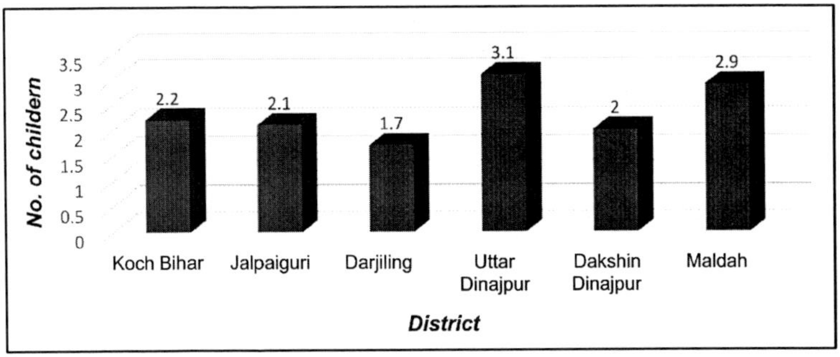

Fig. 2: Total Fertility Rate of North Bengal

Source: Census of India, 2011

3.3 Demographic characteristics:

Population density is highest in Maldah, with 1069 people per square kilometre, followed by Uttar Dinajpur, Koch Bihar, and Dakshin Dinajpur. The lowest population density is found in the Darjeeling district as most of the part of this district is characterized by hilly terrain and mountains; however, the density is far higher (586 per/sq. km) than the national average of 382 persons per sq. km. Uttar Dinajpur and Maldah secured their position at the top of the list in terms of growth rate. These two districts show relatively higher decadal growth between 2001 to 2011. Dakshin Dinajpur, Koch Bihar, Jalpaiguri districts show comparatively lower decadal growth rates. Literacy among the people of north Bengal also enormously varies between districts. Darjeeling has the highest literacy rate among north Bengal, 79.6 percent, followed by Koch Bihar, Jalpaiguri, and Dakshin Dinajpur. Uttar Dinajpur again shows the worst position in terms of literacy too. In terms of work participation, there is no such massive difference among districts. It is 41.9% in Dakshin Dinajpur, followed by Koch Bihar and Jalpaiguri; other districts have comparatively lower work participation rates. The crude birth rate has been calculated to determine the fertility differences; Table 3 shows that the CBR is highest in Uttar Dinajpur and Maldah. Darjeeling and Dakshin Dinajpur show an improved CBR.

Table 2
Demographic characteristics of North Bengal

District	Density (km/sq.)	Decadal growth rate (%)	Literacy rate (%)	Work participation rate (%)	Crude Birth Rate
Koch Bihar	832	13.7	74.8	40	15.22
Jalpaiguri	622	13.9	73.3	39.1	14.80
Darjeeling	586	14.8	79.6	37	12.78
Uttar Dinajpur	958	23.2	59.1	35.8	18.57
Dakshin Dinajpur	755	11.5	72.8	41.9	13.80
Maldah	1069	21.5	62.71	38.6	18.59

Source: Census of India, 2011

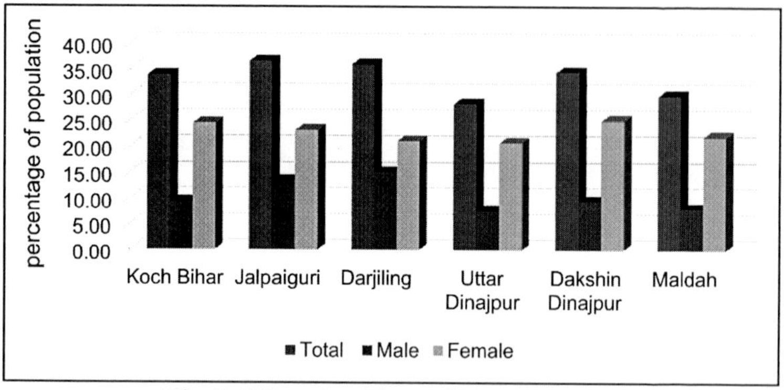

Fig. 3: Migration Rate of North Bengal
Source: Census of India, 2011

Migration is one of the essential factors of democratic change because of its effects on population composition and structure, and migration interacts with other demographic factors and other aspects of social and economic change and differentiation. Migration based on the last residence place reveals that the total migrants of a specific area with a point of time those places of enumeration and place of the last resident are different in the census enumeration time. Almost one in three persons in North Bengal consider as a migration based on the place of the last residence. Among male migrants, Darjeeling (14.98%) is the higher, followed by Jalpaiguri. Almost two to three out of ten females consider a migrant all over the district of North Bengal.

3.4 Age structure, Mean age and dependency ratio

The mean age is also known as the average age, is just the average age of a group of people. Table 4 depicts that the mean age at Darjeeling, Dakshin Dinajpur, Koch Bihar, and Jalpaiguri are more or less 29 years, whereas Uttar Dinajpur and Maldah have a lower mean age of about 26 years. The median age is higher in Darjeeling, Dakshin Dinajpur, Koch Bihar, and Jalpaiguri (varies from 25.3-26.9 years), and it is relatively lower in Uttar Dinajpur and Maldah (21.42 years and 22.32 years, respectively). The dependency ratio has been calculated to show the ratio between the dependent population (Children and elderly) and the working-age population. It does give an idea of economic dependency and the burden of dependent population on economically active working-age population. From table 4, it can be perceived that the dependency ratio is highest in Uttar Dinajpur, which is 69 dependent persons per 100 working-age people, followed by Maldah, Koch Bihar, Dakshin Dinajpur, Jalpaiguri, and lowest in Darjeeling (44.8).

Table 3

Age structure, Mean age and dependency ratio

District	Mean age	Median age	Dependency ratio	0-14 (%)	15-44 (%)	45-64 (%)	65+ (%)
Koch Bihar	29.00	25.57	50.07	28.55	49.84	16.79	4.81
Jalpaiguri	28.69	25.34	47.83	28.06	51.10	16.54	4.29
Darjiling	29.63	26.92	44.78	26.09	52.50	16.57	4.83
Uttar Dinajpur	25.98	21.42	69.26	37.10	45.37	13.71	3.82
Dakshin Dinajpur	29.45	26.41	49.11	28.06	49.79	17.28	4.88
Maldah	26.36	22.32	63.81	35.05	47.13	13.91	3.93

Source: Census of India, 2011.

Discussion

Changes in population size and composition may occur through the demographic component, namely, fertility mortality and migration. Population growth and distribution are crucial for any developed or developing region because land use pattern changes drastically with the increasing population (Kumar, 2016). The Maldah district shows the most significant share, followed by Jalpaiguri, Uttar Dinajpur, Koch Bihar, Dakshin Dinajpur, and Darjeeling. Our study finds that Uttar Dinajpur and Maldah has the highest population of growth rate in the region. The religious, geographical, political, and socio-economic history of Bengal makes it unique in the context of the Indian sub-continent (Kamal, 2009). This study reveals that Hindu and Muslim communities dominate almost all the districts of North Bengal. Jalpaiguri is the first position in terms of the Hindu population, which is near 82%, followed by Koch Behar. It may be further observed that Uttar Dinajpur and Maldah showed one Hindu and two Muslim populations. Age and Sex Compositions the essential characteristics of any population that affect its demographic and social, political, and economic structure. (Bhende and Kanitkar, 1991). Sex-ratio is the most significant demographic indicator that indicates the nature of population structure and gender-bias trends at any age. It also indicates women's status in society, their involvement in economic pursuits, and measuring the two sexes' gross fertility and relative mortality rates at different ages. The study reveals that the sex ratio is highest in Darjeeling, followed by Dakshin Dinajpur and Jalpaiguri, and lowest in Uttar Dinajpur. However, the child sex ratio is comparatively higher in Dakshin Dinajpur and Jalpaiguri than in other districts. Sex-ratio patterns in a population also measure dependency ratio and work-participation rate and also, directly and indirectly, reflect other social and economic correlates of the community (Banik, 2008). The Child-woman ratio is an essential indicator of reproductive behaviour, determined by the ratio of children under the age of five to per thousand women of child-bearing age, usually as 15 - 44.

One of the crucial findings is that Koch Bihar disclosed the worst position in child sex ratio in north Bengal. Occupation means gainful earning by cash or exchange of labour. Work participation rate and age dependency ratios are the measures for understanding economic life. The preceding analyses have examed that there is no such massive difference among districts in the region.

Moreover, the data shows Dakshin Dinajpur highest work participation rate, followed by Koch Bihar and Jalpaiguri; Other districts have comparatively lower work participation rates. Literacy is most important for any population. It develops employment opportunity and a way of life (Majumdar, 2003). The people of north Bengal also enormously varies in literacy rate. The results suggest that Darjeeling has the highest literacy rate, followed by Koch Bihar, Jalpaiguri, and Dakshin Dinajpur. It is clear from this study that Uttar Dinajpur has the worst position in terms of literacy rate. Fertility is the primary determinant of population change in any area. In our study, the crude birth rate has been calculated to determine the region's fertility differences. The data depicts that the CBR is highest in Uttar Dinajpur and Maldah, and Darjeeling and Dakshin Dinajpur show an improved CBR. We have also examined the mean age of the region, which shows that Darjeeling, Dakshin Dinajpur, Koch Bihar, and Jalpaiguri has higher; on the otherhand, Uttar Dinajpur and Maldah have a lower mean age. The average TFR of North Bengal near about replacement level which is 2.3, but there was much variation among inter-district. Uttar Dinajpur is the highest TFR which is 3.1, followed by Maldah and Dakshin Dinajpur, Darjeeling and Jalpaiguri were the below replacement level.

CONCLUSION

The demographic research may be identified by population growth and decline, population composition, and population distribution in space. Therefore, the fertility rate of North Bengal's population has identified tents to below the replacement level. The significant migration rate of the population in the region tent to decrease population pressure in the region. So it cannot contribute greater regarding population growth in the region. The above discussion concludes that north Bengal's demographic profile is significantly essential and it is necessary to understand the ever-growing population of the region in general and the socio-economic and political systems of the region in particular. Finally, we can suggest improvement from backwardness to mainstream. Therefore, to improve North Bengal, the socio- economic condition needs to more focus on all the region of the region. The government should take policy and awareness and so on.

REFERENCES

1. Banik, S. D. (2008). Demography of the Santals in West Bengal and Jharkhand: A comparative study. *Studies of Tribes and Tribals,* 6(1), 53-58.
2. Bhende, Asha & Kanitkar, Tara (1998). Principles of Population.
3. Bloom, D. E. (2011, January). Population dynamics in India and implications for economic growth. St. Gallen, Switzerland: WDA-Forum, University of St. Gallen.
4. Dey, P. P., & Chowdhury, R. S. (2013). A study on population dynamics and migration. *Journal of Interdisciplinary Mathematics, 16*(1), 37-48
5. Hauer, M., Baker, J., & Brown, W. (2013). Indirect estimates of total fertility rate using child woman/ratio: a comparison with the Bogue-Palmore method. *PloS one,* 8(6), e67226.
6. Kamal, N. (2009). *The population trajectories of Bangladesh and West Bengal during the twentieth century: A comparative study* (Doctoral dissertation, London School of Economics and Political Science (United Kingdom).
7. Kumar, D. (2016). Assessment of Population Dynamics Using Geographical Information System in Faridabad District, India. *International Research Journal of Earth*

Sciences, 4(2), 1-8.

8. Majumder, G. (2003). The Oraons of Barasat: A study on some aspects of demography. *Journal of Human Ecology, 14*(2), 133-136.
9. McGrady-Steed, J., & Morin, P. J. (2000). Biodiversity, density compensation, and the dynamics of populations and functional groups. *Ecology, 81*(2), 361-373.
10. Ranade, P. S. (1990). *Population dynamics in India.* APH Publishing.
11. Saxena, G. B. (1971). The *Indian population in transition.* Commercial Publications Bureau.
12. Studies, Himalaya Publishing House, Mumbai.

8

Evaluation of Rajbanshi Community: A Historical Assessment

Bishnu Barman[1] & Bappa Sarkar[2]

ABSTRACT

The Rajbanshi community of North Bengal is an indigenous tribal category. The Rajbanshi Community in North Bengal have consented in the district of Jalpaiguri, Alipur Duar, Dinajpur, Cooch Behar, and plain region of Darjeeling and some of North Bengal's Rajbanshi have been living in the others parts of West Bengal and Assam. There is much debate about the origin and ethnic identity of the dynasty; nevertheless, most scholars and historians agree that the Rajbanshi originated from Koch and belong to Indo-Mongoloid community. The people of this community generally have the features mixed up with all four human streams or cultures, i.e., Austral-Asiatic or 'Adivasi', Dravidian, Mongoloid, and Aryan. The community belongs to Indo Tibetan and Indo-Aryan Language families.

The Rajbanshi community of North Bengal speaks in a different dialect. The Rajbanshi community has a unique identity, traditional culture, and traditional food habits, traditional dresses.

Key Words : Rajbanshi or Koch Rajbanshi, indigenous tribe,

[1]Research Scholar of Raiganj University
[2]Assistant Professor, Dinhata College.
Email: bappa.geo001@gmail.com

Indo-Mongoloid, Dialect, Traditional Foods, Traditional Culture, Traditional Dresses.

Introduction

Koch Rajbanshis is one of the oldest aboriginal ethnic groups in South Asia. Presently they are found in three South Asian countries viz. India, Bangladesh, and Nepal. In India, they are predominantly found in four Indian states, West Bengal, particularly in North Bengal, Assam, and some parts of Bihar and Meghalaya. There are different views among historians and scholars about the origin of Koch Rajbanshis. But before going to the discussion on the origin of Koch Rajbanshis identity, it would be useful to have a short discussion on the use of the terms Koch and Rajbanshi synonymously as in the present study both the term has been used together. In her work Dynamics of a Caste Movement: The Rajbanshis of North Bengal, Swaraj Basu has given a clear picture of whether the terms Rajbanshi and Koch are synonymous or not. She has shown broadly two lines of argument regarding the origin of the Rajbanshis; one by colonial official-cum-ethnographers broadly, they can be considered orientalizes, and another by the Rajbanshi caste publicists (Basu 2003: 27). In the colonial writings, the Rajbanshis was generally regarded as the purified group of Koch who had adopted Hindu culture, tradition, and caste norms, leaving their traditional cultural practices and social norms. B.H. Hodgson, W.W. Hunter, and Herbert Risley are among the colonial writers who have opined that the Rajbanshis was a purified group of Koch who adopted Hindu culture and social norms during Viswa Singha's reign. The powerful Koch kingdom at the beginning of the sixteenth century. However, E.A. Gait, who also belongs amongst the colonial writer, stated a slightly different view. Based on the census report of 1901, he says that the Rajbanshis of Rangpur did not look like the Koches and sprang from an entirely different source. Gait believes that though there were many racial intermixtures in some places, the Rajbanshis belonged to a Dravidian tribe. In Jalpaiguri, Koch Bihar, and Goalpara in Assam, the people now known as Rajbanshi are either pure Koches who have distinctly Mongoloid features or a mixed type in which the Koch element usually prevails (Basu 2003: 28) 4 (Borah, 2016). Koch Rajbongshi is an ancient tribe originally from the ancient Koch kingdom. The Rajbongshi tribe is referred to as Koch Rajbongshi, or Rajbanshi, or Rajvanshi. The word "Rajbongshi" literally means "royal community." They have a rich cultural heritage and their language (Officials et al., 2021). The Rajbanshis, or the Koch-Rajbanshis, the latter term being more popular in Assam, constitute an important category of people spread over north-east India but especially in the contiguous areas of north Bengal and western Assam. The political boundaries of the present should not make us forget that the Rajbanshis are indigenous inhabitants also of the erstwhile Rangpur district and other adjacent areas of present day Bangladesh, and parts of eastern Bihar and Nepal Terai. In short, they appear to be concentrated during the historical period between 25° and 26°30' North latitudes, and 88° and 92° East longitudes (leaving the higher altitudes of Meghalaya but including the low-lying bordering areas of the Garo hills. It may also be mentioned that the Rajbanshi or Koch-Rajbanshi is an ethnic nomenclature that has been enriched over time through the accretion of members from other communities. The areas inhabited by the Rajbanshi community are included in the past within the kingdom of Kamatapur, which had frontiers on all sides without rigid boundaries, over the ruins of which at a later date emerged Koch Behar as a mighty kingdom challenging the Ahom supremacy to the further east. The discord over succession led to the split of the kingdom into two parts - the senior branch of the royal family continued to rule over the Rajbanshis, as they are known in North Bengal and lower Assam, are one of the oldest ethnic groups of North-Bengal. They are the descendants of Koches with Mongoloid physiognomy. Rajbanshi is an ethnic group found in North Bengal and neighboring areas. Now the question is whether the Rajbanshis are tribe, clan, race, community or caste. Rajbanshis are a bit shy in nature and not always ready to reveal theirs all about to others (Rajbongshi, n.d.). The word "Rajbanshis" literally means "royal community". They have a rich cultural ritual and their own language. Koch and Rajbanshis are actually two different tribes but united by the great king into one, hence named Koch Rajbanshis. They have a very strong history but a shaky present, and this is because of the lack of unity among these tribesmen that they have ceased to flourish in today's world (A. Das Gupta, 1857). According to Census 2001, Hindu Rajbansis are 129,904 in Darjeeling of total individual, 609,172; in Jalpaiguri 811,567 out of 3,401,173; in Cooch Behar 972,803 out of 2,479,155; in Maldah 144,158 out of 3,290,468; in Uttar Dinajpur 405,140 out of 2,441,794 and in Dakshin Dinajpur, 224,988 out of 1,503,178 and there of total 14,724,940 in North Bengal, Rajbansis have a population of 2,688,560 (18%). Rajbanshis are now fallen in the Scheduled Cast category. Rajbanshis talk in several dialects. Similarly, they are of several categories. Many non-Rajbanshi castes live long with the Rajbanshis and sometimes establish a successful marital relationship. These people in Rajbanshi dominated areas talk in Rajbanshi dialects. Rajbanshis are mostly Hindus and Vaishnavites, but it is also possible that many of them have converted to Islam. Tribal affiliations and contact with the mainstream by several means are two historical facts. They have certainly become a huge complex (agrarian cum pastoral) social fold (A. D. A. S. Gupta, n.d.).

1. What are their lives like?

Most of the Rajbanshi are farmers who survive on the produce of their own labour. Although they raise some livestock, they do not seem to consider the animals as a primary source of income. Instead, animal products are used as items to sell to purchase necessities that they can't make or grow themselves. A shortage of suitable arable land, overpopulation, and poor farming methods all contribute to a subsistence level of food production. Some have begun to earn money by weaving (they are excellent weavers), working for the Government, or finding employment in the private sector, but as a whole, they live impoverished lives. They are hesitant to change their lifestyle and struggle in their adaption to different types of work.

Houses made of wood, bamboo, thatch, and mud are clustered in villages ranging from ten to one hundred buildings. As in all patriarchal societies, the father is the undisputed head of the household. Most homes are composed of a basic family unit (parents and their children) until the oldest son marries. He and his wife than live with his parents until the second son marries. When the family head dies, all authority and responsibilities are transferred to the eldest son. Most marriages are arranged and conducted according to traditional Hindu rites and rituals.

The Rajbanshi dress very simply. Men wear knee-length dhotis, and languages (loincloths) and women wear *paetanis* (pieces of cloth wrapped around their bodies that provide a covering down to their knees). Western style clothing is slowly becoming more common (Language & Religion, 2021).

2. What are their beliefs?

The Rajbanshi are Hindus who worship millions of gods and goddesses. Every village has a separate hut dedicated to worshiping the goddess Kali (the goddess personifying creation). Festivals are called Pawni. Though they celebrate the Hindu festivals of Dasai and Tihar, the Rajbanshi do not observe them the same way Hindus do in India (Language & Religion, 2021).

3. What are their needs?

Nepal's Government is fiercely opposed to any form of evangelism and has implemented severe restrictions that result in harsh penalties for those who profess to be Christian. The tiny handful of Rajbanshi believers struggle against overwhelming odds, and many have been imprisoned for their beliefs. The Bible has not yet been translated into their language; the Jesus film is not available, and no Christian radio broadcasts are being aired in this region. There are currently no mission agencies working among these people.

With the minute number of Rajbanshi believers, the suppression of churches, and the lack of Bibles, Christian broadcasting, and missionaries in Nepal, the Rajbanshi have little chance of hearing the Gospel of Jesus Christ. Their isolation also makes it difficult for outsiders to reach them. In addition, people such as the Rajbanshi, who practice pantheism (the worship of many gods), find it very difficult to lay aside such beliefs and put all of their faith into one God (Language & Religion, 2021).

4. Actual Population of Koch Rajbongshis or Rajbongshis

Accurate data on the population of the Rajbongshi community cannot be made available now. Almost a century, the identity of Rajbongshis has become so confusing that no actual figure of their population could be finalized. This community never bothered about its actual population. As per survey reports of the British officials, initially, Rajbongshis were considered as a part of the mainstream caste Hindu Bengalis. After independence, the ground realities for the Rajbongshis turned into a quagmire as they became scattered in different states of India and neighboring countries, Bangladesh. When the question came for the annexation of Cooch Behar with West Bengal, that time too, Bengali leaders considered Rajbongshis as their integral part; thus, becoming a part of Bengal was an easy affair. But, over the years, this very idea has proved to be wrong. Rajbongshis could not be fully absorbed in the mainstream Bengali populace, as there remained certain basic differences. On the ground, their population surpasses almost ten million, but they are losing their existence literally on record. Nowhere in the literary circle or socio-economic-political circles names of Rajbongshis are heard of except that little mention made in some general knowledge books that too made obliquely, which is taken as derogatory by the educated and elite group of the community. To make a mention, we can refer to what is given in ManoramaYear book about this community."...The states of UP, West Bengal, Bihar, Tamil Nadu, and Andhra Pradesh account for more than 50% of the SC population, with UP and West Bengal having more than 20% of its population from SCs. Members of the SC earn their livelihood through their own labour, either on land belonging to others or in an occupation like scavenging, flaying and tannery of leather...". Such information can be contested as far as West Bengal is concerned. In North Bengal, the rural population mainly consists of Rajbongshis, who are farmers owning lands and not engaged in any type of menial professions like tannery or scavenging. They take pride in being *Kshatriyas*. It was sheer circumstantial that the Scheduled Caste (SC) status was given to them against their social standing, and that did cost the community heavily. Only the educational scholarship in the form of a monetary stipend and little job opportunities attract the theRajbongsh, which prevents them from contesting grant of SC status to their community. Most of the rural Rajbongshis, being poor or illiterate, are indifferent on such issues; whether called them SC, ST, OBC, or any category hardly makes a difference to them. Also, during the census, as Rajbongshi or Kamtapuri is not a recognized language, Rajbongshis find it confusing to indicate their spoken language in all the states or countries they reside. So there has been no proper census as far as this community is concerned. The only census that can be taken as authentic was the Rajbongshi population of the erstwhile Rajshahi Division (Now in Bangladesh) with its Headquarters at Jalpaiguri in North Bengal. As per details given, the total population in the Division stood as 9,130,072 in 1905, the majority were Muslims with 62.4%, followed by Hindus with 36.3% and the rest with 1.30%. It was mentioned in p.197, 'Gazetteer of Bengal and North-East India' written by B.C. Allen, E.A. Gait, CGS Allen & H.F. Foreword:'...About half the Hindus are aboriginal Rajbanshi and Koch, and the great majority of the local Muhammadans are the descendants of converts from these tribes. As such, the actual population of Rajbongshis of Rajshahi Division alone, which was Muslim-dominated, stood more than 3 million during that period. If the converted Muslims, who spoke the same language, were taken into account, the number would have doubled i.e., more than 6 million surprisingly, during the 1961 census only 31,472 heads of Rajbongshis were counted in the Darjeeling district of North Bengal, which appeared to be too minuscule keeping in view of the overwhelming majority of these people in its rural areas of Siliguri Sub-division. Another astonishing figure came to light about the Koches in Assam. As per 1961 census, only population of Koches was only 3,522. Today, the population of Koch Rajbongshis in Assam is estimated to be not less than 3.6 million, including around 30,000 original Bodo language-speaking Koch tribal. According to Dr. Girijasankar Ray, a renowned Rajbongshi scholar, the 1961 census total population of Rajbongshis, including Rajbongshi Kshatriyas of NorthBengal Koches of Assam and 'Palias' (a group of Rajbongshis) was 18,83,917. Their number surpasses the population of a number of smaller states of India such as Sikkim (0.05 million), Tripura (0.31 million), Mizoram (0.09 million), Manipur (0.23 million), Nagaland (0.19 million), Meghalaya (0.22 million), Jharkhand (0.62 million), etc. Rajbongshis are in absolute majority in rural areas of all the six districts of North Bengal - Cooch Behar, Jalpaiguri, Darjeeling (except hilly areas where 'Gorkhas' are in the majority), North Dinajpur, South Dinajpur, and Maldah; Purnia and Kishanganj districts of northern Bihar; Dhubri, Kokrajhar, Bongaigaon, Goalpara districts of Assam. In all other districts, especially in the whole Northern range up to Lakhimpur district, up to Nagaon district in the south bank of river Brahmaputra and in Barak valley in south Assam, a substantial population of Rajbongshis is found. In Garo Hills area of Meghalaya State, some parts of Tripura State, foothills of Bhutan and Jhapa and Biratnagar districts of the eastern part of Nepal, a good number of their population is found (Ray, 2013). An estimate of their population can be worked out as follows:

Region	Population
North Bengal	42,00,000
Assam	36,00,000
Bihar	12,00,000
Meghalaya	1,00,000

Nepal	3,00,000
Bhutan	2,00,000
Bangladesh	4,00,000

5. Broken Link with Rajbongshis of South Bengal:

It is generally believed that Rajbongshis of the southern part of West Bengal differ from their counterparts in North Bengal and Assam in many ways. Their similarity remains with the name and a little in physiognomy. They also have the features of Dravidian stock predominant; otherwise, Rajbongshis do have Mongoloid features predominantly. That variation might have taken place during the early period of Aryan culture when a group of *Kiratas and Pundra Kshatriyas* (ancestors of Rajbongshis) from 'Pundra' and 'Barendra' (Maldah and Dinajpur districts of North Bengal and parts of Bangladesh) migrated southwards, crossing the mighty river Ganga to reach the deltaic region of 'Banga' (South Bengal) to make fresh settlements. This was necessitated either due to defeat in the war with invading Aryan warlords from midland India or the spread of the epidemic in the region. As they had the royal link of the Pundra kingdom, naturally, they identified as Rajbongshi. As they were pushed further south in the deltaic region, they had hardly any cultivation and were forced to take up the profession of fishermen and other disciplines. On arrival of the Aryan culture, these people were not given any social status within the four 'Varna' system propagated by the Aryan sage Manu and thus obtained the status of 'Kayastha' that now form the majority of SC or the Other Backward Castes (OBC). Their spoken language is not pure Bengali but got some similarities with that of Rajbongshi language spoken in the Maldah area of North Bengal. Now they have an estimated population of 3,50,000 (Ray, 2013).

6. Origin of Rajbanshis:

The people of this community generally have the features mixed up with all four human streams or cultures i.e., Austral-Asiatic or 'Adivasi', Dravidian, Mongoloid, and Aryan, where Mongoloid features like short height, fair complexion and having flat nose are predominant. Some of them can be seen as tall, appropriate, and having sharp noses like people of north or midland Indians, who trace their origin in Aryan culture; Some of them can be seen as far as Aryan people at the same time some areas dark complexion as Adivasis or Dravidians. This was the region we can term as the eastern gateway of India or a meeting place where all four human streams got amalgamated, which gave birth to the new 'sanskritised' culture of the north-eastern part of India. While the civilization progressed towards modernity, Rajbanshis lagged behind mainstream cultures of Bengal and Assam due to their geographical division, political aberrations, and social degradation. *H.H. Risley,* in his work, *'The Tribes and Castes of Bengal', volume-I, page 491* wrote that Rajbanshis belonged to Dravidian origin. Similar views were expressed by *W.W. Hunter* in his work, *'Statistical Account of Bengal (Volume -X, page 402)*. Their views do have relevance as regards Rajbanshis of South Bengal, southern parts of North Bengal, and Bihar, as their features are predominantly Dravidian. According to Sir Gaits, these people were mixed of both the Mangoloid but Mongoloid features were predominant. Whatever the facts were, this particular community formed a major group of the ancient Indian population. The ancient Indians formed a large group of the population, and it was these people who were born introducing foreign cultures through the ages. The territory of their domain always acts as a buffer area between Australia-Asiatic, Dravidian, Mongoloid, and various human currents Lately Aryan culture. When the Aryanised people advanced to the eastern part of India, They were resisted by the people of Pundra (Eastster Bihar, southern Bengal) And West of Bangladesh, *Banga* (southern part of Bangladesh and South Bengal) and *Kamrup* (North Bengal and western part of Assam) all in a strong axis and delayed main Aryan thrust for centuries. Finally, these aboriginal people gave in to powerful Aryan cultured people who accepted the foreign culture. Subsequently, Aryan cultures overrun the axis to reach Brahmaputra valley in one direction and another to *Surma* valley (Barak valley or Cachar district in Assam and

Sylhet in Bangladesh). Ancestors of the Rajbanshi community were the settlers in semi-hilly terrains and plains of North Bengal, Assam, and their adjoining areas, who embraced the Aryan culture, later took to Hinduism. Here, Hinduism denoted the way of civilized life, following Vedic procedures of rituals and adoption of 'Sanskritised' Maithili Apabhramsa languages, which Aryan culture brought along with its advent into this part of ancient India (Ray, 2013).

7. Dadhhi Kada Festival in Ghailadubba:

Only Peoples from Rajbanshi Community in the world celebrate Dadhi Kado Festival on the occasion of Krishna Janma Asthami- the birthday of Lord Krishna. During this celebration, many games items are played like wrestling in Clay along with Coconut Shell, Tradition Pole Vault in Bamboo Stick, climbing banana tree in reverse posture i.e head down and legs up to get the coconut above the banana tree having approximate height 8 ft. The word Dadhi means Curd, Yoghart and Kad0 Mean Clay. As a belief Lord Krishna during his childhood, he used to play various games and sports and was fond of Curd. He played Dadhi Kado with clay coconut and Curd, so from time immemorial Rajbanshi's Started this celebration as they believe that lord Krishna himself comes to see the event and shower on the very day the blessing to the players. Rajbanshi peoples celebrate this festival playing Dadhi Kada and some calls it only nariyol khel. In these festivals, the youths make an arena full of clay and place one newly plucked coconut in the centre and a resemblance of temple of lord Krishna is kept in one end of the arena. The participants of nariyol khel (coconut game) try to put the coconut inside the temple and other tries to oppose them from entering the coconut into the temple. Crows of hundreds of people gathers to see the dadhi kadda festival. The participant who became able to put the coconut into the temple is declared the winner and is awarded suitable gifts and cash prize. The participants believe that if they win the game, they can get rain of blessing from Lord Krishna throughout their life, and every desire will be fulfilled without any hindrance. Here we have clicked some photos of today's dadhi kada (Nariyol Khel) held in one of the remote village of the Jhapa district of eastern Nepal. A game was held in Village Ghailadubba (Mantribari). According to history, the tradition of celebrating Dadhi kada started from the reign of Naranarayan, the great Koch King (15th century).

8. Recapitulation

Rajbanshis are one of the indigenous peoples in North Bengal who are very rich in their traditional culture. However, the hill to Terai migration has had a negative bearing on their traditional livelihood systems. Their culture is also fast being transformed due to the arrival of different social groups from the hills. Therefore, more efforts are to be made for their detailed holistic study of their traditional culture before its disappearance.

9. Economic System

Rajbanshis predominantly practice agriculture as their profession. They are very laborious. Prior to the 1960s, they, together with the Satars and Dhimals, were the only indigenous farmers of Jhapa. But the eradication of malaria in mid-1960s and the subsequent migration of the clever Brahmins, Chhetris, Rais, and Limbus triggered the grabbing of their traditional land resources through fair or foul means. Indeed, all this had the direct bearing on the reduction of their landholding and landlessness in some cases. The political economy of the state turned many landlords Rajbanshi into tenant farmers. Still, they are eking out their livelihood from their reduced size of landholding and tenanted land. Some even work as agricultural laborers. Of late, some Rajbanshis have turned to be petty businessmen and white-color job holders (Shrestha, 2002). Rajbanshis' main occupation is agriculture. Until the people from mountain areas moved down to Jhapa and Morang, Rajbanshi were both landowners and farmers. But the simple- nature Rajbanshis were entrapped into indebtedness by these settlers from outside and who took away our land. However, some well-to-do Rajbanshis are called deuniya Rest of the Rajbanshis have reached a state where we have to sell our property for buying subsistence level food. The Rajbongshis were traditionally agriculturalists, but due to their numerical dominance in North Bengal, there were significant occupational differences among them. Most were agricultural labourers (*halua*) or sharecroppers (*adhiar*). These often worked for landed cultivators, called dar-chukanidars. Above them were the *chukandiars* and *jotedars*, and at the top were the *zamindars*. Some Rajbongshis were *zamindars* or*otedars* (Adhikary, n.d.).

10. Land Holders of North Bengal

There were different categories of landholders in the northern part of present West Bengal. However, the classes which were eventually recognized in law and by sufferance were four i.e; *jotedar*, *Chukanidar*, *Dar-chukanidar* and *Adhiar.*

Jotedar: A *jotedar* is a person who holds land directly of Government. He is a tenant with a heritable and transferable title in his holding vested in him by the possession with the power to transmit this title to those he sublets. He has the right to resettle the land included in his jote on the expiry of the settlement term but subject to an increase of rent. His title to the possession of the land included in his *jote* is, however, always subject to the superior right of Government as proprietor to resume any portion required for public or other purpose or proportional abatement being made in the rental and compensation allowed for any payment improvement. A jote may be acquired by direct settlement, by purchase, and by inheritance.

Chukanidar: The tenant immediately below the *jotedars* is the *chukanidar* or *mulandar*. The rent payable by him is fixed. His title to his holding is heritable and transferable. He is not allowed under the provisions of the *jotedar's* lease to sublet the whole or any portion of the tenure under pain of immediate forfeiture of such tenure. But he is permitted to employ adhiars. *Chukanidars* cannot be ousted from his holding, except by order of a competent court, notwithstanding the fact that he may not have been twelve years on a *jote*. There is an unwritten land between him and his *jotedar* that he cannot be ousted from his land as long as he pays his rent.

Dar-Chukanidar: This class of tenants holds direct from the *Chukanidars*. The tenure rights of this class of tenants were neither found relevant by the Bengal Government nor approved by it. In a letter sent by the Revenue Department to Mr. Sunder, the settlement officer, it was stated, "The Lt. Governor approves your proposal that the newly created under-tenure of *dar-chukanidar* in the Duars estate should be ignored, as much as these tenures have been made contrary to the express order of the government". The *dar-chukanidar* was the under tenant of *chukanidars*. All these under-tenants had occupancy rights in Cooch Behar but not elsewhere.

Adhiar: *Adhiars* or Prajas are holders on the *metayer* system. They cultivate land immediately under the *jotedars*, chukanidars or a derivative *chukanidar*, but whatever the designation or status of the adhiars immediate superior be, he is known as the *adhiars giri*, half the produce of the land. The giri usually makes an advance of seeds and cash to the adhiar, which is adjusted when the produce is divided. The cattle and plough sometimes belong to the *giri*, sometimes to the adhiars. The legal status of various classes of *adhiars* unfortunately remained uncertain. As the *adhiar*s had to pay half of his produce, he was in a chronic state of debt and had very little means to improve his position. He had to take advance from his landlord to survive, and this the landlord realized with heavy interests during harvest time. There were no doubt variations in the position of *adhiars* in different areas of North Bengal. However, this section of the local peasantry had to bear the major burden of exploitation by the state and the landlord.

11. Migration of Population in North Bengal

Another important reason for land transfer to the non-Rajbanshis was the migration of a large number of outsiders to different districts of North Bengal. At the earlier stage, the attraction of this region was the abundance of land, the possibility of good business, job opportunities in government offices as the local people were not in a position to compete with them, opening of tea gardens which provide job facilities for both the "Babus? as well as labourers. Regular settlement work was undertaken, and the *Duars* had been brought under regular ministration providing security to the inhabitants. However, the most important factors that encouraged the migration of the landed entry were the land price and low rent compared to the situation in other parts of Bengal. Therefore, in the third settlement, a large number of people who were not born to the soil could obtain a lease from the Government as*jotedars* in the settled area. Someones acquired*jotes* through purchase. Escalation of land price caused by migration furthered transfer of*jotes* through sale to outside. In fact, the migrants were controlling many of the *jotes* paying revenue from Rs. 20 to 2000 per annum after the 1895 settlement in Western Duars. 29 Comparing the population statistics of the 1881 Census with that of 1891one finds an increase of 114277 in the population of the Western Duars.

12. Marriage Ceremony

The Rajbanshi community is found to marry according to Hindu traditions. People marry within their own community but outside their lineage. Marriage also does not take place within the three generations of the Mit (fictive kin) and seven generations of Guru (religious preacher). In the past, they had a system called the 'Chumana system' under which bride's parents were given money or articles of wealth-a remnant culture of bridewealth. But now this system has almost disappeared. Arranged marriage is generally preferred in the Rajbanshi community, albeit there is the occasional occurrence of love marriage. In the case of arranged marriage, Karuwa (matchmaker) initiates the marriage proposal and Gasain

Thakur performs the rituals. Once the zodiac of the prospective partners is found to be auspicious, the program of meeting the girl proceeds. Five people, including the groom's father and his relatives, visit the bride's home. The groom's father puts a pair of betel and nut (pansupari) on the bride's hand. At the same time, the groom's father examines the bride's nature, wisdom, and practical knowledge. Likewise, groom visit program by the bride's father takes place at the groom's home. The bride's father puts betel and nut Rs. 101, shirt, dhoti, watch, finger-ring, on the groom's hand. Then the auspicious marriage day is fixed. Marriage is not certain until Darahaguwa ritual is fulfilled. The decision is made on the day of Daraguwa. On this day, the clothes and jewelry as demanded by the bride's father are brought, and the decision is made. On the day of marriage or just before leaving for the marriage procession, the Kasakuta ritual is to be held according to which married sisters, aunts, and sisters-in-law prepare a mixture of turmeric, a bhojo (an herb) and oil and anoint it on the groom's body. Kasakuta is, in fact, a ritual for soul purity. Before leaving for the marriage procession, the Aam Mohaliwa ritual is performed in which the groom has to go around a mango tree five times, and money, betel, nut, and holy grass (dubo) are offered to worship the deities. On the day of the marriage procession, Gashain Thakur takes the groom to a temple of the family god and administers mantras in his ears for soul purification. Along with the preparation of the marriage procession, an object called Jivanchhuri (a full nut with a pierced knife) is placed on the hand of the groom. After this, the procession begins with bands and gunfire by riding buses or elephants in the past. Just before reaching the bride's home, children on behalf of the bride block the path to the people in the procession. They discontinue it only after the groom gives them some money. When the procession reaches the bride's home, the groom and bride get seated on Maruwa (dais or platform). Then, the bride's

Father offering his daughter to the groom, asks-" Have you got my daughter?" and the groom says-" Yes, I have." These sentences get repeated thrice. Then the father-in-law hands over his daughter to the son-in-law and utters him," Sin if killed and piety if cared for". After this, the groom puts vermillion on the forehead of the bride three times. At the time of putting the vermillion, the bride's younger sister and the relatives prevent the groom from doing so by blocking the bride's head with a piece of cloth. When the groom gives them some money, they stop doing it. Thus, the marriage is held. In the evening time, the procession returns home. Then, with much fanfare, the groom's mother makes the entry of the daughter-in-law including the procession to her home. At the marriage party, relatives, neighbors and villagers are invited for a meal. On this day, the newly wed couple serves Haldibhata (yellow rice) especially to the people present there. This practice helps to establish the new bride's identity and social acceptance and be socialized in the new social ambiance (Shrestha, 2002).

13. Death Ceremony

Among the Rajbanshis, the dead body is either buried or cremated according to the Hindu tradition. A baby with no teeth is buried, and there is no observance of the mortuary rite for him/her. Three to five-day long mortuary rite is observed for other minors with teeth. During the death of other people, it is observed for 13 days. The eldest son sets fire to the corpse of father or mother. The eldest or youngest son performs Malaluwa (mortuary rite), and other sons are just considered as ritually impure only. After burial or cremation at the funeral spot, the people in the death procession have a bath in the river and return home. Before a man participating in the procession enters his home, the dung or hay fire has to be placed in front of the main gate to his house for ritual purification. Along with it, a pot full of water with Tulasi (a holy plant) leaves is placed. All the men who have taken part in the funeral procession wash their hands and legs, touch fire and enter their homes. All the participants in the procession are served tea and lunch. The person who observes all the mortuary rites has to return home with a piece of white cloth tied to his neck. He observes ritual pollution for 13 days (Shrestha, 2002).

14. Family Structure

There is the existence of two types of family, namely, nuclear family and joint family. Slightly more than half of the families (53%) are nuclear, followed by 47 percent joint families. Gradually, there are now the preference of nuclear families as a function of the fragmentation of the landholdings, education of the youths and quarrel among the daughter-in-laws. These factors of the breakdown of the joint families are also ubiquitous among another caste/social groups in the study district. However, joint families are also equally emphasized due to the agrarian nature of the economy. Relatives in the Rajbanshi society have been classified into categories. These include the relatives by blood as 'Guthiyar', and (ii) relatives by marriage as 'Kutumba'.'Guthiyar includes the relations such as grandfathers, fathers, parental uncles, sons, nephews (brother's sons), grandsons, and great-grandsons. 'Kutumba' includes daughters-in-law and sons-in-law, nephews and nieces (sister's children), maternal uncles and aunts, brothers-in-law and sisters-in-law, father-in-law and mothers-in-law, etc. Besides these relations, there are other relations made by the society or social elites such as Mit, Mister, Mita, Gharamabapa, Dharamputra, and Danguwa Dhokar Beta (Shrestha, 2002).

15. The lineage of the Rajbanshi Communities

The Rajbanshis call themselves the descendants of Suryabansi and reveal their lineage (gotra) to be Kashyap. They follow Chhetri character and customs and add Singh and Rajbanshi to their names.The Koches call themselves the Rajput Chhetris. It is also said that Koch, Bhadai, Paliya, and Deshi, including the Rajbanshi caste, are the Dravidian castes of north-east and East Bengal. They are also thought to be a mixture of Mongolian blood, but they use Brahmins as priests in some of their religious rituals and follow the Hindu religion. There is no discrimination by status and level in their community. They can marry their co-lineage partners under the conditions of a seven generations' gap if the prospective partner is from the same village and 3-4 years' gap in the case of distant village. In the Rajbanshis community, 'Poruwa' is significantly emphasized. They take 'Poruwa' as their family god (ancestral deity). Such 'Poruwas' are of 16 types, namely, Chaitan, Nityananda, Aadit, Satguru, Ramaut, Thunthunia, Lakhigadhadar, Chaturmaria, Bholoram, Chanatkhela, Udit, Jagbandhu, Dhadigar, Kabir, Sitaudit, and Tulsia. There are different kinds of Rajbanshis such as Koch Rajbabshi, Poundra Rajbabshi, Mech Rajbabshi, Newar Rajbanshi, and Khataha Rajbanshi.

16. Food Habit of Rajbanshi Communities

As the Rajbanshis people became Hindus, so they ate everything in accordance with the Hindu religion, but some special food or items are consumed by the Rajbanshis of which Chheka Shak' is one of the delicious food of the Rajbanshis which is cooked by different types of vegetables especially mixing with one kind of soda. Another delicious food is eaten by the Rajbanshis people locally known as Sutka and Sidal. Sutka means dry fishes, and sidal is made by crashing of small dry fishes, spices, turmeric, and chilly, and all these are crushed in a husk locally called chham and Gain. Pelka', one kind of delicious vegetable item to the Rajbanshis, is one kind of traditional food which is mainly cooked with vegetables, specially Lapha shak'. Dai and Chira are favorite to the Rajabanshi people. Rajbanshis like to eat very much pan and supari locally known Gua pan', gua' means raw betel nut. They honored their guest by offering gua pan at the initial stage of receiving. Many of them always keep this gua pan in their pocket or small container, and gradually they eat this after some duration. Later on, after the huge number of people migrated to North Bengal, many indigenous foods were taken as the food of the migrated people; on the other hand, the indigenous people were habituated with the food habit of the migrated people. Not only that, the indigenous people accepted the process of cooking and spices from the migrated people. Besides these, after independence and partition, the spread of education accelerated, many schools, colleges, institutions were established, as a result of which many indigenous people came under the education. They became educated, and many of them got services, the number of employees increased day after day. These educated people went out of the house, settled into different places, and started to live different places of the country. As a result, they gradually became habituated with the food habit of multi-character dishes. The food habit of the educated people automatically influenced the other people of the villages. For example, many people of Rajbangsi Community used burning fishes as their food, but the new generation people including educated people, do not use various types of spices, simply they used turmeric, cumin, coriander etc. dusting in the traditional husking machine, nowadays they use various types of spices purchasing from the market. In this regard, Sitangshu Prosad chakraborty stated, Relating food habit they also habituated with modern food habit at present, particularly, the educated Rajbanshis and the Rajbanshis of urban areas use modern food instead of taking their traditional food habit such as pelka, chheka, sidal- sutki (Shrestha, 2002). They sometimes eat their traditional food like pelka, sutka sidal, chheka etc. But usually they use all the food which is eaten by other Bengali people. There are no vast differences between our food habit and the food habit of other Bengali people. The Rajbanshi people are habituated with the modern food habits and the food habits of Bengali people (Bhawal, 2015).

17. Dress of the Rajbanshi

Upendra Nath Barman stated, "it is known that the women of Rajbanshi community wearied a dress called Buki (Bukali) and it was prevailing since ancient time. Apart from this the two parts of dress named Riya and Mekhla were used by the women. It should be mentioned here that the men of poor families wearied small dhoti from the upper side of the knee and the very poor men wearied a piece of cloth called Nengti'. At the time of continuing, social reforms movement Thakur Panchanan Barma propagated to wear dhoti instead of

Nengti'and sari of women instead of Buki'.17 Advance group among the Rajbansis whom we may refer to in the absence of a better term as the Rajbansi elites', followed the upper caste Hindus of the region in dress, lifestyle, marriage customs, and religious practices. 'According to C.C. Sanyal,-Discarding their traditional clothes, both men and women dressed in the fashion of the upper castes in society. All the indigenous people started slowly to wear a modern dress like other people of mainstream. The young generation, both male and female, are habituated with the modern dresses they started to wear pant, shirt, shoe, etc. The girls and female wear churidar or salwar kamij, frok, sarees etc, not only that, presently, the female also wear the dresses of the male such as pant, shirt etc. The old men wear Dhoti, Punjabi also pant, shirts etc. Nowadays, almost all the indigenous people have been wearing the modern dress, no differences are followed in terms of dresses between the indigenous people and the immigrated people. For the emergence of global culture, no man can deny accepting the global culture. So, now a day's no man can be identified of which community they belong to with their dresses because of the abolition of traditional dresses except few instances and increasing the modern dress-habit.

18. Language and Dialects of Rajbanshi

Kamtapuri/Rajbanshi, also called Rajbanshi is a Tibeto-Burman cum Indo-Aryan language spoken in India, Bhutan Bangladesh, and Nepal. Rajbanshi belongs to the combined language family of Tibeto-Burman cum Indo- Aryan language family. According to a 1991 census, it was spoken by 5 million people. This language is not a dialect of Bengali language or Assamese Language. It has its own identity. "Kamtapuri" language would be included soon under the eighth schedule of the constitution of India. This is the native language of Cooch Behar, Lower Assam, Jalpaiguri, North Dinajpur, South Dinajpur, Terrai of Darjeeling, Upper Maldah, a portion of Bihar, Some parts of Bhutan, Bangladesh & Nepal. Other names of the language are Rajbangsi, Rajbansi, Rajbanshi, Tajpuri, Surjyapuri, Kamrupi, Deshi Bhasha.

Recently "Kamtapuri Bhasha Academy" (2017) is formed by West Bengal Government. **Rajbangshi**, **Rangpuri** or **Kamatapuri**, is a Bengali-Assameselanguage spoken by the Rajbongshi people in India and Bangladesh. Many are bilingual in either Bengali or Assamese. Together withRajbanshi, it forms the KRNB lects. George Abraham Greearson published his research report in 'Linguistic Survey of India' in 1927 where he mentioned 'when we cross the river (Brahmaputra) coming from Dacca, we meet a well-marked form of speech in Rangpur and the districts to its north and east. It is called Rajbansi and, while undoubtedly belonging to the eastern branch', it still has points of difference that lead us to class it as a separate dialect. He also wrote 'The dialect is usually known as Rajbansi, from the tribe of that name already alluded to'. It is also frequently called Rangpuri from one of the districts in which it is spoken. In the Darjeeling Terai, the dialect is influenced by the neighboring Northern Bengali and has a special name, as a sub-dialect viz Bahe. The Rajbanshi language is a dialect of main Bengali language. Provat Ranjan sarkar stated the language of Rajbansis of North Bengal as Rangpuri Bangla.Upendranath Barman stated that the Rajbanshi language is a pure Aryan language supported by scholars like Hodson, etc. Dr. Charu ch.Sanyal wrote, The Rajbansis speak Bengali, but it is a local dialect sometimes widely away from standard Bengali. The main dialects are Western Rajbanshi, Central Rajbanshi, Eastern Rajbanshi, and the dialect of the Rajbanshi of the hills, also known as Koch language. The Central dialect has the majority of speakers and is quite uniform. The Western dialect has more diversity. Lexical similarity is 77% to 89% between the three dialects. But the dialect spoken in the hills has some influence of the local tribal languages. Koch Rajbonshi Sahitya Sabha has given the emphasis on bringing a unique identity of the Rajbonshi language (Officials et al., 2021).

CONCLUSION

Koch **Rajbongshi** is an ancient tribe originally from the

ancient Koch kingdom. The Rajbongshi tribe is referred to as Koch Rajbongshi, or Rajbanshi, or Rajvanshi..Rajbanshi is an ethnic group found in North Bengal and neighboring areas. Now the question is whether the Rajbanshis are tribe, clan, race, community, or caste. Rajbanshis are a bit shy in nature and not always ready to reveal theirs all about to others (Rajbongshi, n.d.). The word "Rajbanshis" literally means "royal community". They have a rich cultural ritual and their own language. Koch and Rajbanshis are actually two different tribes but united by the great king into one, hence named Koch Rajbanshis. Rajbanshi in north Bengal are the tribal community. They have a unique identity, traditional food habits, traditional culture. **Kamtapuri/Rajbanshi**, also called Rajbanshi, is a Tibeto-Burman cum Indo-Aryan language spoken in India, Bhutan, Bangladesh, and Nepal. Rajbanshi belongs to the combined language family of Tibeto-Burman cum Indo- Aryan language family. The main dialects are Western Rajbanshi, Central Rajbanshi, Eastern Rajbanshi, and the dialect of the Rajbanshi of the hills, also known as Koch language. The Central dialect has the majority of speakers and is quite uniform. The Western dialect has more diversity. Lexical similarity is 77% to 89% between the three dialects.

REFERENCES

1. Adhikary, M. C. (n.d.). Socio-Economic Transformation of North Bengal in Post Colonial Era: A Case Study of the Rajbanshis. 1-13.
2. Bhawal, P. (2015). Evolution of Rajbanshi Society: A Historical Assessment. 20(10), 56-61. https://doi.org/10.9790/0837-201015661
3. Borah, P. (2016). Ethnic Movements in Assam: A Study of Koch Rajbanshis Submitted by. 1-139.
4. Das Gupta, A. (1857). Culture survival for the indigenous communities with reference to North Bengal, Rajbanshi people and Koch Bihar under the British East India Company.

5. Gupta, A. D. A. S. (n.d.). Indigenous Peoples of Sub- Sub - Himalayan North Bengal with Special Reference to the Rajbanshis Indigenous Peoples of Sub- Sub - Himalayan North Bengal with Special Reference to the Rajbanshis.

6. Language, M., & Religion, L. (2021). Rajbansi (Hindu traditions) in Nepal. 1-9.

7. Message, S. (2021). Rajbanshi. 2021, 1-7.

8. Officials, K., Projects, U., Message, W. Y., Gallery, P., Links, W., Us, A., ... Sanmilani, K. R. (2021). The Portal of North Bengal Development Department Koch Rajbongshi people The Portal of North Bengal Development Department. 2-3.

9. Rajbongshi, T. (n.d.). Rajbongshi people.

10. Ray, N. R. (2013). Koch Rajbanshi and Kamtapuri. 1-137.

11. Shrestha, K. K. (2002). Ethnography of Jhapali Rajhbanshi. Nepal Journal Online, 11, 38-47.

9

Indigenous Medicinal Plants of Cooch Behar District Used in The Treatment of Skin Diseases: A Review

Aninda Mandal[1]* & Debarun Chakraborty[2]

ABSTRACT

Since ancient times indigenous people are dependent on their surrounding plants for their livelihood, especially for ethnomedicine. In India, plant resources have been used to treat various diseases since the Buddhist era. Skin diseases are a major health problem affecting people of all ages. A systematic web search analysis using Google scholar, PubMed, Google, AJOL, Research Gate etc. was performed on research articles pertaining to medicinal plants used for treatment of skin diseases in Cooch Behar district of West Bengal, India. Based on published ethnobotanical reports, the present review is conducted to document the use of medicinal plants in treating skin diseases by the ethnic people of Cooch Behar district of West Bengal, India. A total of 29 medicinal plants representing 17 families are documented for their therapeutic use against 16 different types of skin problems. Asteraceae has the highest number of plants (5). The dominant life form

[1]Department of Botany, A.B.N. Seal College, Cooch Behar-736101, West Bengal, India

[2]Department of Botany, Cooch Behar Panchanan Barma University, Cooch Behar-736101, West Bengal, India.

*Email: mandal:aninda@gmail.com

Mobile: +91-9434602182

recorded to be herb (58.62%) while the preferred mode of preparation is paste (30.43%), along with leaf (51.52%) as the most used plant part. The present review revealed that the ethnic people of Cooch Behar district are primarily dependent on ethnomedicine for the treatment of skin diseases. More research is needed to assess active constituents as well as any other beneficial plant products available from the local flora for the benefit of mankind's future generations.

Key Words : Cooch Behar, Ethnic group, Ethnomedicine, Medicinal plants, Skin diseases.

Introduction

Since immemorial, ethnic people have depended on medicinal plants for the treatment of diseases and disorders (Singh, Tripathi, & Shukla, 2003; Sofowora, Ogunbodede, & Onayade, 2013) and the most ancient records of ethnomedicinal uses of plants are available in the form of Vedas, Samhitas and Epics like Ramayana and Mahabharata (Mandal et al. 2020a). India has a vast emporium of ethnobotanical and folklore wealth (Thomas, Arumugam, Veerasamy, & Ramamoorthy, 2014) and the ethnic communities of the rural area are still dependent upon the wild plant species for the treatment of diseases. About 65% of Indians are directly dependent on the folk medicine (Bhatt, Mitaliya, Patel, & Ant, 2002). As per the World Health Organization (WHO) more than 80% of the world population is dependent on traditional medicine for their primary health care (WHO, 2003).

Skin diseases are very common human health problem. Skin, being a sensitive organ and due to its continuous exposure to the environmental stress, millions of people of all ages are affected by skin diseases annually (Tripathi & Srivastava, 2010) of which rural people are mostly affected due to poor hygienic conditions, poor sanitation facility and use of contaminated water (Buragohain & Konwar, 2007; Panthi & Singh, 2013; Policepatel & Manikrao, 2013). Dermatological problems have been considered as the fourth leading cause of nonfatal disease burden worldwide (Hay et al., 2014). Skin diseases associated with unfavorable looks pushes a patient into psychic conditions (Dawid-Pa?, 2013). Various skin diseases like eczema, leucoerma, ringworm, scabies, etc. are treated completely with herbal medicines (Policepatel & Manikrao, 2013). Skin diseases caused by bacteria, fungi and viruses are treated with hundreds of medicinal plants worldwide (Prashant Kumar & Vidyasagar, 2008) and 80% of the Indian population uses ethno-medicines to treat skin problems (Tabassum & Hamdani, 2014).

Now-a-days, use of modern medicine is a common practice in the modern world to get relief from the diseases but they have severe side effects also. On the other hand, the herbal medicines are cost effective and ingredients of these formulations are easily available to the ethnic people. Ethnic people are a rich depository of indigenous traditional knowledge on medicinal plants and the knowledge is exclusive to them only and rarely documented and most of the knowledge passed down from one generation to another by verbal communication. In-spite of several advantages of herbal medicines, the younger generations of ethnic communities showing less interest on traditional knowledge due to modernization (Uniyal, Singh, Jamwal, & Lal, 2006; Mandal et al., 2020b). In recent years, the natural habitat of medicinal plants and traditional culture of India are facing threat of extinction due to various anthropogenic activities (Bhattacharjee, 2001; Mandal et al., 2020b). So, it is utmost necessary to document the traditional knowledge on medicinal plants before they become lost forever.

The review is a small endeavor to record the medicinal plants which are safely used by the ethnic communities of Cooch Behar district of West Bengal for the treatment of different types of skin diseases.

Cooch Behar, a district of north-eastern part of the state of West Bengal (Fig. 1), situated at the foothills of Eastern Himalayas (26°22'N 89°29'E) is in the under developing status and mostly the rural people depend on medicinal plants in the treatment of common physical ailments (Mandal et al., 2020a). Major ethnic groups are Rajbanshi, Rava, Santhals, Oraon, Kheria, among others (Bandyopadhyay, 2017). Scientific documentation of medicinal plants was done earlier by several workers in the district (Bandyopadhyay & Mukherjee, 2005; Bandyopadhyay & Mukherjee, 2006; Chowdhury & Das, 2007; Bandyopadhyay & Mukherjee 2010; Bandyopadhyay, Mitra, & Mukherjee, 2014; Datta, Patra, & Dastidar, 2014; Roy, 2015; Bandyopadhyay, 2017; Bandyopadhyay, 2018; Pala et al., 2019; Mandal et al., 2020a). The present work encompasses all the records exclusively the plants used for the treatment of different types of skin diseases published earlier from the district.

Data collection

Published articles were retrieved from the online bibliographical database Ethno-botanical and/or ethnomedicinal surveys reporting on medicinal plant species used for traditional skin diseases treatment in Cooch Behar district were gathered. Search engines includes Google scholar, PubMed, Google, AJOL, ResearchGate, etc. Literature search was performed using the keywords like ethnomedicinal plants for skin, ethnobotany of Cooch Behar district, ethnomedicinal plants of Cooch Behar, plants used for dermatological problems, indigenous plant knowledge, traditional knowledge, traditional healer, herbal remedies, folk medicine, skin diseases, ethnomedicine, ethnic people and tribal people.

More web searches were performed at the Google search engine using more general keywords like skin diseases, dermatological problems, medicinal plants, herbal medicine, ethnic communities, tribal communities, traditional medicine, ethnobotany, etc. combined with either Cooch Behar district, North Bengal or West Bengal.

Screening and criteria

Screening of web search outputs was performed only by focusing on the plants with the potential traditional usage against various skin diseases. At first the title and the abstract of the relevant research articles was examined and then the articles were downloaded and carefully scrutinized for inclusion in the present review.

Inclusion and exclusion criteria

Only full-text original research articles published in peer-reviewed journals and books on ethnomedicinal plants used in the treatment of skin diseases in Cooch Behar district written in English and up to date were considered.

Results and discussion

The present review exhibited ethnomedicinal use of 29 plant species belonging to 29 different genera and 17 families (Table 1) used by different ethnic communities of Cooch Behar district of West Bengal to treat various skin diseases. Plants are arranged in alphabetical order according to families and then according to genus and species within - each family. Information regarding vernacular name(s), scientific name, family, habit, parts used, ethno-preparation, folk claim and ethnic community using them for each species have also been provided.

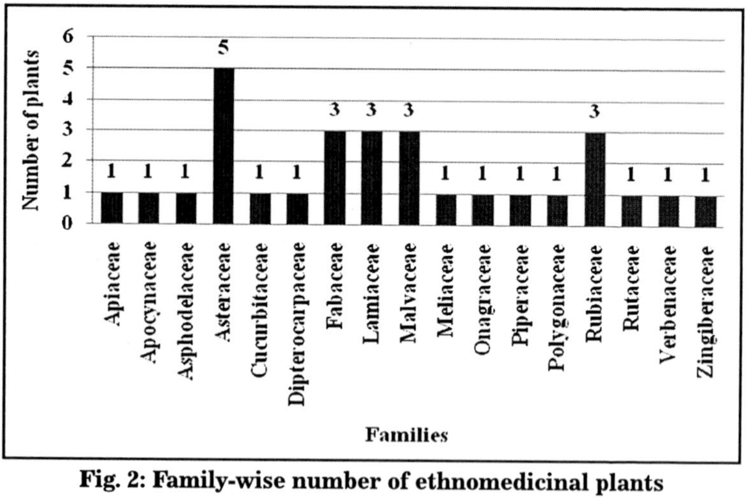

Fig. 2: Family-wise number of ethnomedicinal plants

A total of 17 families (Fig. 2) have been documented in this review of which the plant family Asteraceae (17.24%; 5 species) is represented by highest number of ethnomedicinal plant species followed by Fabaceae, Lamiaceae, Malvaceae andRubiaceae (10.34%; 3 species each) and the rest 12 families represented by single species (3.45%). Asteraceae, the most diverse plant family with a large number of species (Barker et al., 2008), contain effective bioactive compounds to treat several diseases (Tariq, Musarat, & Adnan, 2015) and are used

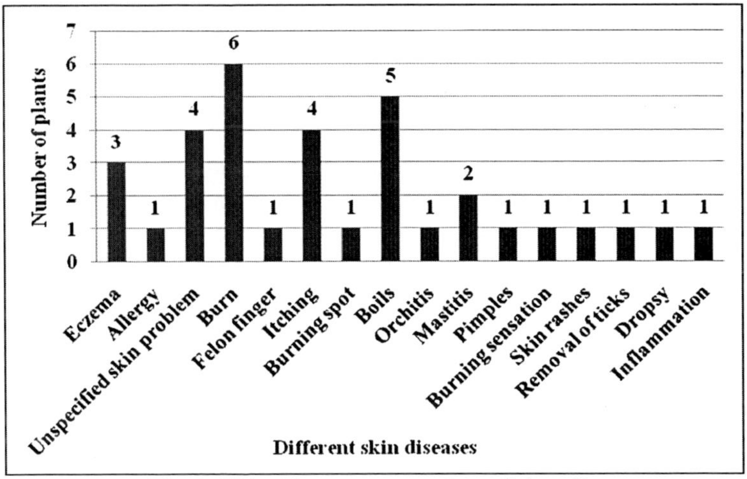

Fig. 3: Skin diseases treated traditionally

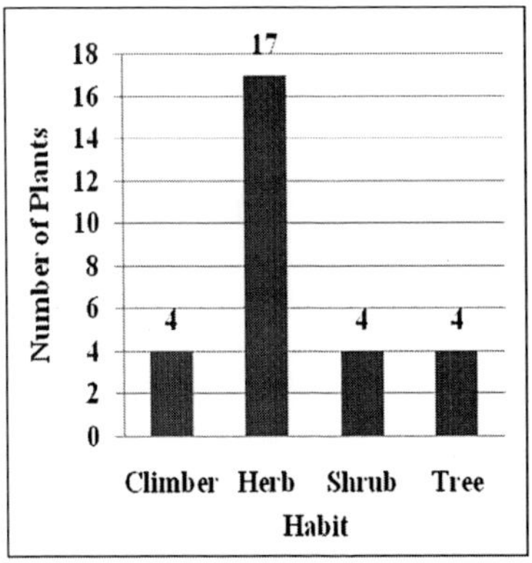

Fig. 4: Growth habit of plants

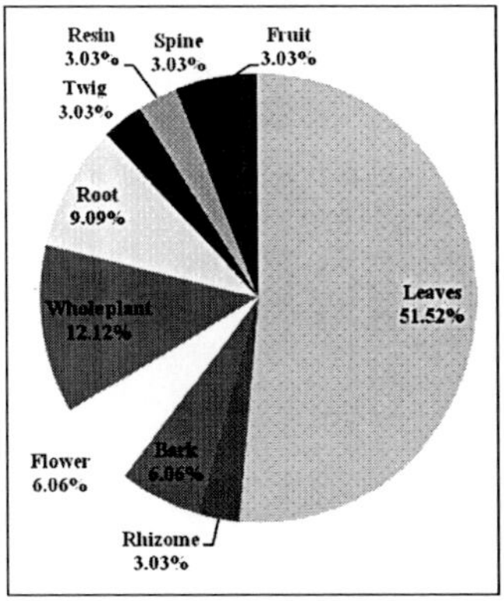

Fig. 5: Parts used for herbal Preparation

frequently in ethnomedicine (Kumar, Sharma, Manhas, & Bhatia, 2015).

Altogether 16 different types of skin problems (Fig. 3) are recorded to be treated using medicinal plants. Most common of them are found to be burns (17.65%) followed by boils (14.71%), itching (11.76%), eczema (8.82%), mastitis (5.88%), allergy, felon finger, burning spot, orchitis, pimples, burning sensation, skin rashes, removal of ticks, dropsy and inflammation (2.94% each). In case of four species (11.76%), particular category of skin diseases are not mentioned in the surveyed literature.

Growth habit (Fig. 4) of the plant species shows that herb (17 species, 58.62%) dominates among the plant type followed by climber, shrub and tree (4 species each, 13.79%). Herbs mostly used in ethnomedicine in most areas of the world due to their abundance and easy collection method (Ahmad, Qureshi, Arshad, Khan, & Zafar, 2009).

Ethnomedicines for skin diseases mostly prepared from leaves (51.52%) followed by whole plant (12.12%), root (9.09%), bark and flower (6.06% each), and spines, rhizome, fruit, twig

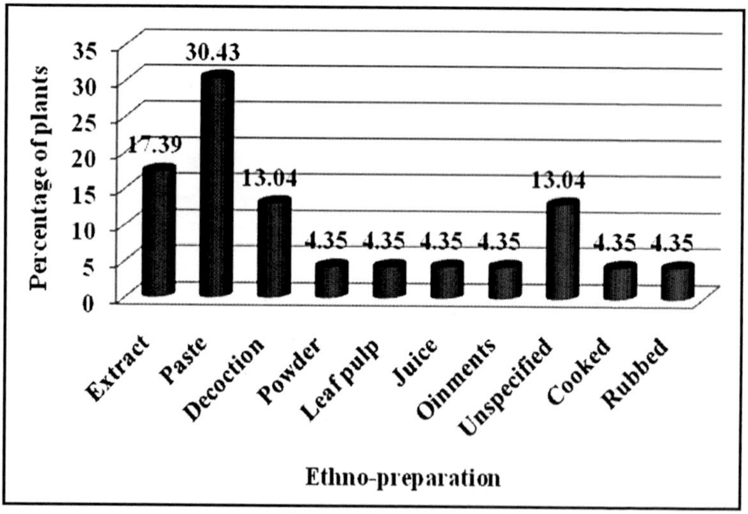

Fig. 6: Mode of preparation of plants.

and resin (3.03% each) (Fig. 5). Leaves are the most commonly used plant part used in the preparation of ethnomedicine (Raj et al., 2018; Mandal et al., 2020a, 2020b).

Mode of preparation (Fig. 6) of the ethnomedicine includes paste (30.43%), extract (17.39%), decoction (13.04%), powder, juice, leaf pulp, ointments and cooked (4.35% each) while, ethno-preparations in few cases (13.04%) are not clearly mentioned in the literature. In a single case, wet twig (4.35%) of a plant is rubbed over the body of cattle to remove tick from the skin. The herbal medicines are commonly administered topically but in most cases mode of administration is not clearly mentioned in the literature. Depending upon the skin problem different types of plant part and ethno-preparation are used to treat the diseases (Watt & Breyer-Brandwijk, 1962). Topical application is common and beneficial because it ensures direct interaction of the plant's active constituents with the skin and gives instant relief (Felhaber, 1997). The reviewed articles do not give any proper information regarding the dose of the medicine.

CONCLUSION

The present review reveals that a number of species are used by the different ethnic groups of Cooch Behar in the treatment of skin diseases. These plant species may disappear from the locality in near future due to anthropogenic activities. Therefore, immediate measures should be taken to protect these important medicinal plant species as well as the traditional knowledge as day-by-day the knowledge is vanishing due to modernization of ethnic people. Majority of the studies have not documented the dose of ethnomedicine. So, comprehensive ethno-pharmacological studies should be carried out to establish a safe dose range.

ACKNOWLEDGEMENT

The authors are thankful to the Principal, A. B. N. Seal College and Head, Department of Botany, A. B. N. Seal College, Cooch Behar for providing necessary facilities. This work is supported by the grant (Memo No: 682/(Sanc.)/BT/

Table 1
Medicinal plants used by ethnic people of Cooch Behar district in treating skin diseases.

SN	Vernacular name(s)	Scientific name	Family	Habit	Part(s) used	Folk claim	Ethno-preparation	References
1.	Thankuni (Ra), Khudaman amoni (Sa)	*Centella asiatica* (L.) Urban	Apiaceae	Herb	Leaves	Eczema	Leaf extract is used to cure Eczema.	Datta et al., 2014
2.	Chatim, Chhatni (Ra), Chhatiani (Sa)	*Alstonia scholaris* (L.) R.Br.	Apocyna-ceae	Tree	Bark	Skin problem	Bark paste is smeared against the infected part of the body.	Pala et al., 2019
3.	Aloe vera, Ghritakumari (Ra, Sa)	*Aloe vera* (L.) Burm.f.	Asphode-laceae	Herb	Leaf pulp	Burn	Leaf pulp is applied to the burnt skin.	Pala et al., 2019
4.	Darya-arak (Sa), Kuksim(Rj)	*Cyanthi-llium cinereum* (Carl Linnaeus) H.Rob	Asterac-eae	Herb	Leaves	Felon Finger	Paste of leaf is used externally in "Anguthora" (Felon Finger).	Bandyopa-dhyay et al., 2014

SN	Vernacular name(s)	Scientific name	Family	Habit	Part(s) used	Folk claim	Ethno-preparation	References
5.	Keshoot (Rj), Kala Kesuri(Kh), Kekuria (Sa)	*Eclipta prostrata* (L.) L.	Asterac-eae	Herb	Whole plant	Itching	The paste of the plant is fried in mustard oil and is applied externally in itching.	Bandyopa-dhyay & Mukherjee, 2005a; Bandyopa-dhyay et.al., 2014
					Leaves	Burning spot	Leaves used to remove Burning spot.	Roy, 2015
6.	Hinchya, Helencha (Rj)	*Enydra fluctuans* Lour.	Asterac-eae	Herb	Whole plant	Itching	The juice of the plant is slightly warmed and is given cure (2 full teaspoons) twice daily for itching.	Bandyopa-dhyay et al., 2014

SN	Vernacular name(s)	Scientific name	Family	Habit	Part(s) used	Folk claim	Ethno-preparation	References
7.	Gada, Ganda (Ra, Or)	*Tagetes erecta* L.	Asteraceae	Herb	Leaves	Burn	Freshly prepared leaf extract is used to heal burnt area.	Mandal et al., 2020a
8.	Tridaksha	*Tridax procumbens* L.	Asteraceae	Herb	Leaves	Boils	Paste of leaves is applied externally on boils for suppuration.	Bandyopadhyay et al., 2014
9.	Chal-kumra	*Benincasa hispida* (Thunb.) Cogn.	Cucurbitaceae	Climber	Fruit	Burn	-	Bandyopadhyay & Mukherjee, 2010
10.	Saulo Fung (Ra)	*Shorea robusta* Roth.	Dipterocarpaceae	Tree	Dry resin	Burn	-	Chowdhury & Das, 2007

SN	Vernacular name(s)	Scientific name	Family	Habit	Part(s) used	Folk claim	Ethno-preparation	References
11.	Lajjawati, Lajnu (Sa)	*Mimosa pudica* L.	Fabaceae	Herb	Leaves	Burn	-	Bandyopa dhyay, 2018
					Leaves and Bark Orchitis.	Orchitis	Decoction of leaf and bark is used to control	Pala et al., 2019
12.	Kurali (Rj)	*Grona triflora* (L.) H. Ohashi & K. Ohashi	Fabaceae	Herb	Whole plant	Boils	-	Bandyopa-dhyay, 2018
13.	Barachakar (Kh)	*Senna alata* (L.) Roxb.	Fabaceae	Shrub	Leaves	Itching	-	Bandyopa dhyay, 2018
14.	Madhuful (Or)	*Leucas aspera* (Willd.) Link	Lamiac-eae	Herb	Leaves	Itching	Mature leaves are boiled in oil and then applied to treat itching.	Mandal et al., 2020a

SN	Vernacular name(s)	Scientific name	Family	Habit	Part(s) used	Folk claim	Ethno-preparation	References
15.	Ram tulsi	*Ocimum gratissimum* L.	Lamiaceae	Herb	Leaves	Skin problem	Decoction of leaves is given to cure skin problems.	Pala et al., 2019
16.	Nishinda (Kh)	*Vitex negundo* L.	Lamiaceae	Shrub	Root	Mastitis in cattle	Root paste is applied to the infected area.	Bandyopadhyay & Mukherjee, 2005b
17.	Shimuli (Rj)	*Bombax ceiba* L.	Malvaceae	Tree	Spine	Pimples	Spine used like sandal to cure pimples.	Roy, 2015
18.	Joba(Ra, Sa)	*Hibiscus rosa-sinensis* L.	Malvaceae	Shrub	Leaves	Burning sensation	Leaves used to treat burning sensation and other skin problems.	Datta et al., 2014; Pala et al., 2019

SN	Vernacular name(s)	Scientific name	Family	Habit	Part(s) used	Folk claim	Ethno-preparation	References
					Flower	Eczema, Allergy	Flower extract (freshly prepared) is used to treat eczema and allergic problems.	Mandal et al., 2020a
19.	Boriari (Or)	*Sida acuta* Burm.f.	Malvaceae	Herb	Root	Boils	Root extract is used against boils.	Datta et al., 2014
20.	Neem	*Azadirachta indicia* A.Juss	Meliaceae	Tree	Leaves	Burn	Leaves are boiled with water and then the affected takes a bath in that water.	Chowdhury & Das, 2007

SN	Vernacular name(s)	Scientific name	Family	Habit	Part(s) used	Folk claim	Ethno-preparation	References
						Skin rashes	Sun dried leaves are crushed and then pan fried and taken with food to treat skin disease.	Pala et al., 2019; Mandal et al., 2020a
21.	Bonlobongo	*Ludwigia perennis* L.	Onagraceae	Herb	Leaves	Skin problem	-	Bandyopadhyay & Mukherjee, 2005a
22.	Pan	*Piper betle* L.	Piperaceae	Climber	Leaves	Skin problem	-	Bandyopadhyay & Mukherjee, 2010

SN	Vernacular name(s)	Scientific name	Family	Habit	Part(s) used	Folk claim	Ethno-preparation	References
23.	Biskanthali (Kh) L. H.Gross	*Persicaria* chinensis L.H. Gross	Polygonaceae	Climber	Twig	Remove tick from the skin of cattle	Wet twig of the plant is rubbed over the body of the cattle.	Bandyopadhyay & Mukherjee, 2005b
24.	-	*Spermacoce mauritiana* Gideon	Rubiaceae	Herb	Leaves	Mastitis	Paste of the leaves is applied to the infected area.	Bandyopadhyay & Mukherjee, 2006.
25.	Bania	*Hedyotis scandens* Roxb.	Rubiaceae	Clim ber	Whole plant	Dropsy	-	Bandyopadhyay & Mukherjee, 2010
26.	Gima sak	*Dentella repens* (L.) J.R.Forst. & G.Forst.	Rubiaceae	Herb	Leaves	Boils	-	Bandyopa dhyay & Mukherjee, 2005a

SN	Vernacular name(s)	Scientific name	Family	Habit	Part(s) used	Folk claim	Ethno-preparation	References
27.	Datmajon	*Glycosmis pentaphylla* (Retz.) DC.	Ruta-ceae	Shrub	Root	Eczema	Root powder is used to cure Eczema.	Datta et al., 2014
28.	Koi okhra	*Phyla nodiflora* (L.) Greene	Verben-aceae	Herb	Flower	Boils	-	Bandyopadhyay & Mukherjee, 2005a
29.	Jhangli halud	*Curcuma aeruginosa* Roxb.	Zingibe-raceae	Herb	Rhizo-me	Inflam-mation	Rhizome paste is applied to the affected area.	Pala et al., 2019

Ra- Rabha, Rj- Rajbanshi, Sa- Santal, Kh- Kheria, Or- Oraon

ST/P/S&T/2G-01/2020 dated 04/01/2021) from the Science & Technology and Biotechnology Department, Government of West Bengal.

REFERENCES

1. Ahmad, M., Qureshi, R., Arshad, M., Khan, M. A., & Zafar, M. (2009). Traditional herbal remedies used for the treatment of diabetes from district Attock (Pakistan). *Pakistan Journal of Botany, 41*(6), 2777-2782.
2. Bandyopadhyay, S., & Mukherjee, S. K. (2005a). Diversity of aquatic and wetland vascular plants of Koch Bihar district, West Bengal. In: A. K. Pandey, J. Wen, J. V. V. Dogra (Eds.), *Plant Taxonomy : Advances and Relevance* (pp. 223-244). New Delhi: CBS Publishers & Distributors.
3. Bandyopadhyay, S., & Mukherjee, S. K. (2005b). Ethnoveterinary medicine from Koch Bihar district, West Bengal. *Indian Journal of Traditional Knowledge, 4*(4), 456-461.
4. Bandyopadhyay, S. (2017). Observation on the traditional herbal remedies of pain from Koch Bihar district, West Bengal. *World Journal of Pharmaceutical Research,* 6(16), 1497-1509.
5. Bandyopadhyay, S. (2018). Diversity of the family Leguminosae in Koch Bihar district, West Bengal. *International Journal of Tourism Research, 10,* 32-41.
6. Bandyopadhyaya, S. & Mukherjee, S. K. (2010). Diversity of climbing plants in the Koch Bihar district of West Bengal, India. Pleione, 4(1), 82-89.
7. Bandyopadhyay, S., Mitra, S., & Mukherjee, S. K. (2014). Traditional uses of some weeds of Asteraceae by the ethnic communities of Koch Bihar district, West Bengal. *International Journal of Pharmacology Research,* 4(1), 31-34.
8. Bandyopadhyay, S., & Mukherjee, S. K. (2006). Traditional medicine used by the ethnic communities of Koch Bihar District (West Bengal - India). *Journal of Tropical*

Medicinal Plants, 7(2), 303-312.

9. Barker, M. S., Kane, N. C., Matvienko, M., Kozik, A., Michelmore, R. W., Knapp, S. J., & Rieseberg, L. H. (2008). Multiple paleopolyploidizations during the evolution of the Compositae reveal parallel patterns of duplicate gene retention after millions of years. *Molecular Biology and Evolution, 25*(11), 2445-2455.
10. Bhatt, D. C., Mitaliya, K. D., Patel, N. K., & Ant, H. M. (2002). Herbal remedies for renal calculi. *Advances in Plant Sciences, 15*(1), 1-3.
11. Bhattacharjee, S. K. (2001). *Hand book of medicinal plants* (pp. 18-25). Jaipur: Pointer Publishers.
12. Buragohain, J., & Konwar, B. K. (2007). Ethnomedicinal plants used in skin diseases by some Indo-Mongoloid communities of Assam. *Asian Journal of Experimental Sciences, 21*(2), 281-288.
13. Chowdhury, M., & Das, A. P. (2007). Folk medicines used by the Rabha tribe in Coochbehar district of West Bengal: a preliminary report. In: A. P. Das, A. K. Pandey (Eds), *Advances in Ethnobotany* (pp. 289-296). Dehra Dun, India: Bishen Singh Mahendra Pal Singh.
14. Datta, T., Patra, A. K., & Dastidar, S. G. (2014). Medicinal plants used by tribal population of Coochbehar district, West Bengal, India-an ethnobotanical survey. *Asian Pacific Journal of Tropical Biomedicine, 4*(4), S478-S482.
15. Dawid-Pac, R. (2013). Medicinal plants used in treatment of inflammatory skin diseases. *Post?py Dermatologii i Alergologii, 30*(3), 170-177.
16. Felhaber, T. (1997). *South African traditional healers' primary health care handbook.* Cape Town, South Africa: Kagiso Publishers.
17. Hay, R. J., Johns, N. E., Williams, H. C., Bolliger, I. W., Dellavalle, R. P., Margolis. D. J., Marks, R., Naldi, L., Weinstock, M. A., Wulf, S. K., Michaud, C., Murray, C. J. L., & Naghavi, M. (2014). The global burden of skin disease in 2010: an analysis of the prevalence and impact of skin

conditions. *Journal of Investigative Dermatology, 134*(6), 1527-1534.

18. Kumar, K., Sharma, Y. P., Manhas, R. K., & Bhatia, H. (2015). Ethnomedicinal plants of Shankaracharya Hill, Srinagar, J&K, India. *Journal of Ethnopharmacology,* 170:255-274.
19. Mandal, A., Saha, P., Begum, A., Saha, A., Chakraborty, B., Dutta, S., & Roy, K. K. (2020a). Ethnomedicinal plants used by the ethnic people living in fringe villages of Rasikbil of Cooch Behar District, West Bengal, India. *Indian Journal of Science and Technology, 13*(16), 1676-1685.
20. Mandal, A., Adhikary, T., Chakraborty, D., Roy, P., Saha, J., Barman, A., & Saha, P. (2020b). Ethnomedicinal uses of plants by Santal tribe of Alipurduar district, West Bengal, India. *Indian Journal of Science and Technology, 13*(20), 2021-2029.
21. Pala, N. A., Sarkar, B. C., Shukla, G., Chettri, N., Deb, S., Bhat, J. A., & Chakravarty, S. (2019). Floristic composition and utilization of ethnomedicinal plant species in home gardens of the Eastern Himalaya. *Journal of Ethnobiology and Ethnomedicine, 15*(1), 1-16.
22. Panthi, M. P., & Singh, A. G. (2013). Ethnobotany of Arghakhanchi district, Nepal: plants used in dermatological and cosmetic disorders. *International Journal of Applied Sciences and Biotechnology, 1*(2), 27-32.
23. Policepatel, S. S., & Manikrao, V. G. (2013). Ethnomedicinal plants used in the treatment of skin diseases in Hyderabad Karnataka region, Karnataka, India. *Asian Pacific Journal of Tropical Biomedicine, 3*(11), 882-886.
24. Prashantkumar, P., & Vidyasagar, G. M. (2008). Traditional knowledge on medicinal plants used for the treatment of skin diseases in Bidar district, Karnataka. *Indian Journal of Traditional Knowledge, 7*(2), 273-276.

25. Raj, A. J., Biswakarma, S., Pala, N. A., Shukla, G., Vineeta, Kumar, M., Chakravarty S., & Bussmann, R. W. (2018). Indigenous uses of ethnomedicinal plants among forest-dependent communities of Northern Bengal, India. *Journal of Ethnobiology and Ethnomedicine, 14*(1).

26. Roy, S. (2015). An ethnobotanical study on the medicinal plants used by Rajbanshis of Coochbehar district. *Journal of Medicinal Plants Studies,* 3(5), 46-49.

27. Singh, S. P., Tripathi, S., & Shukla, R. S. (2003). Ethnomedicinal heritage for Bio-prospecting and Drug development in North-Eastern States of India. *Journal of Economic and Taxonomic Botany,* 26, 384-395.

28. Sofowora, A., Ogunbodede, E., & Onayade, A. (2013).The role and place of medicinal plants in the strategies for disease prevention. *African Journal of Traditional, Complementary and Alternative Medicines, 10*(5), 210-229.

29. Tabassum, N., & Hamdani, M. (2014). Plants used to treat skin diseases. *Pharmacognosy Review, 8*(15), 52-60.

30. Tariq, A., Musarat, S., & Adnan, M. (2015). Review on ethno medicinal, phytochemical and pharmacological evidence of Himalayan anticancer plants. *Journal of Ethnopharmacology, 164,* 96-119.

31. Thomas, B., Arumugam, R., Veerasamy, A., & Ramamoorthy, S. (2014). Ethnomedicinal plants used for the treatment of cuts and wounds by Kuruma tribes, Wayanadu districts of Kerala, India. *Asian Pacific Journal of Tropical Biomedicine, 4*(Suppl 1), S488-S491.

32. Tripathi, S. C., & Srivastava, M. (2010). Ethnomedicinal flora of Euphorbiaceae used in dermatological problems. *Indian Journal of Traditional Knowledge, 9*(2), 318-320.

33. Uniyal, S. K., Singh, K. N., Jamwal, P., & Lal, B. (2006). Traditional use of medicinal plants among the tribal communities of Chhota Bhangal, Western Himalaya. *Journal of Ethnobiology and Ethnomedicine, 2*(1), 14.

34. Watt, J. M., & Breyer-Brandwijk, M. G. (1962). *The Medicinal and Poisonous Plants of Southern Africa: Being*

an Account of their Medicinal Uses, Chemical Composition, Pharmacological Effects and Toxicology in Man and Animal. Edinburgh: E. and S. Livingstone.

35. WHO. (2003). *Diet, nutrition and prevention of chronic diseases.* In: Report of the Joint WHO/FAO Expert Consultation. Geneva: World Health Organisation (WHO).

Agrodiversity

10

Mushroom cultivation practices for Upliftment of Rural economy and Women Empowerment in North Bengal

***S. Barman*[1] *& B.N. Chakraborty*[2]**

Work skill development of rural people, directly and indirectly contributes to the nations' development. As in North Bengal, the rural population mostly comprises of marginal and landless farmers, there is a need for a low cost and maximum profit plan to enhance both their income as well as socio-economic status. One such plan is to set up a small-scale mushroom production unit which requires by-products of the agricultural farm as input and occupy less agricultural land space. Mushroom cultivation is a minimum input maximum output venture proving to be an additional source of income. The vegetarian population residing in the urban areas of our country has now accepted mushrooms in their diet because of its nutritional values so the mushroom produced from the nearby rural areas has a good market of selling their products easily and at a good price. Thus, the mushroom is a boon to both producer and consumer giving it the status of superfood. Mushroom cultivation can also be a way to empower the rural women, provide additional income for the sustenance of farming families and tackle the problem

[1]Department of Botany, Tufanganj Mahavidyalaya, Tufanganj, New Town, Cooch Behar.
Email: sbmarch1990@gmail.com
[2]Department of Biological Sciences, Aliah University, New Town, Kolkata.

of lack of nutritional requirement of the rural people. Rural women are the most productive workforce in the economy, raising the need to strengthen and improve their socio-economic status. A low-cost small-scale mushroom production unit can generate income through the sale of spawns, in addition to the sale of fresh mushroom in a sustainable approach by utilizing farm by-products as their raw material. Mushroom production can play a significant role to eradicate malnutrition, alleviate poverty and create employment opportunity for unemployed farm women in rural area.

Introduction

North Bengal comprises of seven districts out of the twenty districts of West Bengal, namely Darjeeling, Jalpaiguri, Uttar Dinajpur, Dakshin Dinajpur, Malda, Coochbehar, and Alipurduar (25th June 2014). North Bengal comprises of about 18.35% of the state's total area. North Bengal's economy is pre-dominantly farm-based, although many tertiary activities are carried out in the region. Recent years have witnessed a rapid growth of manufacturing industries in North Bengal whose geographical location makes the region a potential candidate for a vibrant economic centre with both agriculture and non-agricultural activities. North Bengal is predominated by the rural areas and most of the population workforce resides in rural areas (Aayog *et al.*, 2017). The projection of population also showed that India will carry on to be predominated by the rurals up to the year 2050 and preceding which it will be overtaken by the urban (Desa *et al.*, 2014). It is generally observed that there is an unplanned migration of rural people to the urban area primarily for better economic opportunities which as a result inflict a scathing pressure on the urban amenities which in turn subjects these rural migrants to work under low wages and live in cruddy, unhygienic, and impoverished conditions. Therefore, in the sight of this unplanned migration of rural people to urban areas and to embellish the socio-economic settings, there is an urgent requirement of setting up strategies to bolster the rural economy and creation of employment opportunities in the rural background. In addition to this, the upliftment in economic conditions of rural communities is also imperative to reduce the incongruity in per capita urban and rural income that has stayed high consistently. Thus, there is a significant requirement of higher growth in the rural economy in comparison to the urban economy in north Bengal. Another important issue that has emerged in the recent past is women empowerment. It is being surmised that the economic empowerment of women will have a way in the country's development process and hence the contention is of paramount importance. Women are thought by the reformers, thinkers, and social scientists as a major factor in national development (Nigmare *et al.*, 2016). The rural women are far less literate than the rural men in North Bengal region as there is a negative behaviour of the family towards the education of a girl child or them as a whole. The major portion of women residing in rural areas not only suffer from economic poverty but also from the "information poverty". They are the crucial and constructive workers in our national economy, but there has been statistical biased by underestimation of rural women role in the developmental process (Bhattacharyya 2015). Even though the women work for more time span than the men and dispense consequentially in the income of the family, they are not recognized as productive labours (Dey *et al.*, 2020). They remain as a muted force who struggle to fulfil their household duties from dawnto dusk. Self Help Group (SHG) is a recent milestone in the upliftment of women. Since women are a vital part of the Indian economy constituting onethird of the national labour force and a major contributor to the survival of the family, they need to promote and enhance participation on an equal basis with men in social, economic and empowerment process of rural development. Rural women bring income with productive activities ranging from traditional work in fields to working in agro based industries. The efficient role of SHGs proved through various results of entrepreneurial training as better entrepreneurs and development managers in any kind of human development programmes. Most micro-finance institutions (MFIs) in India are built upon the grassroots infrastructure of SHG. Deeply embedded cultural and institutional characteristics are the primary drives of national entrepreneurial activity. Govt. institutes like North Bengal University, Krishi Vigyan Kendra (Pundibari) at this region is shouldering this responsibility by training women SHG members to take up income generating activities like mushroom production, preparation of value-added products and composting technologies.

From the ancient time, rural women are known to play an important role in the development of agriculture and its allied field through crop and livestock production, horticulture and its post-harvest operations, fisheries, mushroom production, bee-keeping etc. Furthermore, rural women are also employed in other agri-based allied enterprises such as animal husbandry, floriculture, post harvest processing, value-addition, fruit preservation, fisheries, rabbit rearing, poultry etc. Millions of agricultural labourers are rural women indulged in all these agricultural activities but their role and work go invisible in statistics and it is less conjecturable that they will secure propitious outcomes for themselves in household decision-making process (Dey, *et al.*, 2020).

According to the UNDP Report, 67 per cent of the world's total work is done by women but only a marginal 10 per cent of the global earning is attained by them and an utterly insignificant 1 per cent of the global property is owned by them (Singh, *et al.*, 2007). An expedient approach for the empowerment of women is thought to be by the entrepreneurship development. As from ancient times, agriculture has been the prime dimension of the rural economy and rural employment, rural women empowerment can be achieved by the adoption of agricultural enterprises at individual and/or community level (Awasthi N, 2015). The incorporation of agro-allied sectors in the composition of output and occupation is considered as a potential source of economic growth and transformation in the rural and total economy. In the rural areas of North Bengal, agro-waste and organic materials are available in plenty amount, which often end up in waste thus contributing to the pollution woes. The major part of North Bengal including Terai and Dooars are located in the foothills of the Himalaya and having large and small sized tea gardens in both banks of river Tista. Tea plantations are abundant in this region and form a major part of the economy of this region. The people of rural ethnic groups of this region are very much dependent on tea gardens for their economy. Besides tea garden, paddy cultivation is one of the most important crops in North Bengal. The economy of southern part of North Bengal is basically based on paddy crop. So a huge amount of paddy straw as well as pruned tea leaves is produced every year in North Bengal. Depending on the crops grown, cropping intensity and productivity in different regions of India, there is a large variability in generation and management of these crop residues. In some part of West Bengal paddy straw and husk is used as domestic fuel or in boilers for parboiling rice. Paddy straw as well as wheat straw is being used for compost preparations which are generally utilized for mushroom cultivation.

Present status of mushroom in India

Even though the cultivation of mushrooms had been started in other parts of the world many centuries ago, the origin of its cultivation in India is comparatively recent. The first attempt of mushroom cultivation is known as that by Thomas and his colleagues in Coimbatore by trying to cultivate Paddy straw mushroom. The first scientific attempt to cultivate Button mushroom is credited to the Government of Himachal Pradesh in collaboration with ICAR under the scheme "Development of Mushroom Cultivation in Himachal Pradesh" in 1961 which was later taken up as an enterprise by the progressive farmers of Himachal Pradesh and Jammu and Kashmir in the late 1960s (Dey *et al.*, 2020). The cultivation of mushroom spread to other hilly areas of Uttar Pradesh and Tamil Nadu in the early 70s. It was adopted by the farmers of Haryana, Uttar Pradesh and Punjab in the late70s and early 80s as a seasonal crop. The country's capital Delhi and the economic capital Mumbai together formed a big market for the utilization of fresh mushrooms to the magnitude of 10 to 12 tonnes per day. Today one of the biggest units of mushroom cultivation in India is located in Madras. There are very result-oriented with exhilarating figures of mushroom trade in India at the present time. The corporate houses have set up many export-oriented units encompassed with advanced technology and machinery throughout the country for enhanced mushroom production. In the past decade, there has been a many-fold increase in mushroom production in India (Karthick K, 2017).

Present scenario of mushroom cultivation in different states of India

There was spread of white button mushroom from Jammu and Kashmir and Himachal Pradesh to all over the country after 1980. A remarkable improvement in the production scenario has been witnessed as mushroom cultivation has now spread its shadow from north to south and east to west region of India (Dey *et al.*, 2020). The production of mushroom alone in Himachal Pradesh has crossed 8000 tonnes ever since the two commercial-oriented units have been established at Paonta Sahib and Nalagarh which jointly produce 4500 tonnes per annum of the total (Karthick K, 2017). Many of the cold storages in Punjab has been transformed into the units for production of mushroom. The medium-sized commercial units at Hissar, Kalka, Panipat, and Gurugram has atotal production of 8000 tonnes of fresh mushrooms from Haryana (Karthick K, 2017). Many commercial companies are aspiring to familiarize the production of mushrooms in Madhya Pradesh. Upon being introduced into Chattisgarh, oyster mushroom is being cultivated in the tribal areas around the Raipur in particular with a production of more than 1500 tonnes on an annual basis. In Gujarat and Rajasthan, the cultivation of white button mushroom is on an experimental basis but the cultivation of oyster mushroom has been taken up by the cultivators. In Bihar and Jharkhand, small scale mushroom enterprises are well functional and are underprogress. In Maharashtra, the cultivation of mushroom is confined to Mumbai and Pune with 8000 tonnes production on annual basis and 12-15 tonnes annual production is from one export-oriented unit in Panaji, Goa (Karthick K, 2017) Presently, more than 85 per cent of the total mushroom production is of white button mushroom followed by the oyster mushroom.

Dimension of mushroom in India

Mushroom is generally defined as the fleshy, spore-bearing fungal body which is produced typically above the ground surface or its source of food (substrate). There are different meanings to the word "mushroom" among different people residing in different countries (Dey *et al.*, 2020). They were regarded as the "food of gods" by the Romans in the ancient era and Greeks believed them as a source of strength for the warriors in military warfare (Zhang Y, 2014). Mushrooms are widely used among the world population as a food item and are very often considered as luscious and nutritive food. They contain a distinct range of nutrients and various other natural phytochemicals which possesses an extensive array of health and nutritional benefits (Cheung P, 2010), which includes healing of wounds, enhancement of immunity, and retardation of tumours (Dai YC, 2009). In recent studies, the medicinal mushrooms have shown very promising and encouraging results in their trails against HIV/AIDS having people in Africa. There are more than 2000 reported species of fungi which are edible in the world and out of which India has the availability of 200 species. From all these species, only eight are utilized in the cultivation process among the countries for commercial purposes among which are *Agaricusbisporus* (Button mushroom), *Pleurotus spp.* (Oystermushroom), *Volvariella spp.* (Paddy strawmushroom), *Lentinus edodes* (Shiitake mushroom), *Calocybe indicus* (Milky mushroom), and *Flammulinavelutipes* (Enokitake mushroom) (Chauhan SK,

2015).

Mushrooms cultivated in North Bengal

Oyster mushroom cultivation

Oyster mushrooms of the genus *Pleurotus* known as valuable edible mushrooms which are broadly cultivated in North Bengal. These are the second most popular mushroom after button mushroom all over the world (Adejoye *et al.*, 2006). Among the oyster mushrooms *Pleurotus ostreatuswas* first cultivated in Germany during the first World War and is now grown commercially around the world for food.Due to the high nutritional value, delicate taste, and variable vitamins and minerals content, oyster mushrooms rank second in terms of industrial cultivation worldwide after a white button mushroom, *Agaricusbisporus* (Baars *et al.*, 2008). A wide range of substrates including wheat straw, barely straw, sinar straw and saw dust banana leaves, bean straw is used for P. ostreatus cultivation (Iqbal *et al.*, 2016). The substrates used for cultivation of oyster is used again for other mushroom cultivation. The reused of substrates that contained additional supplements exhibited better growth on both pasteurized and sterilized substrates (Tesfaw *et al.*, 2015).

Milky mushroom(Calocybe indica)

The milky mushroom (*Calocybe indica*) is a potentially new species to the world mushrooms growers. This was reported first time from West Bengal in India and its edibility was confirmed later by Purkaystha, (1976). It is suitable for hot humid climate. This edible mushroom has a long shelf life (5-7 days) compared to other commercially available counterparts. It can grow at temperature range of 25-40°C. Its productivity is influenced by substrate and environment factors (Kumar *et al.*, 2015). Its robust size, sustainable yield, attractive colour, delicacy, long shelf-life, moderate protein content and lucrative market value have attracted the attention of both mushroom consumers and prospective growers.

Button mushroom

Agaricusbisporus (Lange) Imbach is the most cultivated edible mushroom and presents more than 40% of world mushroom production followed by *Lentinula edodes, Pleurotus spand Flammulinavelutipes* (Sharma *et al.*, 2016). *A. bisporushas* delicious taste, high nutritional value, high aroma or flavoring taste and is used as a food and in food industries (Mattila *et al.*, 2010).

Table 1
Productive rate of six edible Mushrooms in different zones of North Bengal

Month	Dooars region of North Bengal					
	Types of edible mushroom					
	Agaricus-bisporus	Calocybe indica	Pleurotus djamor	P. ostrea-tus	P. sajor-caju	P. florida
January	High	-	High	High	Yes	Mode-rate
February	High	-	High	High	Yes	High
March	High	Slow growth	High	High	Yes	High
April	Slow growth	Slow growth	High	High	Yes	High
May	Slow growth	Moderate	High	High	Yes	Mode-rate
June	-	High	Low	Moderate	Yes	Mode-rate
July	-	High	Low	Moderate	Yes	Low
August	-	High	Low	Moderate	Yes	Low
Septe-mber	Slow growth	High	Low	Mode-rate	Yes	Low
October	Low	Low	Yes	High	Yes	High
November	Low	Low	Yes	High	Yes	High
December	High	-	Yes	High	Yes	High
	Hills region of North Bengal					
January	High	-	High	Low	Low	Mode rate
February	High	-	High	Low	Low	Mode-rate
March	High	-	High	Mode-rate	Mode-rate	Mode-rate
April	High	-	High	Mode-rate	Mode-rate	Mode-rate

May	Moderate	Low	High	Moderate	Moderate	Moderate
June	Moderate	Low	High	High	High	High
July	Moderate	Low	High	High	High	High
August	Moderate	Low	High	High	High	Moderate
September	Moderate	-	High	High	High	Moderate
October	High	-	High	High	High	Moderate
November	High	-	High	Moderate	Moderate	Moderate
December	High	-	High	Low	Low	Moderate

- No growth,
* The data is based on village level production units and survey in North Bengal area. (source: thesis submitted by Barman S, 2018)

Small-scale mushroom production unit as a catalyst for the upliftment of rural economy and women empowerment

In India, the majority of the rural agrarian population is composed of marginal and landless farmers, mushroom production can be a significant enterprise for employment and income generation. Mushroom production is a remunerative and profitable small enterprise for rural households having the low income (Dey *et al.*, 2020) and it is able to provide part-time and/or full-time employment to urban, rural, and marginal population of in many developing countries (Dey *et al.*, 2020. The unemployment is recently increasing to a much higher magnitude in both the developing and the developed countries which leaves us with the option of self-employment as the only way to sustain the rural economy and the national economy as a whole. The cultivation of mushroom will help to reduce the vulnerability of rural people to poverty and bolster up their livelihood through fructification of a nimble source of nutritious food and reliable income (Rachna *et al.*, 2013). Mushroom is an indoor crop which is lightindependent and does not require any fertile land for its cultivation. In addition to this, it can be grown on a small scale and does not require any substantial monetary investments (Muthuramu *et al.*, 2015), thus making it a potential candidate for improvement of the socio-

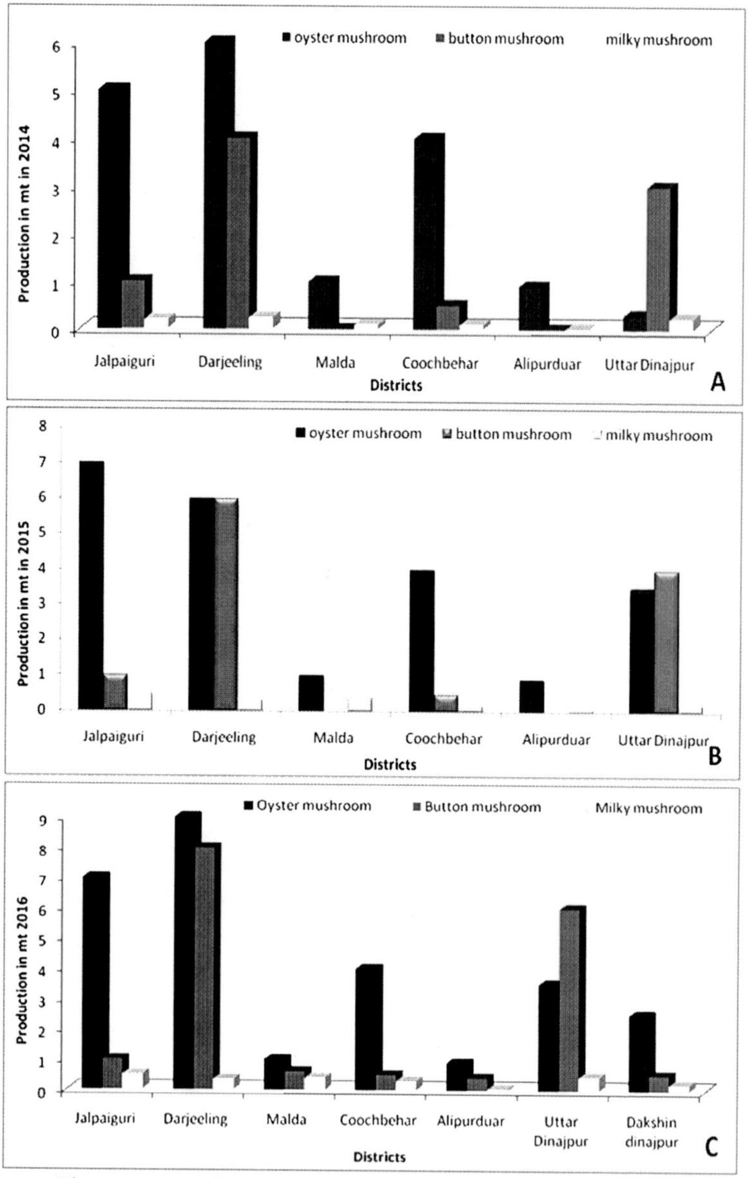

Fig. 1 (A-C): District wise mushroom production in three successive years, A. 2014, B. 2015, C. 2016 (source: thesis submitted by Barman S, 2018)

economic condition of farmers, farming community, rural youth, and solving the problem of unemployment for both the literate and illiterate people from rural and urban communities and most especially rural women. Mushroom cultivation is a women-friendly pursuit and is an agricultural enterprise which can be taken up by them in their leisure periods without renouncing their household liabilities (Shahi *et al.*, 2018). A promotion of mushroom cultivation enterprises would relieve the pressure on land, increase the supply of food, provide nutritional security, and lead to status upliftment of women by generating additional income (Manju *et al.*, 2012). As per a study conducted in Kurukshetra, Haryana; almost 50 per cent of the trained landless rural women belonging to schedule caste adopted the small-scale mushroom production activity after the Krishi Vigyan Kendra organized a training programme. It provided them with additional income and made them an integral part of the socioeconomic developmental process. Almost 60 per cent of the farm women socially accepted the mushroom production model in Rudapur, Aurangabad after a training programme was organized by Krishi Vigyan Kendra (Awasthi N, 2015). This enterprise can be taken up on a part-time basis as little maintenance is required for mushroom cultivation and can provide women employment in semi-urban and rural areas (Nigmare SS, 2016). In a similar trend, a 54.44 per cent adoption level of scientific cultivation of oyster mushroom was observed in Bhatni, Salempur, and Bhatparrani blocks of Deoria district (Kumari *et al.*, 2018). Mushroom production training to the rural farm women in Patna, Bihar also showed an acceptance level of 61 per cent as it aided to their economic empowerment along with an increase in their knowledge regarding the intricacies of technology which would lead them to empower the next generation of farm women (Singh *et al.*, 2018). An NGO, Dhristee while working in Korba city of Chattishgarh brought about changes in livelihood and fortune of rural women by helping them to take up mushroom cultivation through self-help groups (Elango J, 2017). Women have the innate ability to become a micro-entrepreneur only if this ability of theirs' is ignited and harnessed through training and providing them with the confidence to take up the job. Through this entrepreneurship, they would be able to handle the monetary affairs directly and affirm their legitimate position in the family and in the society. The cultivation of mushroom is proved to be one such microenterprise which has a potential for monetizable output even from the utilization of agricultural waste additionally being women-friendly. Small scale mushroom production units can play an influential role in the sustenance of rural economy through its contribution to nutrition and food security, additional income and employment generation, national and regional trades, and expiating opportunities for the processing and value addition enterprises attached to mushroom production like pickling, drying, chips etc.

Impact on the rural economyand women empowerment

There are various impacts of this small-scale low-cost mushroom production unit on the rural economy as well in empowering the farm women. Various aspects of these impacts have been discussed below:

Gain in Knowledge: The exposure to the cultivation of mushroom and its sub-components of the rural people leads to sufficient gain in the knowledge base in regard to its food value, different kinds of mushroom, composting of mushroom, spawning or filling, casing, fruiting, harvesting, and pooling of harvested produces. This will result in the improvement of skills and knowledge proficiency of the rural people, rural youth, and rural women. The exposure to these knowledge bases would thus help in the upliftment of rural economy and the national economy as a whole (Singh *et al.*, 2014).

Change of attitude: There would be a change in the attitude among the rural men and women towards the cultivation of mushroom. There is general negativity related to the production of mushroom in the Indian rural people and it is not well accepted as a source of food. Through these low-cost small-scale production units, the rural population may take up this enterprise and also acquire it in their food habit. These changes in the attitude are expected to come through this technique (Manju *et al.*, 2012).

Change in the Standard of Living of Rural Households: The low-cost small-scale mushroom enterprise can be taken up as the subsidiary source of income with the least technological and economic investments with an appreciable net profit. This net profit will add on to the income of the rural households and will lead in the upgradation of their standard of living and especially to the rural women it will serve as an engine for the upliftment of their status in the family and ultimately their empowerment (Shahi *et al.*, 2018).

Health Benefits: Mushrooms have good nutritive and medicinal values. They have a good content of dietary fibres which prevents diabetes, constipation, hypertension, obesity, arteriosclerosis and colon cancer. The vitamin B and D present in them prevents diseases such as beriberi, rickets, corneal vascularization etc. which are caused due to the deficiency of these vitamins. They have certain medicinal properties and works as immune-modulator, liver protectant, anti-diabetic, anti-viral, and antifibrotic agents (Ooi VEC, 2000). Through all these properties, the mushroom can serve as the agents of good health for the rural people which in turn means that the workforce generated by them will always be in its prime state and contribute to the rural economy.

CONCLUSION

From all the above stated assessment it can be concluded that the low-cost small-scale mushroom production unit can help to bolster the rural economy and provide empowerment of the rural women of North Bengal. The inclusion of mushroom in their daily diet will supplement additional nutrition to the rural people thus, would help them in living a healthy and prosper life. The health benefits from mushroom is always in its prime condition and in turn be an additional benefit for the rural economy upliftment. The additional income from mushroom cultivation will have positive impacts on the economic condition of farm women residing in rural areas. All these together will serve as an agent of empowerment of rural women. The mushroom production could also serve as machinery for providing self-employment in rural backgrounds and add to the rural economy. In brief, it can be said that mushroom cropping would work as a machinery for the elevation of rural economy and empowerment of rural women through reduction of poverty and improvement in the lifestyle of the rural population in North Bengal.

REFERENCES

1. Aayog NI. Changing structure of rural economy of India implications for employment and growth. National Institution for Transforming India, Government of India; 2017.
2. Adejoye OD, Adebayo Tayo BC, Ogunjobi AA, Olaoye OA and Fadahunsi FI. Effect of carbon, nitrogen and mineral sources on growth of *Pleurotus florida* a Nigerian edible mushroom. *African Journal of Biotechnilogy,* 5: 1355-1359, 2006.
3. Anwesha Dey, Shubhi Patel and Md. Mahtab Rashid. Small-scale Mushroom Production Unit for the Upliftment of Rural Economy and Women Empowerment in India: A Review. *Current Journal of Applied Science and Technology.,* 39(2): 38-46, 2020.
4. Awasthi N, Sahu A and Sahu RP. Mushroom production for economic empowerment of rural women in district Rama Bai Nagar, Kanpur. Advances in Social Research. 1(1):31-33, 2015.
5. Awasthi N, Sahu A and Sahu RP. Mushroom production for economic empowerment of rural women in district Rama Bai Nagar, Kanpur. *Advances in Social Research.,* 1(1): 31-33, 2015.
6. Baars J, Sonnerberg A, Mikosch T and Griensven L. Development of a sporeless strain of oyster mushroom Pleurotus ostreatus. In: *Proceedings of the 15th international congress on the Science and cultivation of*

Edible fungi, Rotterdam, 317-323, 2008.

7. Bhattacharyya A. Rural women in India: *The invisible lifeline of rural community.*10: 2015.
8. Chauhan SK and Sharma PG. A study on production potential economic viability and marketing system of varied size mushroom units in Himachal Pradesh; 2015.
9. Cheung PC. The nutritional and health benefits of mushrooms. *Nutrition Bulletin.,* 35(4):292-9, 2010.
10. Dai YC, Yang ZL, Cui BK, Yu CJ and Zhou LW. Species diversity and utilization of medicinal mushrooms and fungi in China. *International Journal of Medicinal Mushrooms.,* 11(3), 2009.
11. Desa UN. World urbanization prospects, the 2011 revision. Population Division, Department of Economic and Social Affairs, United Nations Secretariat; 2014.
12. Elango J. How mushroom cultivation is changing the fortunes of women in rural India. The Better India Blog; 2017. Available:https://www.thebetterindia.com/8 9391/ how-organisation-use-mushroomcultivation-empower/
13. Iqbal B, Khan HS, Khan I, Shah B, Naeem A., Ullah W., Khan N., Adnan M., Shah SRA, Junaid K., Ahmed N and Iqbal M. Substrates evaluation for the quality, production and growth of oyster mushroom (*Pleurotus florida*) *Journal of Entomology and Zoology Studies,* 4(3): 98-107, 2016.
14. Karthick K and Hamsalakshmi H. Current scenario of mushroom industry in India. *International Journal of Commerce and Management Research.,* 3(3):23-6, 2017.
15. Kumar R, Singh G and Mishra P. Influence of different substrates abd environmental factors on yield of two strains of *Calocybe indica. J. Mycopathology Res.,* 53(1): 75-82, 2015.
16. Kumari AR, Singh DP, Singh A, Laxmikant and Kumari M. Adoption level and constraints in scientific mushroom cultivation among rural women. *International Journal of Current Microbiology and Applied Sciences.,* 7:1280-1287,

2018.

17. Manju, Varma SK, Rani S. Impact assessment of mushroom production for rural women. *Rajasthan Journal of Extension Education.*, 20: 78-80, 2012.
18. Mattila P, Konko K, Eurola M, Pihlava JM, Astola J and Vahteristo L. Formation of flavor of dry champignons *AgaricusbisporusL. J ApplBioch Micro.*, 46 (1): 108-113, 2010.
19. Nigmare SS, Fule UW and Chore VP. Empowerment of rural women through agriculture. *International Journal of Researches in Bioscience, Agriculture and Technology*, 2016.
20. Ooi VEC. Medicinally important fungi. In: Van G. (Edt). *Science and Cultivation of Edible Fungi. Balkema.*, 41-51, 2000.
21. Purkayastha RP and Chandra, A. A new technique for in vitro production of *Calocybe indica:* an edible mushroom of India. *Mush J.*, 40:112-3, 1976.
22. Rachna RG and Sodhi GP. Evaluation of vocational training programmes organized on mushroom farming by Krishi Vigyan Kendra Patiala. *Journal of Krishi Vigyan.*, 2(1): 26-9, 2013.
23. S Muthuramu*, V K Paulpandi, S Sakthivel*, K Ramakrishnan and R Karthik. Empowerment of Self-Help Group Members of Virudhunagar District Through Vocational Trainings on Mushroom Production. *J Krishi Vigyan.*, 3: 23-26., 2015.
24. Shahi V, Shahi B, Kumar V, Singh KM and Kumari P. Impact study on mushroom cultivation for micro-entrepreneurship development and women Empowerment. *Journal of Pharmacognosy and Phyto-chemistry.*, SP4. 1-4, 2018.
25. Sharma SK and Gautam N. Evaluation of nutritional, nutraceutical and antioxidant composition of eight wild culinary mushrooms from the northest Himalayas. *International Journal of Medicinal Mushroom,* 18: 539-

546, 2016.

26. Singh BD, Verma M, Kumar R, Gupta PC and Aditya. Economic empowerment of rural farm women through mushroom production-A case study of Patna district, India. *International Journal of Current Microbiology and Applied Sciences.,* 7(5): 348-351, 2018.
27. Singh I, Kumari U. Rural development and women empowerment. Kurukshetra. 55(5):3-8, 2007.
28. Singh J, Chahal VP, Rathee A and Singh K. Economic empowerment of Scheduled Caste (SC) landless rural women through mushroom cultivation: A case study. *African Journal of Agricultural Research.,* 9(52): 3811-5, 2014.
29. Tesfaw A, Tadesse A and Kiros G. Optimization of oyster (Pleurotus ostreatus) mushroom cultivation using locally available substrates and materials in Debre Berhan, Ethiopia. *J App Biol Biotech,* 3 (01): 015-020, 2015.
30. Zhang Y, Geng W, Shen Y, Wang Y and Dai YC. Edible mushroom cultivation for food security and rural development in China: *Bio-innovation, technological dissemination and marketing. Sustainability.,* 6(5): 2961-73, 2014.

11

A Closer Look at The Black Gold of Mountain Agriculture – Large Cardamom – A Collection of Observation and Insights

Pushpanjali Ray[1]

ABSTRACT

Large cardamom is an important crop in the eastern Himalayan states of India like sub Himalayan West Bengal, Sikkim, Arunachal, Nagaland and Manipur as well as in neighbouring countries like Nepal and Bhutan. Large cardamom (*Ammomumsubulatum* Roxb.) is a perennial herbaceous monocotyledonous plant belonging to the family Zingiberaceae. Capsules of large cardamom are held together in the spike type inflorescence. In each spike 10-25 capsules are produced. From qualitative chemical examination of large cardamom capsules it was found out that carbohydrate, flavonoid, amino acids, glycosides, tannins, triterpenoids, steroids are present in the capsules. It was found out that volatile oil is the main aroma giving compound in large cardamom and 1, 8 - cineole is the major active compound of the volatile oil. Large cardamon oil is used in traditional medicines because of its therapeutic properties. The oil has antiseptic, antispasmodic, carminative, digestive, diuretic, expectorant, simulative, stomachic properties. Being a shade loving tree it is also useful in Alnus based agro-forestry. The common cultivers of large cardamom are Sawaney, Ramsey,

[1]Department of Botany, Ananda Chandra College, Jalpaiguri, West Bengal, India.

Dzongu Golsey, Varlengey, Ramla and Seremna. Propagation is done from seeds or by sucker multiplication. The crop after hervesting is dried or cured by using either direct sunlight or in modified klins called vatties. After curing the product is marketed according to farmers need.

Key Words : Ammomumsubulatum Roxb., agro-forestry, 1, 8-cineole, volatile oil

Introduction

Large Cardamom (*Amomum subulatum* Roxb) a prominent Spice and also an important crop for mountain agriculture, is a member of family Zingiberaceae. The crop was cultivated in the sub Himalayan state of Sikkim and Darjeeling district of West Bengal. However, in recent times it is also cultivated in parts of Uttarakhand and also in other North Eastern Hill states like Arunachal Pradesh, Nagaland and Manipur. Nepal and Bhutan are the two neighbouring Himalayan countries with the same agro-climatic factors where large cardamom cultivation is being done and are emerging as competitors. The State of Sikkim is till date the largest producer of large cardamom and constitutes the major share of Indian & world market. This crop is believed to be originated in the small Indian State of Sikkim (Bhandari, Negi, Bisht, Baunthiyal and Sundriyal, 2011).

Spices have played an important role in shaping the history of agricultural trade and likewise Large cardamom has been playing a pivotal role in the rural economy of the Stakeholders engaged in mountain agriculture. It is the one of the prioritized cash remunerative crop that can be grown in the steep terrains of the Himalayan belts.

Large cardamom is locally called "*thuloalaichi*" in the hills of Sikkim and Darjeeling, and is called "Badi elaichi" or "Kali Elaichi" in hindi by most consumers and traders. Though for trade the term Bada Dana; chota Dana, Pan type is mostly used.

The Large Cardamom Plant:

Large cardamom is a perennial herb with leafy stem called a pseudo stem, and can have dimension of 90 to 100 cm, large coarsely striated fruits are brown to dark red brown in colour, measuring 2 to 3 cm in length and 1.5 cm in width in most cultivars. The plant consists of subterranean rhizomes and several leafy aerial shootsor tillers that can be 1.5 to 2.5 m in height. Depending upon the origin of cultivers the size of capsules varies. Capsules are 20 to 25 mm in length, oval to globose and contain 30 to 55 seeds on most, but can grow upto 65 to 70 in released varieties. Capsules of large cardamom are held together inside the spike with viscous sugary pulpandare 20-25mm long and oval to globular in shape (Thomas, Sabu and Gupta, 2009)

Researchers have also described, Large cardamomas on evergreen, herbaceousmonocot plant (Gopal, Baby and Mohammed, 2012). Height of this plant ranges from 1.5-3.0 m (Bisht, Negi, Bhandari and Sundriyal, 2011) but varies as per cultivar and leaves are found at the upper portion of the stem. The rhizomes are of dull red colour and flower buds protrude from the base of the rhizome. The peduncleis short in some, longer in other sand the buds are encasedintightred bracts. Individual flowers remain open for three days and more. At the same time, new ones open successively. The inflorescence remains intact with flower for over amonth (Sharma, Sharma, Sharma and Singh, 2000)

Flowers:

The flowers are mainly bisexual, zygomorphic, bracteate, epigynous. Some variations can be found in different varieties. The yellowish perianth is differentiated into calyx, corolla and anther crest (Vijayan et al. 2018). Anthesis is said to be dependent on climatic factors and are at varying durations of day (Gupta & John, 1987). The inflorescence is a condensed spike on a short peduncle bearing 40-50 flower buds un acropetal succession. This is essentially a cross pollinated crop. Flowering starts from March- April at low altitudes (970 m) and continue up to July at High altitudes (1515 m) depending on the type of cultivars. Flowering in single spike of Large cardamom is completed within 60 days. Each Spike bears 40-50 flowers and depending upon cultivar and management practices anaverage of 10 - 25 capsules are set per spike. (POP Spices Board 2013)

Constituents of Large Cardamom capsules:

Bhandari, Bisht, Negi and Baunthiyal (2013); reported that there have been many Qualitative chemical examinations of various extracts of *A. subulatum* which revealed the presence of carbohydrates, flavonoids, amino acids, steroids, triterpenoids, glycolsides and tannins (Bisht, Purohit, Negi and Bhandari, 2010). Quantitative chromato-graphic analysis of essential oil of large cardamom wasalso carried out (Nigamand Purohit, 1960). Shankaracharya, Raghavan, Abraham and Sankaranaryana (1990) reported that the seedsof large cardamom do contain moisture (8.5%), protein (6%), volatile oil (2.8%), crudefiber (22%), starch (43.2%), ether extract (5.3%) and alcohol extract (7%), further it has been reported that 100 g of cardamom contains 666.6 mg calcium, 412 mg magnesium, 61 mg phosphorous and 14.4 ppm fluoride (Bhandary, 2013).

Large cardamom seeds are arid, bitter andaromatic. It is credited with curative propertiesin Ayurvedic and Unani systems of medicine (Mukherjee 1972; Singh 1978). The flavour and odour of large cardamom is dependent on the composition of aromatic compounds. It is used as a spice as well as in many Ayurvedic preparations. It contains 2-3% essential oil and is stomachic, carminative,diuretic and cardiac stimulant, and a goodremedy for throat and respiratory trouble. It isused for the treatment of indigestion, vomiting, biliousness, abdominal pains and rectal diseases. (Vijayan et al. 2017)

Gautam, Bhattarai, Khanal and Oil (2016) have also reported that Volatile oil (2-4%) is the principal aroma-giving compound in large cardamom and 1,8- cineole is the major active compound, in an extent of 60 to 80% of the total volatile oil. Alcohol and aqueous extract of largecardamom have been reported to contain allopathic, analgesic, anti-inflammatory, antimicrobial, antioxidant, antiulcer, cardio-adapto genic and hypolipidaemic activities. Large cardamom also posseses curative properties, and is one of the major spices which has been mentioned in Ayurveda and Unani medicine (Chempakam and Sindhu, 2008).

Some common facts about large Cardamom:

Large cardamom contributes a lot to the human being for good health. It contains many compounds that are known to have antioxidant, disease preventing and health promoting properties. The seeds of large cardamom are good source of minerals like potassium, calcium, magnesium, manganese and iron. Potassium is an important component of cell and body fluids that help to control heart rate and blood pressure. Manganese is a co- factor for the enzyme superoxide dismutase which is a very powerful free radical scavenger. Iron is required for red blood cell formation.

Large cardamom is also said to be rich in many vital vitamins including riboflavin, niacin, vitamin-C that are essential for optimum health. The therapeutic properties of large cardamom oil has found application in many traditional medicines as antiseptic, antispasmodic, carminative, digestive, diuretic, expectorant, simulative, stomachic and tonic to heaat and liver. It promotes elimination of bile and is useful in congestion of the liver. Large cardamom is very effective in treating tooth abscesses, gum infection, tuberculosis, throat infection, lung congestion etc. It is also useful in curing many disorders related to digestive system. Essential oil, oleoresin, flavoured biscuits and flavoured liquors are some of the products developed for diversifying its uses. Medicinally, those seeds have diuretic, antidote for snake and scorpion venome, stimulant, stomachic, alexipharmic and astringent properties (Gopal *et al.*, 2012).

Agro forestry:A system unique to Large cardamom cultivation:

Large cardamom (*Amomum subulatum*) a crop that has immense economical relevance in mountain agriculture is a shade loving plant and since a long time it is cultivated under the shade of trees, even agro shade nets are being used at the farmers field for proper plantation maintenance and output as such. It is believed to perform well under humid conditions and has to have moist soil for optimum growth and production. It is observed to have robust growth in soil having good organic content.

Though now Large Cardamom cultivation has become more of scientific cultivation, earlier it was more like wild cultivation. planting was done inside forest area, loamy soil sufficient tree canopy. The Large cardamom clumps grow well under trees of *Alnusnepalensis* called Utis in nepali. There is evidence that *Alnus* provides shade and nitrogen to Large cardamom plantations and the trees also provide with litter and wood for the farmers. Other trees are also used by farmers for the same.

Earlier practices had been to undertake planting at areas near perennial water source like stream (Jhoras) where the soil was moist throughout the year. However, with uptake of commercial cultivation use of irrigation pipes too have become a prominent feature.

Singh (2002) hasfound it out that Himalayan alder (*Alnus nepalensis*) based agro forestry is useful for supplying nutrients such as nitrogen and phosphorus to the plantations or croplands located downstream. The agroforestry practice supports highly diverse tree species and tree diversity index in cardamom agroforestry is higher compared to other agroforestry practices in the region (Sharma, Sharma and Purohit, 1997).

Scientific system of Large Cardamom cultivation practices:

Agro Climate: Large cardamom prefers humid, subtropical, semi evergreen forests on steep hills of eastern sub-Himalayan region. It is a shade loving plant (Sciophyte) grown in tracts with well distributed rainfall spread around 200 days with a total of about 3000- 3500mm/year.

Soil: Deep well-drained soils with loamy texture are best suited. Soils of large cardamom growing area are generally acidic in nature with pH ranging from 4.5-6., rich in organic carbon and nitrogen; medium in available phosphorus and potassium.

Prevalent Cultivars and their features

S.No.	Cultivar	Altitude adaptability	Attribute
1.	Sawaney	Medium-High	Robust cultivar, wide adaptability, medium to bold capsules, high yielder
2.	Ramsey	High (>1500m amsl)	Robust cultivar, cultivated on steep slopes, small capsules, high yielder
3.	Dzongu Golsey	Low	Plant is not robust, specific for Dzongu area of North Sikkim, tolerant to chirke but susceptible to foorkey and leaf streak diseases
4.	Varlengey	Medium - High	Robust cultivar, performance is good at high altitude, high yielder with bold capsules
5.	Ramla	High	Robust cultivar, medium yielder with bold capsules
6.	Seremna	Low	Plant is not robust but high yielder, 2-3 spike/tiller

PROPAGATION

Nursery: The propagation is both through seeds as well as suckers. The propagation by seed though is time consuming, has an added advantage as the seedlings are said to be disease free from viral infections Chirkey and Foorkey. It takes four to five years for seedlings from seed nursery to be productive. For sucker propagation a single pseudo stem along with part rhizome, some root system and two buds is used.

FROM SEED

Primary Nursery: Seeds are mostly sown during September - October. Seedbed of 15-25 cm height, three feet width and convenient length is to be prepared and should be well drenched. Decomposed compost mainly Farm Yard Manure or enriched compost is mixed with the soil and the surface of the bed leveled to fine tilt. About 3 kilogram of seed is required to make one unit of Nursery, and about 80-100gm of seeds per bed is sown in lines across the bed at a distance of 10cm and the bed is covered with leaf mulch or paddy straw as per availability. Sprinkling of water is done at regular intervals to keep the surface of the bedmoist.

The emergence of leaves from the seeds commences from March onwards. When average germination is noticed, the mulch is removed carefully. The inter space between the rows is then covered with chopped paddy straw or leaves. Shade is provided using bamboo mats, thatch grass or agro shade nets on overhead structure. When the seedlings attain 3-4 leaf stage, they are transplanted to secondarynursery.

Secondary Nursery:

i) **Poly bag Nursery:** Secondary nursery can be prepared in poly bags or raised beds. Polythene bags of 15x15cm size are filled with a potting mixture (soil, sand and cow dung, 4:1:1). Seedlings are planted in April and May and watered regularly and kept under shade. They become ready for field planting in 10-12 months.

ii) **Bed Nursery:** Nursery beds are prepared as suggested for primary nursery. Seedlings with 3-4 leaves are transplanted in beds during May-June with a spacing of about 15cm between them. The inter space is mulched with chopped paddy straw or dried leaf. Overhead pandal is erected for providing shade. The soil is kept moist by regular watering. Once the seedlings attain 45-60cm height and have 2-3 tillers, they are planted in the main field during June-July of the subsequent year.

Sucker Multiplication Nursery: Suckers are multiplied with adequate precautions to ensure that, mother plants are free from viral diseases. The site for such a nursery should be located at least 500m away from main plantations. Trenches of 30x30 cm are prepared at convenient length with an inter space of 30cm. Well decomposed compost is mixed with soil and filled into the trenches. Planting units (suckers) with one grown up shoot and a vegetative bud are planted at 30cm distance, in the trenches during April-May. After planting the plant base is mulched with dried leaves.

Main field Preparation: Main field is cleared from old seedlings, weeds and layout for foot path, irrigation/drainage channel, compost pit and curing unit (bhatti) are made. Pits of size, 30 x 30 x 30 cm are prepared on contour, at a spacing of 1.5x1.5m (1.8 x 1.8m for robust cultivars) before the onset of monsoon showers. The pits are filled with topsoil and compost/ FYM/ vermin compost @ 4-5kg per pit. The ideal time for planting the large cardamom is May to July. Suckers with one mature tiller with 2 vegetative buds is used for planting. Deep placement of suckers must be avoided and stacking must be ensured after planting to avoid lodging. After planting, base of the plant must be mulched with dried leaves to conserve soil moisture.

Shade: Crop performs well under partial shade (50%). It is necessary to establish shade prior to planting of cardamom. Generally *utisis* widely used as shade tree due to its nitrogen fixing and nutrient recycling ability. Other popular shade trees are *Panisaj, Mailto, Argeli, Asare, Bilaune, Kharane, Siris,*

Faled, Jhingani and Chillowne. Shade trees are planted at a spacing of 10-15m between plants for even shade distribution. However excess shade affects the crop adversely. So timely lopping of branches and tree height is necessary.

Nutrient Management: For sustained productivity it is necessary to apply well decomposed farmyard manure @ 4-5kg per plant during April-May or 500g mustard cake per plant.

Irrigation: Large cardamom being shallow rooted crop, issensitive for moisture stress. During the dry period (November-March) crop is supplemented by irrigation water coupled with surface mulching.

Weeding: Generally, weeding is carried out 3 times a year for effective control of weed growth. After weeding, dried shoots and other thrashed materials can be used as mulch around the base of the plant. During flowering period, weeds or thrashed materials should not cover the inflorescence which limits the visit of pollinators.

Harvesting: When the seed of topmost capsule turn brown to black it is right stage for harvesting. To fasten the maturity process the bearing tillers are cut at a height of 35-45cm when the seed of top capsule becomes brown and left for another 10-15 days for complete maturity. Yield of 300-1000kg of dry cardamom per ha can be expected in fourth year after planting, depending upon management and growing conditions of plantations. Well-managed plantation can yield profit even up to 15 years. However, in low to moderate management plantations economic yield can be achieved up to 8 years.

Curing: The harvested capsule has 72-80% moisture, curing is done to reduce it to 11% level. Traditionally cardamom is cured in kilns called Bhatti, where capsule are dried by direct heating. This turns the capsule into dark brown colour which has low market preference. Using alternative curing or drying without direct heating the seeds with pinkish colour can be produced. Scientifically cured pinkish capsule are preferred in market and fetches higher price.

(Extracts from Package of practices for scientific system of large cardamom cultivation, Spices Board)

SWOT ANALYSIS

Strengths

- Profit is relatively higher
- Suitable topography and agro-climate.
- Cultivating in marginal land.
- Less capital investment required to cultivate in comparison to other crops.
- Traditional knowledge and experience
- Generate rural employment forwomen

Weaknesses

- Shortage of disease free saplings
- Very old Plantations.
- Dependency on traditional Bhattis (Dryer)
- Declining productivity due to disease and other factors
- Lack of value addition
- Low production, productivity & management
- Lack of price information mechanism

Opportunities

- Potential for land expansion/extension
- Production and distribution disease free seedlings/ saplings
- Potential for research, development/training
- Increasing awareness in post harvest value addition
- Exploitation of International market and domestic Market Opportunities.
- Establish industry for extraction of essential oil
- Develop variety according to altitude, disease & pest tolerant variety
- Branding as per niche market

Threats/ Challenges

- Drying/decreasing irrigation water sources

- Adulteration and mixing wild cultivars
- Propagation through mother rhizome only.
- Declining international reputation
- High price fluctuation
- Augmenting the existing supply chain to value chain

Quality Parameters

*BIS specifications IS 13446:2009

Requirements	
Odour and Taste	Capsules & seeds shall be characteristic and fresh. Shall be free from foreign odour and taste, including rancidity and mustiness.
Freedom from Insects and moulds, etc.	Large cardamom capsules and seeds should be free from live and dead insects and moulds.
Extraneous Matter	Large cardamom capsules and seeds should be free from dirt or dust.
Empty and malformed capsules	These shall not be more than 2 percent of capsule.
Immature and shrivelled capsules	The proportion of Immature and shrivelled capsules shall not be more than 2 percent (m/m).
Light seeds	The proportion of light seeds shall not be more than 3 percent (m/m).
Insect damaged matter	This includes large cardamom, capsules and seeds exhibiting definitive evidence of insect feeding or containing one or more whole insects or equivalent.

Grades at Domestic Markets (seed size)		
	Grade Name	Specifications
A	Extra Bold Hand pick	> 1.5 cm
B	Extra Bold Tail cut	> 1.4 cm < 1.5 cm

C	Medium tail cut	> 1.3 cm < 1.4 cm
D	Chotta Tail cut	> 1.2 cm < 1.3 cm
E	Pan variety	> 1.1 cm < 1.2 cm
F	Pan dana tail cut	

Grades for Export (seed size)		
Trade Name	Grade Name	Specifications
Bada dana (A)	Grade I	> 1.5 cm
Bada dana	Grade II	> 1.4 cm < 1.5 cm
Medium dana	Grade III	> 1.3 cm
Chota Dana	Grade IV	> 1.2 cm
Pan Elaichi	--	> 1.2 cm

*POP Spices Board of India

The Supply Chain

The large cardamom supply chain has been a simple model wherein farmers are at the base of the whole system as producers and the sale is staggered throughout the year. The farmers sale their produce as per their need for ready cash, and the peak is mostly during harvesting season in Sikkim and North Bengal where in the period coincides with Dasai and tihar festivals.

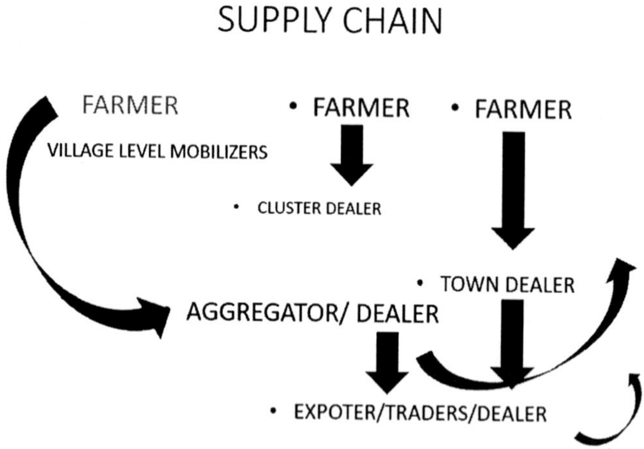

Fig. 1: Supply Chain

ACKNOWLEDGEMENT

Due acknowledgement to the collaborators of the Package of Practices of Large Cardamom 2013, published by Spices Board from where the major understanding of cultivation aspectwere looked into. I would also like to thank all the farmer friends with whom I interacted for better understanding specially Mr. Pawan koyu (Rai) and G.S. Rai of Polok, South Sikkim.

REFERENCES

1. Bhandari A.K., Bisht V.K., Negi J.S., & Bauthiyal M. (2013). 1,8-Cineole: A predominant component in the essential oil of Large cardamom (*Amommumsubulatum* Roxb.) Journal of *Medicinal Plants Research,* 7 (26),1957-1960.
2. Bhandari, A.K., Negi, J.S., Bisht, V.K, Baunthiyal, M, & Sundriyal, R.C. (2011). An assessment introduction of *Amommumsubulatum*Roxb. (Large Cardamom) in Uttarakhand. Proceedings of Uttarakhand 6th USST Cong., India p 13.
3. Bisht, V.K, Kandari, L.S, Negi, J.S, Bhandari, A.K, & Sundriyal R.C (2013). Traditional use of medicinal plants in district Chamoli, Uttarakhand, India. *Journal of Medicinal Plant Research.*7(15), 918-929.
4. Bisht, V.K, Negi, J.S, Bhandaru, A.K, & Sundriyal R.C. (2011). *Amommumsubulatum* Roxb. Traditional, phytochemical and biological activities - An overview. *African Journal of Agricultural Research.* 6(24), 5386-5390.
5. Bisht, V.K, Purohit, V., Negi, J.S., & Bhandari, A.K .(2010). Introducton and advancement in cultivation of Large Cardamom (*Amomum subulatum* Roxb.) in Uttarakhand, India. *Research Journal of Agricultural Sciences 1*(3), 205-208.
6. Chempakam, B., & Sindhu, S. (2008). Large Cardamom. In Parthasarathy V.A, Vhempakam B and Zachariah T.J (Eds.), *Chemistry of Spices*. Wallingford, United Kingdom

CAB International, 59-69. DOI: 10.1079/9781845934057.0059

7. Gautam, N., Bhattarai, R.R., Khanal Sharma B. K., & Oli, P. (2016). Technology, chemistry and bioactive properties of large cardamom (*Amomum subulatum* Roxb.) An overview. *International Journal of Applied Sciences and Biotechnology, 4*(2), 139-149.
8. Gopal, K., Baby, C., & Mohammed, A. (2012) *Amomum subulatum* Roxb: An overview in all aspects. *International Research Journal of Pharmacy, 3*(7), 96-99.
9. Gupta U, John T.D (1987). *Floral biology of Large Cardamom.* Retrieved from Agris.fao.org
10. Mukherjee, D .K. (1972) Large cardamom. World Crops 25, 31-33
11. Nigam, S.S., & Purohit, R.M. (1960). Chemical Examination of the Essential Oil Derived from the seeds of *Amomumsubulatum* Roxb. *Perfumery and Essential Oil Record, 51*(3), 121-123
12. Rao, Y.S, Kumar, A., Chatterjee, S., Naidu, R & George, C.K.G; Large cardamom (*Amomumsubulatum* Roxb.) - a review. *Journal of Spices & Aromatic Crops* 2(1&2), 1-15.
13. Shankaracharya N.B, Raghavan B, Abraham K. O., and Shankaranarayana, M.L. (1990) Large Cardamom Chemistry, technology and uses. *Spice India,* 3(8), 17-25.
14. Sharma, E., Sharma, R., Sharma, G., and Singh K.K. (2000). A Boon for Mountain Populations Large Cardamom Farming in the Sikkim Himalaya. *Mountain Research and Development, 20* (2), 108-111.
15. Sharma, G., Sharma, R., & Sharma, E. (2009). Traditional Knowledge systems in Large cardamom farming: biophysical and management diversity in Indian mountainous regions. *Indian Journal of Traditional Knowledge 8*(1), 17-22.
16. Sharma, R., Sharma, E., & Purohit, A.N. (1997). Cardamom, mandarin and nitrogen fixing trees in agroforestry systems in India's Himalayan Region I. Litterfall and decomposition. *Agroforestry Systems, 35,*

239-253.

17. Singh, G.B (1978) Large cardamom. *CARDAMOM 10,* 3-13.

18. Singh, S.P. (2002). Balancing the approaches of environmental conservation by considering ecosystem services as well as bio diversity. *Current Science, 82,* 1331-1335.

19. Thomas, V.P, Sabu, M. and Gupta, U. (2009). Taxonomic studies on cultivars of *Amomumsubulatum, Rheedea, 19,* 25-36

20. Vijayan, A. K., Leela, N.K., Dhanalakshmi, M., Akshitha, H. J., Rahul, R., Utpala, P. & Babu, K.N. (2017). Volatile oil composition of four popular varieties of large cardamom (Amomum subulatum Roxb.) *Journal of Spices and Aromatic Crops, 26*(1) , 37-43.

21. Vijayan, A.K., Bhat, S.K., Gudade, B., Bora S.S., Mary Mathew, K., and Remashree, A.B.(2018). Crop cultivars and varieties with emphasis on nursery propagation of large cardamom (Amomum subulatum Roxb.) in India. *International Journal of Agricultural Science, 10*(20), 7364-7368.

12

Arbuscular Mycorrhizal Fungi: A biostimulant for regeneration of plant

S. Allay[1]

ABSTRACT

Arbuscular Mycorrhizal Fungi (AMF) commonly known as bio-fertilizer help impart the plants to tolerate stressful conditions relating to both biotic and abiotic factors. They help the plants to uptake minerals and maintain soil stability. They also help to restore vegetation in degraded lands otherwise imperilled by the climate change and soil erosion. Darjeeling mandarin (*Citrus reticulata* Blanco), Darjeeling tea (*Camellia sinensis* var. sinensis), and ginger (*Zingiber officinale*) are important cash crops in Darjeeling and Kalimpong hills. But sadly, there has been a decline in their health and production causing a threat to the farmers. This review helps to understand the role of AMF as a biostimulant and help in sustainable horticulture and agriculture bringing about environmental and economic justice.

Introduction

"Universal Plant Symbiosis" is what AMF is described as. It is due to the fact that they have colonized practically all group of plants excluding the members of the mustard family

[1]Sambhu Nath College, Labpur, West Bengal-731303
Email: sanjiava@gmail.com

(Brassicaceae). Since the advent of terrestrialization, AMF have had wide spread distribution both in terms of habitat and host species symbiotic relationship (ENVIS newsletter: Himalayan ecology 1, 2004).

AMF has a crucial connection with the plant and soil structure. Mycorrhizae contribute greatly to soil stability by increasing the root proliferation and hence play an important role in soil erosion. Glomalin, a glycoprotein is produced by AMF. It cements the soil particles and protects them forming an aggregated structure. These aggregates reduce soil erosion and compaction facilitating nutrient and water uptake (Pal and Pandey, 2014). It also contains a large amount of organic carbon contributing to the terrestrial carbon pool (Singh *et. al.*, 2013). Glomalin helps in soil aeration and drainage and productivity (Nichols and Wright, 2004).

They have very fine hyphae which is able to penetrate smaller pores (Allen, 2011). Therefore they make a direct contribution to plant growth, plant protection, disease suppression, crop yield and soil fertility (Chakraborty *et. al.*, 2012). Positive outcomes on plant production in both controlled and field applications have been observed by various authors (Chakraborty *et. al.*, 2013; Berruti *et. al.*, 2016).

AMF also increase plant tolerance to different environmental stresses. They help to improve the absorption of phosphorus, a relatively immobile nutrient that is mobilised by the fungus especially in low nutrient soils or under drought conditions (Fusconi and Berta, 2012).

Phosphorus uptake and Plant growth

Several studies have shown that extensive root colonization have positively affected the host plant species (Jamsa *et. al.*, 2008) and can greatly increase the uptake of phosphorus and nitrogen (George *et. al.*, 1995). Dual application of *G. mosseae* and *G. fasciculatum* decreased total phosphate content of soil (Allay et. al., 2012). Joint inoculation of *G. mosseae* with *T. hamatum* led to an increase in the growth of citrus seedlings (Allay and Chakraborty, 2010). In other studies, AMF inoculation increased the concentration of phosphorus in cotton plant leading to the growth, yield and fibre quality (Gao *et. al.*, 2020). Chakraborty *et. al.*, (2014) has stated that in addition to phosphorus, nitrogen is also of great importance for plant growth and that *Glomus* sp. can metabolise both organic and inorganic sources of nitrogen maybe by glutamate synthetase activity. AMF inoculation has also had a direct impact on maize growth and biomass content (Song *et. al.*, 2020), yield of tomatoes (Nedorost and Pokluda, 2012) and increased plant biomass of pepper and parsley and root biomass of carrots (Regvar *et. al.*, 2003).

Disease suppression

Fusarium solani and *F. oxysporum* are among the few notorious soilborne fungi that causes great loss to agricultural as well as horticultural crops. Several studies to mitigate the yield losses and suppress disease with AMF either single or in consortium with other beneficial fungi and rhizobacteria have been done (Caron *et. al.*, 1986; Allay and Chakraborty, 2010; Hu *et. al.*, 2010; Chakraborty *et. al.*, 2011a; Khastini *et. al.*, 2012; Shukla *et. al.*, 2015; Shabbir *et. al.*, 2021;). The population density of the pathogen, *Pseudomonas syringe* in soybean rhizosphere was suppressed by using *Glomus mosseae* preventing the infection of soybean plants (Shalaby and Hanna, 1998). Replant disease is a poorly understood problem where new plantings fail to establish themselves when they are placed into soil previously occupied by a related species. AMF reduced the incidence of grapevine replant disease by reducing the number of fluorescent pseudomonads on the rhizosphere (Waschkies *et. al.*, 1994). Otto and Winkler, 1995 also reported the suppression of actinomycetes causing replant disease in apple alongwith an increase in root colonization by AMF. Tobacco plants, infected by Tobacco Mosaic Virus (TMV) and cucumber plants infected by Cucumber Green Mottle Mosaic Virus (CGMMV) colonized by Rhizophagus irregularis showed reduced disease symptoms and virus titre when compared to non-mycorrhizal plants (Stolyarchuk *et. al.*, 2009). Preinoculating grass plants with AMF decreased nematode colonization and reproduction but the suppression was not because of systemic plant response but through local mechanisms (de la Pena *et. al.*, 2006).

Stress tolerance

Plants are exposed to many of the biotic and abiotic stresses such as extreme temperature, drought, flooding, toxic metal and soil pathogens. AMF colonization increase the activity of soil enzymes such as dehydrogenase, phosphatase and urease helping the plant to be stronger against stress conditions (Ortas, 2012). Chlorine was found to be higher in Mycorrhizal treated citrus plants (Hartmond *et. al.*, 1987). Flooding decreases the rate of absorption of macronutrients probably due to root mortality and loss of Mycorrhizae and salinity inhibits the growth and alters plant morphology and anatomy (Kozlowski, 1997). Liu et. al. (2014) reported that ATP concentration and expression of plasma membrane ATPase genes were increased by AMF inoculation which maybe by lowering the H_2O_2 accumulation in the roots of cucumber. AMF inoculated wheat plants also showed higher activities of key carbohydrate metabolism enzymes in low temperatures (Li *et. al.*, 2020).

Present scenario of Darjeeling mandarin, tea and ginger in Darjeeling and Kalimpong Hills

Orange is not only consumed for its sweet taste but is an excellent source of vitamin C and other important phytochemicals which helps build the body immune system and prevent arteriosclerosis, cancer, stomach ulcers and kidney stones thereby promoting overall human health (Etebu and Nwauzoma, 2014). However recently there has been a decline in quality fruit production of mandarin probably due to various biotic and abiotic factors (Gurung *et. al.*, 2017). Many factors like Citrus Tristeza Virus (Biswas, 2008; Ghosh *et. al.*, 2013), nematodes (Thapa and Mukhopadhyay, 1994), old and nutrient-exhausted farms, root rot, powdery mildew and low soil nutrient content (Roy *et. al.*, 2018) has contributed to the decline of mandarin in Darjeeling hills. AMF consortium has had a positive impact on the growth of *C. sinensis* seedlings (Sharma and Kayang, 2017). Phytophthora root rot caused by *Phytophthora nicotianae* in Shogun orange could be reduced by treating the plants with either *G. etinucatum* or *A. tuberculata* where shoot die back symptoms was lowered followed by restoration of healthy young shoots (Wataranojanaporn *et. al.*, 2011). Several work has been done on the efficiency of AMF in reducing the disease severity and plant resistance of Fusarium root rot and Fusarium wilt caused by Fusarium (Al-Askar and Rashad, 2010; Jun-Li *et. al.*, 2010; Chakraborty *et. al.*, 2011b). Studies have shown that AMF also have the ability to reduce parasitic nematodes in a root system (Elsen *et. al.*, 2008).

Tea is an aromatic beverage consumed worldwide. Darjeeling tea has a reputation for its flavour and quality. It has many health benefits as it provides essential antioxidants which help to neutralize harmful chemicals and eliminate toxins, reduces the risk of cancer, provides hydration, relieves stress and boosts cardiovascular health. Red rust and blister blight in tea is increasing gradually (Sarkar and Kabir, 2016) which is posing a problem for the tea gardens. Bhujel *et. al.* (2016) has recorded a number of pests and diseases prevalent in Darjeeling tea plantations. AMF inoculation has had positive effects on leaf food quality which maybe due to up-regulation of relevant gene expression in the seedlings (Shao *et. al.*, 2019). Various cultural practices have a negative impact of AMF diversity at the genus level in tea plantations of the colder regions (Singh *et. al.* 2008). The AMF population in tea plants increased during the dormant period but over application of NPK fertilizer has a negative impact on AMF population (Toman and Jha, 2011). Sharma and Kayang (2019) also studied the effect of AMF on teas and stated that AMF could be a promising resource for sustainable tea cultivation.

Ginger whose rhizome is widely used as spice and medicine is a herbaceous perennial. Even though the agro-climatic condition of Kalimpong favours the production of ginger, the crop has failed to make any significant progress during the past few years (Bera and Moktan, 2006). Incidence of rhizome root rot and wilt disease in ginger has been spotted in the major growing areas of Darjeeling hills (Sharma *et. al.*, 2016) and have caused huge loss to the farmers who are now slowly shifting their focus to other remunerative crops like chillies and vegetables (Darnal and Bandyopadhya, 2014). Studies have shown that Mycorrhizal treatment on ginger increases the plant height, number of leaves, number of tillers and fresh weight of ginger rhizome (Samanhudi *et. al.*, 2014) and conjunctive use of AMF with Trichoderma could enhance yield upto 25 percent (Sudha *et. al.*, 2020). The root, shoot and biomass production of ginger under post vitro conditions were considerably greater than control plants after application of AMF either singly or in combination with phosphorus (Santos *et. al.*, 2010). Similarly, AMF colonization with single AMF species or in combination with PGPR induced plant disease resistance and improved ginger growth and yield (GuiMeng *et. al.*, 2017) and plants enhanced well developed root system without disease incidence (Bhai, *et. al.*, 2005). Ginger yellow disease caused by ***Fusarium** oxysporum* f. sp. *zingiberi* was effectively managed using a combination of *Gigaspora margarita*, pine needles and *Trichoderma harzianum* (Sharma *et. al.*, 1997). A study has also shown that ethanol extract of AMF treated ginger could barrier T47D breast cancer cell lines indicating that it can be used as potential herbal medicine for cancer-related ailments (Suharty *et. al.*, 2018).

CONSLUSION

AMF have demonstrated a great potential to reduce crop damages from infectious organisms to a large extent but its application in agriculture has not been substantially applied (Singh and Giri, 2017). AMF as a biofertilizer can be used as a good prospective for agricultural productivity and at the same time maintaining the balance of the ecosystem. It can be used as a good substitute for chemical fertilizers as it reduces the input of chemical fertilizers. Chemical fertilizers do help in increasing the crop yield and suppression of diseases but its unrestrained and superfluous use has caused much damage to the environment and human health and also causes the death of soil flora (Ghosh, 2017). Chemically produced plant cumulate toxic chemicals in the human body which can be fatal (Chandini *et. al.*, 2019). The demand of agricultural products is great but at the same time we should make sure that the food we produce should be safe for consumption. Hence chemical inputs and fertilizers ought to be replaced by biofertilizers which is non-toxic and remains out of harm's way to the environment as well as human health (Suharty *et. al.*, 2018).

REFERENCES

1. Al-Askar AA and Rashad YM (2010). Arbuscular Mycorrhizal fungi: A biocontrol agent against common bean Fusarium root rot disease. *Plant Pathology Journal* 9(1): 31-38
2. Allay S and Chakraborty BN (2010). Activation of defense response of mandarin plants against Fusarium root rot disease using *Glomus mosseae* and *Trichoderma hamatum. J. Mycol. Pl. Pathol.* 40(4): 499-511
3. Allay S, De UK and Chakraborty BN (2012). Root colonization of mandarin plants grown in orchards of Darjeeling hills and plains with Arbuscular Mycorrhizal fungi and their effects on plant growth. *NBU Journal of Plant Sciences.* 6(1): 41-47
4. Allen M F (2011). Linking water and nutrients through the vadose zone: a fungal interface between the soil and plant systems. *Journal of Arid Land* 3(3): 155-163
5. Bera BK and Moktan MW (2006). Economics of ginger cultivation in the hill region of West Bengal. *Journal of Crop and Weed* 2(2): 11-13
6. Berutti A, Lumini E, Balestrini R and Bianciotto V (2016). Arbuscular Mycorrhizal fungi as natural biofertilizers: Lets benefit from past successes. *Frontiers in Microbiology.* 6, 1559

7. Bhai RS, Kishore VK, Kumar A, Anandaraj M and Eapen SJ (2005). Screening of rhizobacterial isolates against soft root rot disease of ginger (*Zingiber officinale* Rosc.). *Journal of Spices and Aromatic Crops.* 14(2): 130-136

8. Bhujel A, Singh M, Choubey M and Singh M (2016). Pest and disease management in Darjeeling tea. *International Journal of Agricultural Science and Research* 6(3): 469-472

9. Biswas KK (2008). Molecular diagnosis of citrus tristeza virus in mandarin (*Citrus reticulata*) orchards of Darjeeling hills of West Bengal. *Indian J. Virol.* 19(1): 26-31

10. Caron M, Richard C, Fortin JA. 1986. Effect of preinfestation of the soil by a vesicular-arbuscular mycorrhizal fungus, Glomus intraradices, on Fusarium crown and root rot of tomatoes. *Phytoprotection.* 67:15-19.

11. Chakraborty BN, De UK and Allay S. (2014). Molecular detection of Arbuscular Mycorrhizal fungi and their application for plant health improvement. In: Biology of Useful Plants and Microbes (ed.) Arnab Sen, Narosa Publishing House, New Delhi, India pp. 13-31

12. Chakraborty U, Chakraborty BN, Allay S, De U and Chakraborty AP (2011) (a). Dual application of *Bacillus pumilus* and *Glomus mosseae* for improvement of health status of mandarin plants. *Acta Horticulturae* 892: 215-229

13. Chakraborty BN, Chakraborty U, RAi K, Allay S, and Dey PL (2011) (b). Molecular detection of fungal pathogens of Citrus reticulata grown in Darjeeling hills and their managenment. *Acta Horticulturae* 892: 189-206

14. Chandini, RK, Kumar R and Prakash O (2019). The impact of chemical fertilizers on our environment and ecosystem. In book: Research Trends in Environmental Sciences, 2nd Edition Chapter 5 69-86

15. Darnal R and Bandhopadhya AK (2014). Assessment of

intervention needs for enhancing ginger production in some selected areas of Darjeeling district, West Bengal. *International Journal of Development Research.* 4(7): 1384-1385

16. De la Pena E, Echeverria SR, Vander Putten W, Freitas H and Mans M (2006). Mechanism of control of root-feeding nematodes by Mycorrhizal fungi in the dune grass *Amnophila arenaria. New Phytologist.* 169: 829-840
17. Etebu E and Nwauzoma AB (2014). A review on sweet orange (Citrus sinensis Osbeck): health, diseases, and management. *American Journal of Ressearch Communication,* 2(2): 33-70
18. Elsen A, Gervacio D, Sivennen R and Waele DD (2008). AMF-induced biocontrol against plant parasitic nematodes in *Musa* sp. a systemic effect. *Mycorrhiza* 18(5): 251-256
19. Fusconi A and Berta, G (2012). Environmental stress and role of arbuscular mycorrhizal symbiosis. - In: Ahmad, P., Prasad, M. N. V. (eds.) Abiotic Stress Responses in Plants: Metabolism, Productivity and Sustainability. Springer, New York, pp. 197-214
20. Gao X, Guo H, Zhang Q, Guo H, Zhang L, Zhang C, Gou Z, Liu Y, Wei J, Chen A, Chu Z, Zeng F (2020). Arbuscular mycorrhizal fungi (AMF) enhanced the growth, yield, fiber quality and phosphorus regulation in upland cotton (*Gossypium hirsutum L.*). *Sci Rep* 10:2084, 1- 12
21. George E, Marschner M and Jakobsen I (1995). Role of Arbuscular Mycorrhizal fungi in uptake of phosphorus and nitrogen from soil. *Critical Reviews in Biotechnology,* 15: 3-4
22. Ghosh A, Das A, Pun KB, Kumar R, Meena R and Baranwal VK (2014). Present status of Citrus tristeza virus infecting Citrus spp. in Darjeeling hills and its detection in different plant parts. *Phytoparasitica* 42: 381-386.
23. Ghosh P (2017). Local AMF and plant health-An instant

effect on human health. *Indian Journal of Biological Sciences.* 23: 58-62

24. GuiMeng L, ShuPeng T, WenXian S and RunJun L. (2017). Effects of Arbuscular Mycorrhizal fungi and plant growth promoting rhizobacteria on bacterial wilt of ginger. *Journal of Fungal Research.* 15(1): 1-7
25. Gurung N, Sarkar S, Allay S, Meena R and Singh B (2017). Problems and future prospects of Darjeeling mandarin in Darjeeling and Sikkim Hills (A Review). *Journal of Agroecology and Natural Resource Management.* 4(3) 228-231.
26. Hartmond U, Schaesberg Nv, Graham JM and Syvertsen JP (1987). Salinity and flooding stress effects on Mycorrhizal and non-mycorrhizal citrus rootstock seedlings. *Plant and Soil.* 104(1): 37-43
27. Shabbir I, Samad MYA, Othman R, Wong M-Y, Sulaiman Z, Jaafar NM and Bukhari SAH (2021), Evaluation of bioformulation of Enterobacter sp. UPMSSB7 and mycorrhizae with silicon for white root rot disease suppression and growth promotion of rubber seedlings inoculated with *Rigidoporus microporus, Biological Control,* 152: 104467,
28. Jansa J, Smith F and Smith S (2008). Are there benefits of simultaneous root colonization by different Arbuscular Mycorrhizal fungi? *New Phytol.* 177: 779-789
29. Jun-Li Hu, Xian-Gui Lin, Jun-Hua Wang, Wei-Shou Shen, Shu Wu, Su-Ping Peng and Ting-Ting Mao (2010). Arbuscular Mycorrhizal fungi inoculation enhances suppression of cucumber Fusarium wilt in greenhouse soils. *Pedosphere.* 20(5): 586-593
30. Khastini RO, Ohta H and Narisawa K (2012). The role of a dark septate endophytic fungus, *Veronaeopsis simplex* Y34, in Fusarium disease suppression in Chinese cabbage. *J Microbiol.* 50: 618-624
31. Kozlowski TT (1997). Responses of woody plants to flooding and salinity. *Tree Physiology.* 17(7): 490

32. Li M, Li S, Wang Z, Liu S, Zhou R and Li X (2020). Abscisic-acid mimicking ligand AMF4 induced cold tolerance in wheat by altering the activities of key carbohydrate metabolism enzymes. *Plant Physiology and Biochemistry.* 157: 284-290

33. Liu A, Chen S, Chang R, Liu D, Chen H, Ahammed GJ, Lin X and He C (2014). Arbuscular Mycorrhizae improve low temperature tolerance in cucumber via alterations in H_2O_2 accumulation and ATPase activity. *J. Plant Res.* 127 (6): 775-785

34. Nedorost L and Pokluda R (2012). Effects of Arbuscular mucorrhizal fyngi on tomato yield and nutrient uptake under different fertilization levels. *Acta Univ. Agric. Et.silvic.* Mendel. Brun; 60 (8): 181-186.

35. Ortas I (2012). Mycorrhiza in citrus: Growth and nutrition. In: Advances in Citrus Nutrition (ed.) A. K. Srivastava. Springer, Dordrecht 333-351

36. Otto G and Winkler H (1995). Colonization of rootlets of some species of Rosaceae by actinomycetes, endotrophic mycorrhiza and endophytic nematodes in a soil conducive to specific cherry replant disease. *Z. Pflanzenkr Planzenschutz* 102: 63-68

37. Pal A and Pandey S (2014). Role of glomalin in improving soil fertility: A review. *International Journal of Plant and Soil Science* 3(9): 1112-1129

38. Regvar M,Vogel-Mikus K and Severkar T (2003). Effect of AMF inoculums from field isolates on the yield of green pepper, parsley, carrot and tomato. *Folia Geobotanica* 38: 223-234

39. Roy R, Kharga BD and Moktan MW (2018). Darjeeling mandarin orange: Reasons for its decline and perceived constraints. *Int. J. Curr. Microbiol. App. Sci.* 7(9): 14-20

40. Samanhudi, A, Pujiasmanto B and Rahayu M (2014). Effect of organic manure and Arbuscular Mycorrhizal fungi on growth and yield of young ginger (*Zingiber officinale Rosc.*). *IOSR Journal of Agriculture and*

Veterinary Science 7(5): 1-5

41. Santos RD, Giarardi CG, Pescador R and Sturmer SL (2010). Effects of Arbuscular Mycorrhizal fungi and phosphorus fertilization on post vitro growth of micropropagated *Zingiber officinale* roscoe. *Revista Brasileira de Ciencia do Solo.* 34: 765-771

42. Santos, Rosilda dos, Girardi, Carla Giovana, Pescador, Rosete, & Stürmer, Sidney Luiz. (2010). Effects of arbuscular mycorrhizal fungi and phosphorus fertilization on post vitro growth of micropropagated Zingiber officinale roscoe. *Revista Brasileira de Ciência do Solo,* 34(3): 765-771.

43. Sarkar S, and Kabir SE 2016. A Field Survey of Tea Diseases and Their Control Measures In Some Tea Gardens of Terai Region, West Bengal, India. *Int J Recent Sci Res.* 7(3): 9810-9813.

44. Shalaby AM and Hanna MM (1998). Preliminary studies on interactions between VA mycorrhizal fungus *Glomus mosseae, Bradyrhizobium japonicum and Pseudomonas syringae* in soybean plants. Acta Microbiol Pol 47: 385-391

45. Shao YD, Zhang DJ, Hu XC, Wu QS, Jiang CJ, Gao XB and Kuca K (2019). Arbuscular Mycorrhiza Improves Leaf Food Quality of Tea Plants. *Notulae Botanicae Horti Agrobotanici Cluj-Napoca,* 47(3): 608-614. https://doi.org/10.15835/nbha47311434

46. Sharma BR, Roy S and Dutta S (2016). Survey of rhizome rot and wilt disease incidence of ginger in major growing area of Darjeeling hill, India. *Direct Research Journal of Agriculture and Food Science.* 4(1): 14-18

47. Sharma D and Kayang H (2017). Effects of Arbuscular Mycorrhizal fungi (AMF) on *Camellia sinensis* (L.) O. Kuntze under greenhouse conditions. *Journal of Experimental Biology and Agricultural Sciences* 5(2): 235-241

48. Sharma D and Kayang H (2017). Effects of Arbuscular

Mycorrhizal fungi (amf) on *Camellia sinensis* (L.) O. Kuntze under greenhouse conditions. *Journal of experimental Biology and Agricultural Sciences* 5(2): 235-241

49. Sharma S, Dohroo NP and Sharma S (1997). Management of ginger yellows through organic amendment, fungicide seed treatment and biological methods. *Ind. Cocoa Arecanut Spice J.* 21: 29-30

50. Shukla A, Dehariya K, Vyas D and Jha A (2015). Interactions between Arbuscular mycorrhizae and *Fusarium oxysporum* f. sp. ciceris: effects on fungal development, seedling growth and wilt disease suppression in *Cicer arietinum* L. *Archives of Phytopathology and Plant Protection* 48(3): 240-252

51. Singh I and Giri B (2017). Arbuscular Mycorrhiza mediated control of plant pathogens. In Ajit Varma, Ram Prasad and Narendra Tuteja (eds): Mycorrhiza-Nutrient uptake, Biocontrol, Ecorestoration. Springer 131-160

52. Singh PK, Singh M and Tripathi BN (2013). Glomalin: An Arbuscular Mycorrhizal fungal soil protein. *Protoplasma.* 250: 663-669

53. Singh S, Pandey A, Chaurasis B and Palni LMS (2008). Diversity of Arbuscular Mycorrhizal fungi associated with the rhizosphere of tea growing in 'natural' and 'cultivated' ecosites. *Biology and Fertility of Soils.* 44(3): 491-500

54. Song Z, Bi Y, Zhang J, Gong Y and Yang H (2020). Arbuscular mycorrhizal fungi promote the growth of plants in the mining associated clay. *Scientific reports* 10:2663,

55. Stolyarchuk IM, Shevchenko TP, Polischuk VP, and Kripka, AV (2009). Virus infection course in different plant species under influence of arbuscular mycorrhiza. *Microbiol. Biotechnol.* 6, 70-75. doi: 10.18524/2307-4663.2009.3(7).103120

56. Sudha B, Jon J, Meera AV and Sajeena A (2020). Growth, nutrient uptake and yield of ginger as impacted by potting

media, foliar nutrition and microbial inoculants. *Journal of Spices and Aromatic Crops* 29(2): 113-121

57. Suharty N, Wahyuni FS, Dachriyanus (2018). Cytotoxic Activity of Ethanol Extract of Arbuscular Mycorrhizal Fungi Induced Ginger Rhizome on T47D Breast Cancer Cell Lines. *Pharmacog J.* 10(6):1133-6
58. Thapa A and Mukhopadhyay S (1994). Studies on the problems of citrus nematode in orchards and nurseries of mandarin orange in Darjeeling hills and their management. *Indian Journal of Nematology.* 24(2): 214-220
59. Toman TS and Jha DK (2011). Diversity of Arbuscular Mycorrhizal fungi associated with the rhizosphere of tea [*Camellia sinensis* (L). O. Kuntze] plantation in upper Assam, India. *Mycorrhiza News* 23(2): 10-13
60. Waschkies C, Schropp A and Marschner H (1994). Relations between grapevine replant disease and root colonization of grapevine (*Vitis sp.*) by fluorescent pseudomonads and endomycorrhizal fungi. *Plant Soil.* 162: 219-227
61. Watanarojanaporn N, Boonkerd N, Wongkaew S, Prommanop P and Teaumroong N (2011). Selection of Arbuscular Mycorrhizal fungi for citrus growth promotion and Phytophthora suppression. *Scientia Horticulturae.* 128(4): 423-433

13

Heritage Crop (Sital Pati) Cultivation of North Bengal

Sumana Saha[1] & Bappa Sarkar[2]

ABSTRACT

Cooch Behar District is famous for its rich cultural heritage. Belonging various handicrafts, Sitalpati is one of the significant products of this area. Such product depicts the Social-cultural, and economic traits of Betkar community. A particular community or a considerable number of rural inhabitants in this district depends on this perennial tropical shrub called Murta or Cane or Pati bet plant, as the raw material of cottage industry. Pati or *Schumannianthas dichotomus* (Roxb.) Gagnep belongs to the family Marantaceae, a forest species grown in the swamp, low-lying wetlands of Cooch Behar district. The Study area are Ghogumari, Tufanganj, and Deochorai village. The study's primary objectives were to determine the techniques for traditional management of cane plantation, seed germination, propagation was from rhizomes, and branch cutting and little intensive management was recorded. Type and quality affect the price and the demand of the product. So, the profit of Betkar community depends on the plantation process and procedure, that also control by the physical and

[1]Research Scholar of Cooch Behar Panchanan Barma University
[2]Assistant Professor of Geography, Dinhata College
Email: bappa.geo001@gmail.com

cultural determinants of this region. The cultivation process of Murta has excellent potential for the rural economy of this District. Therefore, it is the need of the hour to promote marketing of this plant-based small-scale industry as a cash crop cultivation to retain the cultural heritage and a source for sustainability.

Key Words : Pati plant (schumannianthus dichotomus), cultivation process, Sital Pati, indigenous handicraft.

Introduction

India is traditionally a country of artistic handicrafts. The origin of Indian handicrafts dates back to the hoary past when the story of human beings first began to be articulated. Until the advent of British rule in the 18th century, India was much too renowned for artworks worldwide (Maiti, 2017). In collaboration with UNESCO, the government of West Bengal has developed a Rural Craft Hub at Ghughumari, which is just 20 minutes away from Cooch Behar Town. Such product depicts the social-cultural and economical traits of Betkar community. Sital Patihas been a heritage of the North-Eastern part of India (Hossen et al. 2020). Sitalpati (cool mat) is an age-old traditional handicraft item of Cooch Behar, which is sometimes used as an alternative to bed sheets or prayer mats (Basak, et al., 2015). For generations, people living in the North-eastern states in the country, such as West Bengal, Assam (Chowdhuri, 2006) Tripura, have been making the popular craft item by the bark of cane or Murta plants (Schumannianthus dichotomus) (veldkamp et al., 2016). The tradition of Sital Patiweaving was inherent to Bangladesh. Still, it was brought to India by the craftsmen who came to India after partition as refugees and continued with the craft they knew best for earning their livelihood (Chowdhury et al., 2007).

As a traditional craft practice, the making of Sital Patiis championed by families (Das et al., 2018). Cooch Behar district, Cooch Behar Sadar, and Tufanganj showed a high market potential of this production sitalpati is made using the raw material produced from Murta schumannianthus dichotomus (marantaceae) is the scientific name of the plant (Ahmed et al., 2007). The plant is also known as Pati Plant, Pati bet, Murta, mustak, Pati Pata,Patijung, Pati doi etc. in different regions of different states in India and many regions of Bangladesh such as Sylhet, Sunamganj, Maulvabazar, Tangail, Chittagong, Comilla, Noakhali, Jhalokati, Chittagaon, Comilla, Sirajganj and Munshiganj (Rashid et al,1993). The geographically Murta plant is distributed in other countries, Burma, Thailand, Cambodia, Vietnam, peninsular Malaysia, Borneo, and the Philippines (Hussain and Ismail, 2016). This tropical plant is naturally grown in marshy lands, so in this region, Betkar community generally cultivate Murta plant .at present days, all types of soil, high or dry land or marshy land for business (Mandal, *et al.* 2014).The sapling of Murta plant planted in the prolonged monsoon when cultivable lands in the vast low-lying areas go underwater. Pati is generally made by the stem's three-part: *chittor, saloi, maji*. According to Wikipedia (2010), Murta (Schumannianthus dichotoma (Sal.) is the raw material for making Sital Pati, a traditional bed mat of Bangladesh. Murta is a clump-forming rhizomatous shrub belonging to the family Marantaceae (Hooker 1892; Prain 1903). It is dichotomously branched and has green cylindrical stems attaining a height of 3-5 m and a diameter of 2.0 cm with oblong leaves of 8-15 cm length broadly rounded at the base (Mohiuddin and Rashid 1988; Wikipedia 2021). The cylindrical stems of Murta plants are collected as raw materials for Murta-based enterprises. Traditional artisans make strips from outer portion of the stem, including the epidermal part. These split strips are processed and plaited into mats. Murta splits are also used for making prayer mats, wall mats, dining mats, baskets, bags, and novelty items. (Saha 2012). Many industries developed in ancient India. One of those industries is the plant-based industry. The role of the plant in economic activities has been discussed at length in Sanskrit texts. Plants have been an integral part of an Indian culture from time immemorial and when one talks about the Indian culture

(Dwivedi, 2018).

The Sitalpati weavers are organized under the Cooch Behar-I Patishilpo Samabay Samity. The co-operative has 633 members. They have their Common Facility Centre (CFC), which includes a Museum, a space for the weekly market of Sitalpati, and a work space. The collective has celebrated the Annual Sitalpati Mela since 2015 (https://sheatwork.com/shital-pati-rich-cultural-heritage-of-rural-bengal/). The craft item was inscribed on the national list of Intangible Cultural Heritage by the People's Republic of Bangladesh in 2007. The country has also applied to UNESCO for its inscription on the Representative List of Intangible Cultural Heritage of Humanity "Traditional Art of Shital Pati Weaving of Sylhet".

Study Area

The study was conducted at Ghugumari, Deochorai, Uttar Ghogarkuti, Barokodali, and Dholuabari village of Cooch Behar district of West Bengal. The region is in the foothill of Eastern- Himalaya. Many rivers flow in this flat region with a slight southeastern slope; heavy rains often cause strong river current and flooding. The turbulent water carries huge amounts of sand, slit, and pebbles, which adversely affect crop production. Alluvial soil is common in this area, and it has low levels of nitrogen with a moderate levels of potassium and phosphorus. Deficiencies of boron, zinc, calcium, magnesium, and Sulphur are high. The soil depth varies from 15 to 50 cm. The temperature is maximum 32.2° in August and minimum 9.4° in January in this area. It is highly humid region with average annual rain fall is 3,562mm. Monsoonal rainy season lasts June to September month. (IMD, 2020).

Objectives

1. To find out the controlling factors and the favorable conditions for cultivating the Cane Plant in Cooch Behar District.
2. To observe the small-scale cottage industry based on cane or Murta plants.
3. To identify the value of Sital Patior cane plant.

4. To find the problems and barriers of cane cultivation and weaving practice.

Methodology

The present study has been carried out on Sital Pati Cultivators and in the Cooch Behar District which constitutes 12 blocks and 1140 mouzas covering an area of 3387 km^2. Samples were taken from the sampled village according to the Cultivators. To obtain the primary data at the household level, 5 village have been selected from the 3 Sital Pati dominating blocks of the district. The villages are Ghugumari, Deochorai, Uttar Ghogarkuti, Barokodali, and Dholuabari. Standard questionnaires investigated the species potential, an interview schedule was designed to collect the primary information for the selected respondents. These collected data were again verified consulting available literatures, research papers, articles, and the internet. Finally the data was tabulated and analyses by descriptive statistical method.

Result and discussion

Murta can be readily cultivated on land that remains under water for a long period during the rainy season and remains wet even in dry season. Hence, it is not suitable for the the cultivation of other cash crops. Sustainability of Sital Patimaking depends on a continuous supply of suitable raw materials, financial support, skilled artisans, effective market channels and efficient pricing system, and reliable demand. Lack of capital constraints artisans is another form of increasing problems restricting their capabilities. Now-a-days Murta-based small-scale enterprises are under threat mainly due to the acute shortage of raw materials lack financial support for producers and weak marketing and pricing systems. Moreover, the return from Murta cultivation is comparatively higher than the traditional rice cultivation (Mohiuddin and Rashid 1988). However, it is a labour-intensive enterprise. In Cooch Behar, 130 Sital Patiis made by the Murta plantation of 1 bigha field area.

Botanical Aspects

The cane plant or schumannianthus dichomus (Roxb.) Gagnep belongs to the Marantaceae family. One Mature Pati plant height is 4-5 m, the green branches are 1-2 m in length, the leaves (10-15 cm length) are lanceolate with petiolar sheath at the base and dichotomously branched stems 3-5 m high, and basal diameter of 2-5 cm (Prain 1903; Anon1950; FMP 1992). It has a tuberous rootstock (Hooker 1892) with stem buds on culms (new shoot buds). Rhizomes are tough and fibrous, with 10-24 tillers or shoots erect (Chowdhury and konwar, 2006). These shoots are cut and used as propagating part of this plant. It appears in April-May month and Octobar-November, it has a deep roots in the soil (Mandal, *et al*, 2014). Flower length is 3 to 4 cm, purely white, bisexual, having three calyx and irregularly lobed corolla, in this the pollination is entomophilic, which have three celled basally tabular ovary (Gupta *et al*, 2020).

Method of Cultivation

'Murta' is one of the non-woody forest species; swampy wetlands is the most favorable ambiance for the growth of the plants. Seed germination or rhizome-based farming procedure is kept in many cases based on old plantation fields. It is cultivated like paddy, at first in a small wet area, 'Murta' saplings are planted for few more growth (100 saplings in 400 rupees). After few months, the small plants are grown, gathered with 5 or 6 saplings together, after ploughing and water-logging field. Plantation starts in the rainy season (month of April), flowers blossom in august to September month (Hasan and Mia, 2015). The stems are hard, but the branches are soft than the mature stem of Murta. The leaves of this plant are straight, 10-15cm in length or 5-7 cm width, and after cutting the plant, is is used as fuel. Sometimes people eat the flower of Pati plant. Murta plant prefers clay or clay loam soil with high moisture. The plant propagated from rhizome that were planted in the field (Ahmed *et al*. 2007). It prefers clay or clay-loam soil with high moisture. The plant cannot tolerate direct sun. It is propagated from rhizomes that are planted directly in the field at 1 - 1 m spacing (Merry 2001). The wetlands in which "pati bet" grown naturally, but in Cooch Behar district, it is cultivated both high and lying area to make Pati or trading of raw material, based plant. The Betkar people plant this plant at the rest of their house area. Other agricultural farming is sometimes affected so this type of plantation is is planted separately or in a continuous field area manner of the same plant (Hossain, 2009). Culture holds the heritage and the indigenous techniques of Murta cultivation (Basak and Chowdhury, 2019) in this region by generation. Murta is profitable to cultivate as a family side business (150 rupees per Sital Pati). This plantation need not require more investment, more care, and manpower. The suitable factors are discussed below-

Soil: Soil is the major controlling factor for cultivating cane plants in this area. Sticky- silt or clay is suitable for cultivation. Cooch Behar District is full of cover of alluvial soil. Marshy soil is most favorable for Cane culttivation but now a days its spread in agricultural land also. Plant quality depends on the soil type. Plans that grow in high land are hard in nature, but in the the case of low-lying water logging field, the steams are became soft (Basak, *et al.* 2019).

Climate: A humid climate nourished this tropical-type of plantation farming. Cane plants tolerate high temperatures, heavy rainfall, water -logging roots, cyclone, and flood also. Pre-monsoon months (April-May) are most effective for harvesting (Ahmed *et al.* 2007).

Rainfall: As a tropical plant, it required 150 -200 cm. rainfall. This plant has no issues with heavy rain or water logging in the field; the root of this plant is so strong. Tight binding from in soil texture so that this plant control soil erosion.

Weeding: In this forest-type plantation farming, many other weeds are grown naturally in the field, creeper, climbers. After the rainy season the weeds are removed by laborers once a year, Rs. 300 per day paying (Ahmed, *et al.* 2007). Sometimes medicines are applying to burn weeds. In plantation field, after 30-40 years total plantation is wipeout and plant new plants for good quality of production.

Fertilizer: Some research work clearly indicated that the plantations are limited by either of these nutrients (organic matter, N, P and K). Both organic and inorganic components used as fertilizer (Mia, *et al* 2018). Pit or bog soil is helpful for this type of plant. The respondents use Cow dunk, compost of kochuripana, DAP, and urea used in the agricultural field and maintain a schedule. 1500 Rs. per bigha agrarian field. For the growth of Murta plant N, P, K used in plantation time. Fertilizers are used in dry season (observation in study area).

Pest and disease management

Insect fungi affect the plantation area, so sometimes insecticides are used for the good health of cane. The betker people, rat report no major pests, snakes are common. During the water logging time, some dark spots are formed on the seam of the cane. This stem rot is a permanent disease of pati plant, so it decreases the quality of cane mat (Gupta *et al.*2020). For this Betkar people colour those strips of cane to make the product a good look. Lal pati has a lower price, but sital sadapati is higher than that's quality (Bhattacharjee and Shill ,2017).

Cutting and weaving

In this area, generally male people take part in Murta cultivation, and cutting or collection, and female persons are involved in the making of Sital Pati (weaving). In one day, a cultivator cut the cane stem for weaving 8 or10 pieces of mats, 300 rupees labor cost per day. At the cutting time, Betkar cut the mature stem first from the central areas of the plantation field to free the creeper or to provide a good place for the growth of other stems. For this method, cattle do not enter the field easily. In a year, Murta cane is collected two times. After 1 year or 1.5 years the mature plan is cut down from the single group of the field plantation. The plants or Sitalpati cannot store for more than six months. So, the amount of cutting cane plant is based on requirement or demand in the market. Sitalpati has a smooth glossy waterproof outside, Sital Patiis made by the saloi or outer green layer when cut into finer slips. The inner layer is used for making bukapati, a mat of inferior quality rough on both sides. Based on demand at a low price, the outer layer of the soloi can be used to make motapati and bukapaki (Gupta *et al.* 2020). Some bets are derived from the green younger branches of the Pati plant, which are more flexible and finer quality that is used for dalapati, such as dalamota & dala sital.

Methods of making sital pati

After collecting the Pati bet the stems are washed and cut into three parts for making pati - *chittor* (split into 2 parts), *saloi* (split of chittor), and *maji* (inner most part). Saloi part is used for high-quality Sital Pati, such as *Kamal kosh* (decorative, complex imagery), *bhusnaipati* (made by very fine strips), Dupuni pati (made by small bets), (Gupta, *et.al.* 2020).

List of traditional practices for making Pati using Murta plant along with farming practice

Steps	activity	Tools used	Traditional methods	Result or final product
Nourish-ment of sapling	Tiny plant planted wet place separately	Spade, sickle	For perfect plantation	Growth of plant
Plantation	Plowing & watering before plantation of sapling	Bamboo stick	Spacing between two plantation bunch	Suitable growth and desirable size
Manuring	Application of fertilizer		Cow dunk, urea, DAP use	Perfect height
Harvest	Cutting of mature stem from the base	Sickle		Obtain bet
Cutting	For straight growth of	Sickle	Strips	Make the bet

	plant short brancher are collected			
Processing of bet	Submergence in water and drying		Kept 10-15 days based on maturity and the quality of bark, after that 1-hour drying in sunlight	Making the quality bet
Split of bet	Splitting	Knife	Individual stems are slitted lengthwise into two halves	Making of chittor
Split of chittor	Separation	Bati, by hand		Production of pati and maji
Split of pati	Segmentation		Pati divide into 3 parts from outside to inside depend on stem thickness	Best quality of pati produced
Boiling of pati	Heated with water removal of color	Container	Boilling 1 hr with water, mixinig with boil rice, juice,and for colour, magenta colour	Pati became smooth glossy, remove the raddish colour
Drying of pati	Dry the strips of pati in sun light	By hanging on bamboos	Specific size mat strips bunch together	Good quality of mat bet ready to use
weaving	Gradation or design of pati	Knife	Different size mat weaved	Different type of mat developed.

Sital Patiis famous for its quality. After cutting, the smooth glossy decorative mat or the raw materials and the total plant have been sold in different places or states. This area is a production field of Murta plant for good cultivation (Hasan, 2015). In Betkar community, many of the artisans, either individually or in self-help groups, are engaged in the production. The cane plant is the raw material for making the most important value-added product Sital Pati, a traditional bad mat, prayer seats, hats, ladies handbags, purse, mobile covers, file covers, hand fans, wall matsetc. (Mandal, *et.al.*, 2014).

Future prospect of Murta cultivation

Plantation farming was introduced to impact historical globalization and more profitable activity (Hossain, 2009). For sharing this traditional practice, Betkar people present Sital Pati or other accessories as a gift to their friends, guests, and honorable people to promote their knowledge on a large scale (Chowdury, 2006). In spite of the Bektar people Involved in other occupations, they cultivate this Pati plant, because it has a maximum profit as seasonal cash crop treading. Today, it is a bio-cultural heritage confined in a small place to need more investment or promotion to use this type of product (Gupta *et al.* 2020). In Ghogumari, Swami Vivekananda Swanirvor Prokalpo is available for financial support or subsidy. The government and other organizations should provide their support to the cultivators and the Betkar people for boost their socio-economic standards by bringing the products to the international market and enhance the rural economy through tourism.

CONCLUSION

The study revealed that the cane plant or Murta is a cash crop for the Betkar community of Cooch Behar district. As a plantation farming, this Murta cultivation gives a less Labor consuming and more profitable production for long-term outcome in one time more investment. Bioresource is helpful for the environment, as a raw material for sustainable environmental retainment and eco-friendly plant product give us growth of pollution-free small-scale cottage industry

(Bakri *et.al.*, 2021). The present study also revealed that all physical and social factors are there in the Cooch Behar district region to harvest the Murta plant. This tropical forest species is grown in the same latitudinal extended areas of different countries for similar climatic conditions (Sharma *et al.* 1999). After the partition, people moved from Bangladesh to India so that the cultural heritage moved from one place to another. Therefore, the migrated people of this region (Cooch Behar district) have a legacy of cultivating the plant for generations (Hossen *et al*, 2020). The cultivation process of Murta has great potential for the rural economy of this District. Therefore, it is the need of the hour to promote marketing of this plant-based small scale industry as a cash crop cultivation to retain the cultural heritage and a source for sustainability.

REFERENCES

1. *Al-Hadi AH.* Sylhet District. In Islam S (ed.), *Banglapedia Multimedia CD.* Dhaka, Bangladesh: Asiatic Society of Bangladesh; 2004
2. *Anon. Wealth of India (Raw Materials),* Vol. II. New Delhi: Council of Scientific and Industrial Research; 1950:427
3. Arnold JEM. Socio-Economic Benefits and Issues in Non-wood Forest Products Use. In *Report of the International Expert Consultation on Non-wood forest products. Non-Wood Forest Products 3.* Rome: FAO; 1995:89-123.
4. Bakri, M.K.,Omoregie, A., Rahman "Bamboo and its Bio-composites", ACADEMIA Letters August 2021.
5. *Banik RL.* Economic Importance and Future of Rattan and Patipata in Bangladesh. In Roshetko M and Bose SK (eds), *Propagation and Cultivation of Rattanand Patipata in Bangladesh.* Proceeding of Training Courses held at the Bangladesh Forest Research Institute (BFRI), Chittagong, Bangladesh; 2001: 25-8.
6. *Chowdhury MSH, Uddin MS, Haque F, Muhammed N and Koike M.* Indigenous Management of Patipata (*Schumannianthus dichotoma*) plantation in the rural

homesteads of Bangladesh. *Journal of Subtropical Agriculture Research and Development* 2007; 5(1):202-7

7. Das,T. K., Maity, B., Pradhan, K.,"Socio-Economic status and Constraints of weavers in Sital Pati Production in Cooch Behar District of West Bengal" Volume 2 - Issue 4 Online ISSN: 2582-368X, 2018.
8. Dr. Dwivedi, D. V., "Development of Plant based Industries as Depicted in Sanskrit Texts"Lalita Kavi-Bharati, Vol. IX No: I, 2017, PP. 7-19.
9. Dr. Kasemi, N "*Prospects of Bamboo-based household industries: Case study of Koch Bihar in India*" Zenith International Journal of Multidisciplinary Research, ISSN 2231-5780 Vol.4 (7), JULY (2014) Online available at zenithresearch.org.in
10. FAO. *Non-wood forest products for rural income and sustainable forestry* 7. Reprinted in 1999. Rome:FAO; 1995:1-2
11. *Hooker JD. Flora of British India,* Vol. VI. Kent, UK: L. Reave and Co.; 1892: 257-8
12. Hore D.K., Sharma B.D. "Indian matcane *Schumannianthus dichotomus* (Roxb.) Gagnep: an underutilized fiber plant of India" Indian Journal of Plant Genetic Resources, 1999, Volume: 12, Issue: 3, pp. 376-381.
13. https://ich.unesco.org/en/RL/traditional-art-of-shital-pati-weaving-of-sylhet-01112
14. https://sheatwork.com/shital-pati-rich-cultural-heritage-of-rural-bengal/
15. Hussain, A. Barbhuiya, & Ismail, K ."Effect of fiber length and loading on the properties of Schumannianthus dichotomus (Murta) fiver-reinforced epoxy composites "International journal of polymer analysis and characterization, volume-21, issue-3, 2016.
16. Indira Khurana and Romit Sen, Drinking Water Quality in Rural India: Issues and Approaches, Water Aid.

17. Islam ANMF. The role of Murta-Based Cottage Industry in Socio-Economic Development of Rural People: A Case Study from Sylhet District, Bangladesh. A Project Paper. Department of Forestry. Shahjalal University of Science and Technology, Sylhet, Bangladesh; 2005:47

18. *Kanakalata Mukund and Syamasundari B.,* "The Cotton Handlooms of Andhra Pradesh: Traditional Industry in the New Market Economy", Sage Publications, New Delhi, 2001, Pp. 104 - 105.

19. *Kasemin "Influence of socio-economic factors on the productivity of household industry: a case study of bamboo-work industry in jalpaiguri district, West Bengal",* 2013, geo-analyst, issn 2249-2909

20. *Mahapatro P.C.,* "Economics of Cotton Handloom Industry in India", Ashish Publishing House, New Delhi, 1996, Pp. 74 - 76.

21. Mandal, R.N., Bar, R., and Chakrabarti, p. p. 'pati bet', *schumannianthus dichotomus (Roxb.) Gagnep.-A raw material for preparation of livelihood supporting handicraft, Indian Journal of National Products and Resources. vol.5(4), December-2014, pp-365-370.*

22. *Merry SR.* Propagation Technique of Patipata. In Roshetko JM and Bose SK (eds), *Propagation and Cultivation of Rattan and Patipata in Bangladesh.* Proceeding of Training Courses held at the Bangladesh Forest Research Institute (BFRI), Chittagong, Bangladesh; 2001: 22-4

23. *Mishra, Aswini Kumar,* "Social Impact of Handloom Co-operatives on Weavers in Western Orissa: An Empirical Study", 1994 Journal of Rural Development, Vol.13, No.2, P. 263.

24. Mohiuddin M and Rashid MH. Survival and growth of vegetatively grown pati-pata (*Schumannianthus dichotoma*): an exploratory study. *Bangladesh Journal of Forest Science* 1988;17 (1 & 2): 20-5

25. *Mr. Harish Tigari , Ms. Nazneen Taj S.K,* Economic

activities and livelihood: A case of Beedi Workers, SJIF Impact Factor: 6.093 Volume: 4, Issue: 5, May, 2019 ISSN: 2455-7838 (Online) EPRA International Journal of Research and Development (IJRD) Peer Reviewed Journal.

26. *Ms. Jadhav. Shreya,* Indian Handicrafts: Growing or Depleting? IOSR Journal of Business and Management (IOSR-JBM) e-ISSN: 2278-487X, p-ISSN: 2319-7668 PP 07-13 www.iosrjournals.org
27. Mukul, S A.,"Changing Consumption and Marketing pattern of Non-timber Forest Products in a Competitive World: case Study from an Urban Area of North-eastern Bangladesh"Small-scale Forestry (2011) 10:273-286DOI 10.1007/s11842-010-9147-6
28. *Naga Raju, G. and Viyyanna Rao K.,* A study on the Socio-Economic conditions of Handloom Weavers, Journal of Rural Development, Vol. 33 No. (3) pp. 309-328 NIRD & PR, Hyderabad.
29. *Siddiqi NA, Ara R and Merry SR.* Survival and initial growth of *Schumannianthus dichotoma* (Marantaceae) from four different propagating materials. *Indian Forester* 1998; 24(12):1014-19
30. Veldkamp, J.F. and Turner, I.M., "The correct name for schumannianthus dichotomus (Marantaceae)", Kew Bulletin article number :47(2016) Springer link.

14

Review on Major Eco-Friendly Local Plant Based Protective North East Indian Approach Against Mosquitoes

Somnath Kundu[1]

ABSTRACT

Mosquitoes are one of the major disease-causing arthropod vectors studied so far. It causes a significant disease load and creates considerable harm to humans. Different known chemical measures controls surge of mosquitoes but possess quite a lot of negative impacts starting from generation of resistance to its environmental impact. Owing to these facts and as part of the alternate control strategy, natural plant derived products can be exercised. North Eastern part of India is equipped with a rich diversity of medicinal plants. The native peoples of this region utilizes these sources to heal serious health concerns from long past. Several of such plants have potent mosquitocidal as well as repellent properties and activities. Each and every part of such plant resources has active components that can deter the mosquitoes. Differential solvent extraction procedure can isolate the active ingredients of such plants and these chemical compounds can effectively act against mosquitoes. As part of safe and environment friendly approach these plant-based mosquito control strategies could be the alternative against the most commonly used chemical control strategies.

[1]Assistant Professor, Department of Zoology, Toofanganj Mahavidyalaya.

Key Words : *Environment, Mosquito, Phyto-component, Plants, Repellent*

Introduction

Mosquitoes are the medically significant arthropod vectors that transmit parasites and pathogens which causes disease burden mostly in tropical countries. It spreads many deadly diseases such as filariasis, malaria, dengue, yellow fever, Japanese encephalitis etc. Thus the mosquito borne disease is one of the major health issues and affects the socio-economical status of a country. To control the outbreak of mosquitoes chemical insecticides are being routinely used globally. The repeated use of synthetic insecticides could result into several ecological imbalances, development of resistance against insecticides, harm to other non targeted organisms etc (Brown, 1986). Ethno botanical utilization of plants for maintaining superior health status is known since time immemorial. The ethnic and rural tribal populations from north east India have retained a diversified and rich traditional knowledge about the medicinal importance of the plants growing around them. This local knowledge helped them to treat certain common diseases and conditions. Utilizing such traditional knowledge, a variety of innovative medicines had already been prepared (Kantheti & Alapati, 2017). Thus indigenous botanical products with insecticidal properties can be utilised as part of a control strategy against a variety of insect pests and vectors. Plants usually prevent themselves against plant-eating insects by producing certain chemical repellents, feeding deterrents, toxins, and growth regulators. These compounds can be commercially exploited as these are generally more recyclable, less hazardous, will not cause any notable adverse affect and might develop less resistance against insecticides. Thus, herbal sources have opened up a new edge for discovering eco-friendly insecticides. Therefore biologically active plant materials have attracted considerable attention in mosquito control programmes in the recent time (Ghosh *et al.*, 2012).

Diseases caused by mosquitoes:

Since ancient time, mosquitoes have been reported as the source of various ailments affecting human life. Approximately 3500 species of mosquitoes are found around the world. Among them, human disease causing mosquito genera includes- Anopheles (malaria, filariasis), Aedes (yellow fever, dengue, chikungunya) and Culex (West Nile, Japanese encephalitis, filariasis). During the life span, a female mosquito repeatedly sucks blood as a source of protein to fulfil their egg development. Thus several blood borne human diseases such as Malaria are being easily transmitted by such female mosquito. It is caused by the protozoan parasites *Plasmodium vivax*, *Plasmodium malariae*, *Plasmodium ovale*, *Plasmodium falciparum* etc. transmitted by female *Anopheles* mosquitoes. *Culex quinquefasciatus* causes bancroftian filariasis in tropical and subtropical regions. Approx. 19 millions of Indian population are the sufferers of filarial disease whereas 25 million harbours microfilaria. On an estimate around two-third of our world's population are residing in the dengue infected areas and it infects about 100 million of people every year (Ghosh et al., 2012) (Brown, 1986).

Traditional mosquito control strategies:

Several mosquito borne diseases are very threatening as there is no proper vaccine or treatment. These diseases are caused only due to our carelessness and thus we are creating a danger for ourselves. The only effective way to get rid of from these diseases is to take proper protective measures as early as possible. Several mosquito controlling strategies has been summarized below (Table 1).

Table 1
Important techniques for controlling mosquitoes

Mosquito controlling methods		
Chemical methods	**Non-chemical methods**	**Biological methods**
Synthetic repellents e.g. DEET,	Physical methods e.g. Medicated net, Nonmedicated net,	Using some particular fish species that feeds on mosquito larvae

Permethrin	Mosquito traps	in the water bodies
Natural repellents e.g. Eucalyptus oil, citronella oil	Mechanical methods e.g. Electric mosquito zapper, Mosquito magnet	

Plant based protective strategies:

Many medicinal plants from north east India were tested for their pesticidal and repellent properties which could be used as a crude resource of essential oils or individual active ingredients. Naturally occurring plant-derived compounds contains a broad range of chemically active ingredients that interferes with several biological and life cycle processes of the mosquito. Several important mosquito repelling plants from various north eastern part of India are summarized below (Table 2).

Differential solvent extraction of phytochemicals:

The efficacy of phytochemicals as mosquito repellent can vary significantly depending on plant species, plant parts used, geographical origin of the plant, age of plant parts (young, mature or senescent), extraction procedure, solvent used during extraction, photosensitivity of some of the compounds in the extract as well as upon the available vector species (Shaalan *et al.*, 2005). Solvent polarity has a major role in total extraction of the active phytochemicals from the plant parts concerned. Extraction of polar molecules has been best studied in polar solvents whereas the non polar molecules in non-polar solvents. Hexane, petroleum ether, ethyl acetate, chloroform, acetone, ethanol, methanol and water (Low to high polar solvent) are used with their varying levels of polarity in extraction procedure. Highly polar solvents extract proteins, glycans, etc. somewhat polar solvents extracts steroids, alkaloids, etc. Most extraction experiments exercises to use either highly polar or the solvent with minimum polarity. The moderately polar solvents were also seen to give good results in different studies. Thus, differential use of solvents can extract a diverse range of

Table 2
Overview of mosquito repelling plants and their effective chemical components

S.No.	Plant Family	Plant Name	Location	Active repelling ingredient	Plant parts used	Reference
1.	MYRTACEAE	*Eucalyptus globules*	Different north eastern states mainly in Assam	Eucalyptol, α-Terpenol, Sesquiterpene, Linalool, Thymol, 1,8-Cineole,β-Ocimene,α-Pinene	Leaf extract used as a potent mosquito repellent when applied on skin surfaces	(Sharma et. al., 2012), (Ngo et al., 2020)
		Backhousia myrtifolia	Eastern Himalayan Sikkim	Myrcene, Linalool, Citronellal, Iso-neral, Iso-geranial, Neral,Geranial	Essential oil is used externally as mosquito repelling agent.	(Southwell et al., 2000), (Tangjang et al., 2011)
2.	VERBENA-CEAE	*Lantana Camara*	Phom tribe of Nagaland	α-pinene, Caryophyllene, Cineole, Citral, Eugenol, Geraniol, Linalool, p-Cymene, Terpeneol	Oil extracted from leaf used to repell mosquitoes.	(Pradhan & Badola, 2008), (Zandi-Sohani et al., 2012)

S.No.	Plant Family	Plant Name	Location	Active repelling ingredient	Plant parts used	Reference
		Artemisia nilagirica	Sacred groves of Manipur	Camphor, Alpha-thujone, Germacrene D, Camphene, 8-Cineole, beta-Caryophyllene	Leaf oil acts as poten mosquito repelling agent	(Devi Khumbong-mayum et al., 2005), (Malik et al., 2019)
3.	LAMIACEAE	*Hyptis suaveolens*	Darjeeling Hills	Myrcene, α- and β-Pinene, Limonene, Terpinolene, Germacrene, Sabinene, beta-Caryophyllene	Leaf juice repells insects including mosquitoes	(Pradhan & Badola, 2008), (Gaddaguti, 2012)
		Ocimum sanctum	Tribes of tropical evergreen forest of Mizoram	Linalool, Caryophyllene, p-Cymene, Eucalyptol, Eugenol, Citral, Ocimene, Limonene	Oil extracted from leaf	(Borkataki et al., 2008), (Balasubra-manian, 2014)

S.No.	Plant Family	Plant Name	Location	Active repelling ingredient	Plant parts used	Reference
4.	POACEAE	*Arundo donax*	Manipur	Xanthone, Tetradecane, Phenol	Leaf dry fumigation	(Kantheti & Alapati, 2017), (Pansuksan et al., 2020)
		Cymbopogan citratus	Phom tribe of Nagaland	Citronellal, Citronellol, Neral, α-Pinene, Geraniol, Limonene, Myrcene, Linalool, Geranial, Caryophyllene	Leaf extract	(Ojewumi, 2017), (Pansuksan et al., 2020), (Uraku, 2015)
5.	MELIACEAE	*Azardirachta indica*	Assam, Arunachal Pradesh, Mizoram, Manipur, Meghalaya and Nagaland.	Azadirachtin, Nimbin, Nimbidin, β-Elemene γ-, Elemene, Germacrene D, Caryophyllene, 4-Cymene, α-Terpinene, Salannin	burning leaves, fruits and bark smoke	(Shankar et al., 2012), (Maia & Moore, 2011)

S.No.	Plant Family	Plant Name	Location	Active repelling ingredient	Plant parts used	Reference
6.	ASTERACEAE	*Artimesia vulgaris*	Sikkim Himalayan region	Camphor, alpha-Thujone, Germacrene D, Camphene, 1, 8-Cineole, beta-Caryophyllene	Plant burning fume	(Tangjang et al., 2011), (Maia & Moore, 2011)
		Ageratum conyzoides	Phom tribe of Nagaland	Precocene-II, Precocene-I, Caryophyllene, Germacrene-D	Smoke of dried plant	(Kantheti & Alapati, 2017), (Maia & Moore, 2011)
7.	ZINGIBERACEAE	*Curcuma Longa*	Lepcha community of Sikkim Himalayas	Eugenol, Caryophylline, α-curcumine, α-Pinene, β-Pinene, Myrcene, Linalool, Ocimene, Thymol	Application of rhizome extract as mosquito repellent	(Tangjang et al., 2011), (Maia & Moore, 2011)

S.No.	Plant Family	Plant Name	Location	Active repelling ingredient	Plant parts used	Reference
		Kaempferia galanga	Hill regions of Assam	Totarol, Cembrene, Borneol	Rhizome extract acts as an repellent.	(Kantheti & Alapati, 2017), (Raina & Abraham, 2015)
		Kaempferia rotunda	Tripuran villege areas	Borneol, Naphthalene, β-Phellandrene repellent	Burning smoke of flower and rhizome acts as	(Kantheti & Alapati, 2017), (Maia & Moore, 2011)
8.	Rutaceae	*Clausena anisata*	North Eastern Lepcha community	β-Pinene, Sabinene, Germacrene-D, Estragole, Linalool	Leaf extract as well as burning plant fumes acts as mosquito repellents.	(Kantheti & Alapati, 2017), (Govindarajan, 2021)
9.	Lauraceae	*Litsea citrata*	Meghalayan sacred forests	Geranial, Neral, Borneol, Geraniol, Linalool, Nerol repellent.	Fruit extract of this plant species acts as a potent	(Kantheti & Alapati, 2017), (Madivoli et al., 2021)
10.	Acanthaceae	*Adhatoda vasica*	Different districts of Assam	α-Pinene, Eucalyptol, 5-Caranol, Thymol, α-Terpineol	The whole plant itself acts as an mosquito repellent.	(Kantheti & Alapati, 2017), (Sahi, 2016)

active chemical compound from different plant parts (Chowdhury *et al.*, 2007).

Phytocompounds and integrated mosquito management: Integrated Mosquito Management (IMM) is a comprehensive mosquito control strategy that utilizes all available mosquito control methods singly or in combination to reduce their numbers in tolerable levels while maintaining a quality environment. IMM does not put emphasis on mosquito elimination or eradication rather specially adapted to safely respond to different mosquito life cycle stages. This can be done by affecting immature mosquitoes (larvae and pupae) or as such the adult mosquitoes by utilizing selective bioactive agents. The major approaches of IMM includes: (i) habitat management for protecting larvae contaminated foods, (ii) larval stage destruction utilizing bacteria, insect growth regulators, phytochemicals etc. (iii) destructing adults through active usage of repellents, insecticide impregnated nets, genetic manipulations etc., (iv) disease surveillance, and (v) biocontrol techniques using entomophagous bacteria, fungi and parasites. Thus the application of larvicidal and adult repelling agents from botanical origin was extensively studied as an essential part of IMM (Shaalan *et al.*, 2005).

Mode of action of mosquito repellents:

Excretory products, carbon dioxide, lactic acid etc. present in animal sweat attract female mosquitoes. Mosquito chemoreceptor then takes the perception of the odour. The repellent product used upon the skin block the lactic acid and other receptors and thus the mosquitoes lose its contact with the host. Thus repelling chemical compounds work by covering human scent, or by using a scent which insects naturally stay away from.

Protective measures of using natural repellents:

Inspite of its less toxicity, certain protective measures should be followed during the application of natural repellants. 1) Skin application must corresponds with its correct dose and should not be swallowed or else rubbed into the mucous membranes, 2) user must be aware about its active ingredients to avoid allergic reaction, 3) children, pregnant women and lactating women should avoid such repellents, 4) it should not be applied to the mouth or eyes, cuts, wounds, or on sunburned or irritated skin, 5) before facial application, it is recommended to spray on hands first and then rub on face, 6) can be safely applied to the exposed portions of body, 7) repellent-treated skin must be wash when the purpose is over etc. Direct application of repellents to regular cloths is also recommended.

Advancements in plant based repellents:

The demanding need of protection against diseases caused by arthropod bites necessities the production of safe, pleasant and environment friendly repellent compounds. The major trouble with natural repellents is the volatility of oils or compounds responsible for repellence. To mitigate these issues, combinations of plant-based chemicals with larger molecules that evaporate more slowly have been tagged. In recent years, advancements in nanotechnology has opened a new frontier to increase the duration and potentiality of plant-based repellents. The development of nano-emulsions and improved formulations could be beneficial.

CONCLUSION

To protect the environment against increasing chemical pollution, it is very much essential to introduce some kind of eco-friendly approach that could be able to eliminate mosquitoes. Besides numerous health hazards, chemical insecticides also produces resistance within mosquitoes, which make them vulnerable to cause nuisance towards human-beings. Besides fulfilling their major job, they must be environment friendly. Botanical insecticides can thought as an alternative as it is easily available locally, cost effective and relatively safe for the environment. GCMS analysis of these North East Indian plant parts have found many such potent ingredients that can effectively act against mosquitoes. Different plant derived chemicals such as terpenoid, ocimene, linalool, thymol, eucalyptol, eugenol, alpha-pinene, geranial, neral etc. has a great share to repel mosquitoes. Utilizing different biochemical and molecular mechanisms, these active chemicals could be separately isolated, characterized and formulated for their effective usage in future. To increase the durability and efficiency of these chemicals, several modern devices such as slow releasing essential oil polymeric device could be used. Utilization of such locally accessible medicinal vegetation as mosquito control agent could produce local employment opportunities too. Overall advance research is necessary to develop more competent and dynamic plant derived mosquito repellents in future.

REFERENCES

1. Balasubramanian, S. (2014). GC-MS analyses of Phytocomponents in the Methanolic extract of Ocimum Sanctum (Tulsi). Asian Journal of Pharmaceutical Analysis and Medicinal Chemistry, 2(2), 71-75.
2. Borkataki, S., Chutia, M., & Borthakur, S. (2008). Ethnobotany of biofencing among teagarden and ex-teagarden communities of Nagaon district of Assam. Indian Journal of Traditional Knowledge, 7(4), 666-668.
3. Brown, A. (1986). Insecticide resistance in mosquitoes: a pragmatic review. Journal of American Mosquito Control Association, 2(2), 123-140.
4. Chowdhury, N., Bhattacharjee, I., LASKAR, S., & Chandra, G. (2007). Efficacy of Solanum villosum Mill. (Solanaceae: Solanales) as a Biocontrol Agent against Fourth Instar Larvae of Culex quinquefasciatus Say. Turkish Journal of Zoology, 31(4), 365-370.
5. Devi Khumbongmayum, A., Khan, M., & Tripathi, R. (2005). Sacred groves of Manipur, northeast India: biodiversity value, status and strategies for their conservation. Biodiversity and Conservation, 14(7), 1541-1582.
6. Gaddaguti, V. (2012). GC-MS analysis and in Silico Molecular Docking studies of Mosquito Repellent compounds from Hyptis Suaveolens L. International

Journal of Bioassays, 1(9), 36-41.

7. Ghosh, A., Chowdhury, N., & Chandra, G. (2012). Plant extracts as potential mosquito larvicides. Indian J Med Res, 135(5), 581-598.
8. Govindarajan, M. (2021). Chemical composition and larvicidal activity of leaf essential oil from Clausena anisata (Willd.) Hook. f. ex Benth (Rutaceae) against three mosquito species, 3(11), 874-877.
9. Kantheti, P., & Alapati, P. (2017). Review on tribal medicinal practices of north-east India for mosquito Repellency. Journal of Pharmacognosy and Phytochemistry, 6(5), 1256-1259.
10. Madivoli, E., Gitu, L., & Gumba, E. (2021). Isolation And Identification of Essential Oils From Cymbopogan Citratus (Stapf) Dc Using Gc-Ms and Ft-Ir, 2(4), 13-22.
11. Maia, M., & Moore, S. (2011). Plant-based insect repellents: a review of their efficacy, development and testing. Malaria Journal, 10(S1).
12. Malik, S., de Mesquita, L., Silva, C., de Mesquita, J., de Sá Rocha, E., & Bose, J. et al., (2019). Chemical Profile and Biological Activities of Essential Oil from Artemisia vulgaris L. Cultivated in Brazil. Pharmaceuticals, 12(2), 49.
13. Ngo, T., Tran, T., & Le, X. (2020). The effects of influencing parameters on the Eucalyptus globulus leaves essential oil extraction by hydrodistillation method. IOP Conference Series: Materials Science And Engineering, 991, 012-126.
14. Ojewumi, M. (2017). Analytical Investigation of the extract of Lemon Grass Leaves in Repelling Mosquito. International Journal of Pharmaceutical Sciences and Research, 8(5), 2048-2055.
15. Pansuksan, K., Sukprasert, S., & Karaket, N. (2020). Phytochemical Compounds in Arundo donax L. Rhizome and Antimicrobial Activities. Pharmacognosy Journal, 12(2), 287-292.

16. Pradhan, B., & Badola, H. (2008). Ethnomedicinal plant use by Lepcha tribe of Dzongu valley, bordering Khangchendzonga Biosphere Reserve, in North Sikkim, India. Journal of Ethnobiology And Ethnomedicine, 4(1).
17. Raina, A., & Abraham, Z. (2015). Chemical profiling of essential oil of Kaempferia galangaL. germplasm from India. Journal of Essential Oil Research, 28(1), 29-34.
18. Sahi, N. (2016). Evaluation of Insecticidal Activity of Bioactive Compounds from Eucalyptus citriodora Against Tribolium castaneum. *International Journal of Pharmacognosy and Phytochemical Research*, *8*(8), 1256-1270.
19. Shaalan, E., Canyon, D., Younes, M., Abdel-Wahab, H., & Mansour, A. (2005). A review of botanical phytochemicals with mosquitocidal potential. Environment International, 31(8), 1149-1166.
20. Shankar, R., Sharma, B., & Deb, S. (2012). Antimalarial plants of northeast India: An overview. Journal of Ayurveda and Integrative Medicine, 3(1), 10.
21. Southwell, I., Russell, M., Smith, R., & Archer, D. (2000). Backhousia citriodora F. Muell. (Myrtaceae), A Superior Source of Citral. Journal of Essential Oil Research, 12(6), 735-741.
22. Tangjang, S., Namsa, N., Aran, C., & Litin, A. (2011). An ethnobotanical survey of medicinal plants in the Eastern Himalayan zone of Arunachal Pradesh, India. Journal Of Ethnopharmacology, 134(1), 18-25.
23. Uraku, A. (2015). Determination of Chemical Compositions of Cymbopogon citratus Leaves by Gas Chromatography-Mass Spectrometry (GC-MS) Method. Research Journal of Phytochemistry, 9(4), 175-187
24. Zandi-Sohani, N., Hojjati, M., & Carbonell-Barrachina, Á. (2012). Bioactivity of Lantana camara L. essential oil against Callosobruchus maculatus (Fabricius). Chilean Journal of Agricultural Research, 72(4), 502-506.

15

The Uncertain Future of NH10: Concern and Issues

Sapan Tamang[1]

ABSTRACT

Darjeeling, well known for its bracing climate and scenic beauty has become a fascinating political battle field since later half of the last century. The place designed and crafted with English vigor had grasped the world attention through its charm for many years. But the growing political instability together with the process of modern capitalist development has really made the place from worth living to worse living. Based on the practical evaluation and personal experience, this study is a sincere attempt to highlight the problem associated with NH10, lifeline road connecting the state of Sikkim and Kalimpong district of West Bengal with rest of India. The major objective of the study is to examine the social security, environmental responsibility and Neo liberal development in the small Himalayan region of Darjeeling with special reference to the devastating condition of NH 10.

Key Words : Political Upheaval, Social Security, Environmental Responsibility, Capitalist Development, Disaster Management.

[1]Department of Political Science, Dinhata College, Dinhata-736135, West Bengal
Email: swapna2924sm@gmail.com

Introduction

Darjeeling, a well known tourist destination, endowed with its bracing climate and scenic beauty has become a fascinating political battle field since later half of the last century. The place designed and crafted with English vigour had grasped the world attention through its charm for many years. But the growing political instability together with the process of modern neo liberal development has really made the place from worth living to worse living. Man as a social animal has always liked to live in a social group. Social development takes place when different social animals come into contact with each other. In this process of development, nature and environment have also played an important role. Further, in due course of such socio-anthropological history the same herd of social animals formed communities. One such community is *Gorkha Community* of Darjeeling Himalaya settled in the region since ages. It is also imperative to note that the Gorkha community is heterogeneous in nature. It is the blend of different ethno-racial and linguistic groups' viz. *Tamang, Rai, Lepcha, Limbu, Newar, Sherpa, Gurung, Chettri, Kami etc.* settled in scattered way in different parts of the country called themselves as *Gorkha*. However, a sizable population of such community settled in Darjeeling Himalaya since last many centuries and rigorously raising their voice for the recognition of ethnic identity and the participation in mainstream politics of the nation.

Brief Geo-Political History of Darjeeling

Darjeeling, the small Himalayan region situated in the lap of Kanchenjunga is well known for its bracing climate and mesmerizing scenic beauty. As per the census of 2011, it covers the geographical area of 3149 square kilometers. The region has many mountainous slopes together with numerous rivers such as Tista, Rangit, Balasun, Jaldhaka etc. Hence, the region is very vulnerable in terms natural disasters. If we look back to the political history of the place it has been found that the region faced many ups and downs in regard to its ownership and settlement till the permanent arrival of the Britishers in the place. During the 19th century, this place was a part of the dominions of the king of Sikkim. Two British officers named Captain Llyod and Mr. J.W.Grant stayed in a place for quite few days while heading towards Nepal. These British officers were mesmerized by the bracing climate of the hills and the view of the magnificent Kanchenjunga. They find the place is very ideal for the construction of sanatorium. On the basis of the recommendation made by these two officers, negotiation has been opened between The King of Sikkim and the British government for the cession of Darjeeling. Subsequently, in the month of February 1835, a deed of grant was signed between the Rajah of Sikkim and the British government as a result of which a strip of hill region, 24 miles long and about 6 miles wide was successfully transferred to the British government. This transferred land of Sikkim included the villages of both Darjeeling and Kurseong, and it became Darjeeling District later on. Accordingly, in the 1866, 486 square miles east of the Tista, a hilly tract was annexed from Bhutan and amalgamated in Darjeeling District which subsequently became Kalimpong sub-division. Similarly, Terai and a portion of the Sikkim hills were annexed. The Development and beautification of the place was the major concern when the region was first acquired. Because the major portion of the land was under forest and scantly populated. There was no proper road connectivity. Hence Dr. A. Campbell was appointed the Superintendent of the new hill station. Under his supervision rapid development takes place in the region. Tea Plantation, Construction of Roadways and Establishment of Railways are the major development in the region which led to the employment opportunities hence migration started and population increased.

NH 10 Highway and the associated Issues

The problems associated with NH10 are very pertinent and genuine in regard to social security, human security and perhaps the future of the region. NH 10 as mentioned earlier is the life line road connectivity of the state of Sikkim with the rest of India. It is also an important route for Kalimpong to connect with Siliguri and rest of the country. But from last few years the condition of the road is very pathetic rather would be catastrophic. It is very evident that accidents on this highway occur quite frequently. In fact, the situation becomes worse during the time of Monsoon. Occurrence of frequent landslides and blockade of roads are the normal phenomena in the place. Hence, it is very difficult for both the people of Sikkim and Kalimpong to connect with Siliguri because, it is the only direct connecting road for both Sikkim and Kalimpong. The alternative road is via Kurseong - Darjeeling which is lengthier and time consuming for both Sikkim and Kalimpong.

The second aspect of the crucial discussion is that a sizable population has been settled in the adjoining areas of this NH10 highway. Numerous restaurants, small tea stallsand local vegetable shops are being run by the local people with the purpose of making a decent living. But, with the growing situation of NH10, it is very difficult them to live and run their livelihood in such a vulnerable place. However, these local people are residing in the place since many decades. They are both emotionally and socio-economically attached with the place as a result of which they are still in the place and running their normal life. But inside every household there is a big fear of uncertainty. How will this problem be addressed, who will address this problem, GTA local authority or Sikkim Government or Private Company associated with NHPC is still a big question.

The third aspect which cannot be ignored is geological aspect of the place. As it is already mentioned above that Darjeeling Hills is situated very adjacent to Kanchenjunga and the settlement was made in the mountainous slope areas. No doubt, it was the British vision and vigor which actually carved the adamant mountainous slopes for human habitation. Apart from mountainous slopes the place is traversed by numerous rivers such as *Tista, Rangit, Jaldhaka,*

Balasun etc. Some geologists have argued that Darjeeling hill is situated within the sub Himalayan belt of Eastern Himalayas. It is bounded by the Sikkim Himalaya in the north, Bhutan Himalaya in East and Nepal Himalaya in the West. Darjeeling Himalaya is one of the youngest Himalayas compared to other Himalayas. Hence there is huge possibility of massive geo- morphological activities in the region. As a result of which the place has been often considered as vulnerable and seismic zone. Accordingly, NH10 highway is situated in between the two important natural gifts of the region. On the one side it has the vulnerable mountainous slopes. On other side, deep silent teesta river is flowing in its own rhythm. Hence, this NH10 highway is adjacent to Teesta River. Naturally, it is very difficult for the people to travel at the time monsoon. Because during the rainy season the Teesta River often destroys its normal river bank and becomes quite big in size and strength. Similarly, due to the heavy rainfall there has always been the possibility of occurrences of landslides in mountainous slopes areas. Thus, numerous accidents happened during rainy season in the NH10 highway. Some images of the present study are as follows:

Fig. 1: Landslide on NH-10 cuts off links between Sikkim & Bengal

Fig. 2: NH-10 blocked by multiple landslides

Fig. 3: Landslide on NH-10 cuts off link between Sikkim & Bengal

Fig. 4: Landslide on NH-10 cuts off Bengal-Sikkim Road Link
By IANS 07 July, 2020
TWC India

It is revealed from the above discussion that the problem associated with NH10 is very pertinent and genuine. It has to be addressed as early as possible. But it is indeed essential to discuss about the modern capitalist policy attached with NH10 in the name of NHPC (National Hydroelectric Power Corporation). NHPC limited was the private limited company when it was first incorporated in the year 1975. But from 2nd of April 1986 it was converted into public limited company. The main purpose for the formation of NHPC Ltd is electricity generation and energy trading. Hence with the view of electricity generation and energy trading it negotiated with both Sikkim and West Bengal government and entered in the hill region of Darjeeling and started work in the Teesta

River. The power plant project in the Teesta River, though it is very lucrative in terms of revenue generation, has at the same time damaged the very geological settings of the region. As a consequence, frequent earthquake, river bank erosion, huge landslides have become the common phenomena in the place. Moreover, due to the use of various high technological machines in the river, the river has lost its originality as a result of which not only the river but also the adjoining areas are highly affected by the NHPC project. Hence, it is evident that the project of NHPC Ltd is highly responsible for the pathetic condition of NH10 highway. It is also noteworthy to state that the government of Sikkim has started the construction of railway connectivity in its region. The mountainous slope of NH10 is the only connecting route for this project. Hence, it is a matter of grave concern that this new venture of Sikkim government will definitely exaggerate the problem of NH10 to a mammoth size which will further cause a colossal damage.

Frequent Political Upheaval in Darjeeling Hills

It is also a well known fact that Darjeeling Hills is politically very unstable from last several decades. Establishment of peace and tranquility has become a distant dream in the region. Frequent shut down, strike, gherao are the common things in the region. With the downfall of Subash Ghising, supremo of GNLF party and the chairman of Darjeeling Gorkha Hill Council (DGHC), Darjeeling hills became a total political battlefield. There is neither any fixed political system nor any fixed political party which could restore real peace and well being in the region. The situation is very alarming. Several different political parties are in existence in this small Himalayan region. All political parties are fighting with each other to secure better position in this hollow political battle field. It is also true that these all political parties of Hills are formed with the clear objective to earn and accumulate maximum money in the name of different ethno-political issues. However, general people of the region are busy in watching the doldrums of these different political parties and their leaders. On the other hand, the condition and the situation around NH10 have been worsening. On the basis of some general observation, it has been found that there are only few people involving academicians and Civil Society Activists of the region who are expressing their concern about the situation. They are also trying to address the problem at their best. But the majority of the masses including the leading political parties and its leaders are not very concerned with either the present situation of the place or the possibilities of future disaster associated with the problem.

Some images of political upheaval in Darjeeling

Capitalist Development, Social Justice and Environmental Responsibility

In case of NH10 and adjoining areas, it has been often

considered that the capitalist development in the name of NHPC Ltd is largely responsible for the present condition of NH10. It is indeed important to understand the very idea of sustainable capitalism. Further, it is very essential to make a parallel line between economic development, social justice and environmental responsibilities. Hence every capitalist development should be made on the basis of the 'Triple Bottom Line theory'. According to this theory, capitalist development, social justice and environmental responsibilities should flow in a parallel line. Without being concerned about environment and society, capitalist development cannot be called as inclusive social development. Thus, in case of NH10 there is huge lack of inter connection between capitalist development, social justice and environmental responsibility. It has been observed by some scholars, academicians and general people that the sole objective of NHPC is to increase revenue generation only. It is not concerned with either society or environment. The picture below explicitly elaborates the connection between capitalist development, social justice and environmental responsibility.

Epilogue

From the above discussion it could be contended that the condition of NH10 and the adjoining areas is getting worse by the day. The use of heavy technological equipment and vehicles of NHPC streamlined with nonstop heavy monsoonal rain, the region really aggravates the situation into next level. Hence, it is high time for the people of the region to think and start a movement to preserve and protect NH10 and the adjoining areas. Accordingly, there should be intervention from both the governments Sikkim and West Bengal regarding the degrading condition of NH10 and the surrounding areas. Further, it is recommended that while dealing with the situation, all stake holders of the concerned issues should be taken into account so that the problem should be dealt with and addressed from all perspectives including environment.

REFEREBCES

1. Arora V (2009) They are all set to dam(n) our future: Contested development through hydel power in democratic Sikkim, Sociological bulletin 58(1), Pg. 94-114, Sage publication.
2. Bomjan, D.S. (2008) Darjeeling-Doars People and Place under Bengal's Neo-Colonial Rule. Vikash Jana Sahitya Kendra, Darjeeling-734101
3. Khawas, Bimal (2006). Socio- Economic Condition of Tea Garden Labourers in Darjeeling Hills. Council for Social Development, New Delhi.
4. Lama, Basant. (2008) The Story of Darjeeling.Nilima Yonzone Lama Publications, Dowhill, Kurseong
5. O'Malley, L.S.S (1907). Darjeeling District Gazetteer. Gyan Publishing House, New Delhi-110002
6. Rahaman M. Mizanur & A.Al- Mamun (2020), Hydropower development along Teesta river basin: opportunities for cooperation, Water Policy 22(4),641-65, IWA Publishing
7. Tamlong, D.T. (2012). Darjeeling Diaries: Pub. Mrs. Amina Tamlong, mani Printing House, Darjeeling
8. Wangyal, S.B. (2002). Sikkim and Darjeeling Division and Deception. Pub. Sonam B. Wangyal. KMT Press Pvt Ltd, Phuentsholing, Bhutan.
9. Internet Sources : www.darjeelingtimes.com
10. www.google.com Wikipedia

16

Landuse/Land Cover Change Detection of Matigara Block, Darjiling District: A Case Study

Chandana Singhal[1] & Ranjan Roy[2]

ABSTRACT

Landuse/Land cover mapping is fundamental for assessment, managing and protection of natural resources of a region and the information on the existing land use is one of the prime pre-requisites for suggesting better use of terrain. Landuse/Land cover maps are valuable tools for agricultural and natural resources studies. Due to strength of natural resources, updating these maps is essential. Employing traditional methods through aerial photos interpretation to produce such maps are costly and time consuming. With the growth of population and socio-economic activities, natural land cover is being modified for various development purposes. This has increased the rate of changes on land-use pattern over time and thus, affecting the overall ecosystem health. Landuse/Land cover mapping is an important tool for land management and monitoring. This paper analyzes changes in Landuse/Land cover of Matigara block of Darjiling district, West Bengal with the

[1]Department of Geography, Banwarilal Bhalotia College.
Email: chandana.singha10@gmail.com
[2]Department of Geography & Applied Geography, University of North Bengal
Email: royranjangeo@gmail.com

help of Landsat images which have been processed under Digital Image Processing (DIP) technique, particularly by the supervised classification. Five land use classes have been delineated in this scheme and changes are interpreted over 20years.

Key Words : Change Detection, Landuse/ Land cover, Land Management, Digital Image Processing, Supervised Classification.

Introduction

Landuse refers to man's activities on earth, which are directly related to land, whereas land cover denotes the natural features and artificial constructions covering the land surface. In the present day, Landuse and Land Cover mapping is of great significance in scientific, research, planning and management. Regional land use pattern reflects the character of interaction between man and environment and influence to the mankind's basic economic activities. Due to Advancement in satellite sensors, their analysis techniques are making remote sensing systems fruitful, realistic and attractive for use in research and management of natural resources. Landuse map is a valuable tool for agricultural and natural resources studies, updating of these maps are essential due to strength of natural resources.

Land is becoming a scarce resource due to immense agricultural and demographic pressure. Hence, information on landuse / land cover and possibilities for their optimal use is essential for the selection, planning and implementation of land use schemes to meet the increasing demands for basic human needs and welfare. Remote Sensing (RS) and Geographic Information System (GIS) are now providing new tools for advanced ecosystem management. GIS involves mapping data and interpreting the relationships among that data and making inferences. The collection of remotely sensed data facilitates the synoptic analyses of earth - system function, patterning, and change at local, regional and global scales over time; such data also provide an important link between intensive, localized ecological research and regional, national and international conservation and management of biological diversity (Wilkie and Finn, 1996). This paper analyzes Landuse/Land cover of Matigara block of Darjiling district, West Bengal.

Objective

The main objective is to map the land use changes and to detect the changes in land use categories over 20 years from 1990-91 to 2010-11 in the study area.

Study Area

The study area has been chosen for the present study is Matigara block which lies in the central-east part of Darjiling district of West Bengal. It is located between 26°43' N to 26°57' N of latitude and 88°20' E to 88°30'E of longitude. It has an average elevation of 127 metres having an area of 166.32 sq. km. It consists of one Census Town: Bairatisal and five gram panchayats, viz. Atharakhai, Matigara-I, Patharghata, Champasari, and Matigara-II. There are 79 villages in the block with the total population of 129326 persons. It is bounded on the north by Police Station Kalimpong on the east by District

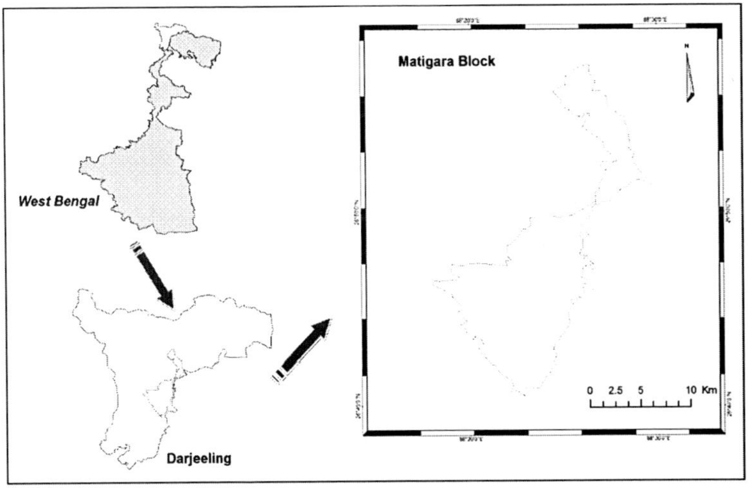

Fig. 1: Location Map of the Study Area

Jalpaiguri on the west by Police Station Kurseong and on the south by Police Station Naxalbari.

Methodology

This paper attempts to classify land use with adequate field validation and change detection analysis. Two types of data have been used in this study. In order to achieve this objective, the following satellite imageries have been used:

I. LANDSAT 7 ETM+ Image acquired in 1991
II. LANDSAT 7 ETM+ Image acquired in 2011

The Landsat ETM image of 1991 and 2011 downloaded from USGS Earth Resources Observation Systems Data Centre. The ancillary data included the ground truth data for the land use classes. The ground truth data in the form of reference points collected using Global Positioning System (GPS), used for image classification.

The above mentioned two Landsat images have been processed using Digital Image Processing (DIP) technique, particularly by the supervised classification. In the Supervised classification technique, two satellite images with different dates are independently classified. A Supervised classification method has been carried out by using training areas. Maximum Likelihood Algorithm was employed to detect the land use types in ArcGIS 10.3.1 version. Five land use classes have been delineated in this scheme. Before the creation of classification of satellite imagery, an extensive field survey was performed throughout the study area using Global Positioning System (GPS) equipment. This survey was performed in order to obtain accurate locational point data for each land use class included in the classification scheme as well as for the creation of training sites and for signature generation.

After land use classification, ground verification has been done in order to check the precision of the classified land use map. Based on the ground verification necessary correction and adjustments have been made. The map from

1991 compared with the map produced at time 2011 and categorical change obtained for all GPs.

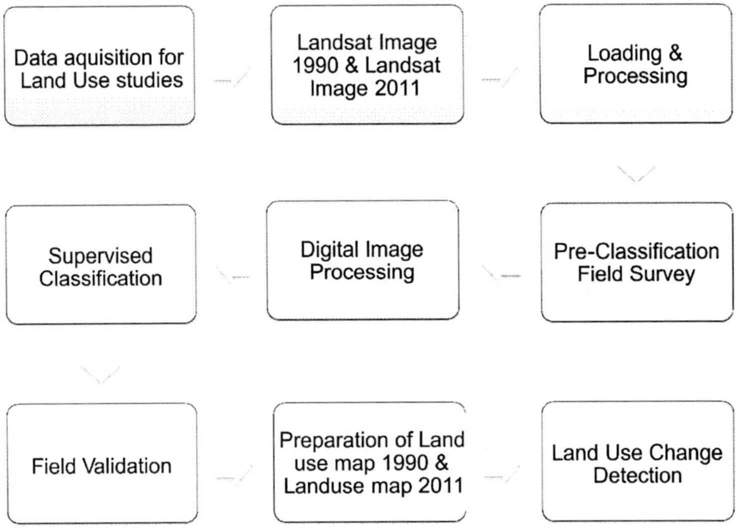

Fig. 2: Flow chart shows the methodology for land use change detection

The detailed methodology adopted for land use classification is given in the figure 3.1

Results and Discussions

In this section attempt has been made to map the land use changes and to detect the changes in land use categories over 20 years from 1990-91 to 2010-11 with the help of remote sensing and GIS techniques. The study area has been classified into five categories of land use which are: agricultural land, forest land, tea garden, built up area and river and water body. Generally, over 20 years of study, the changes in area coverage varied from one class of land use category to another class with built up area experiencing the most increase and agricultural land undergoing the most decrease in area coverage in the study area (Table no. 3).

The land use changes in each category discussed in the following paragraphs:

a) Changes in Agricultural land

The land which is used for growing food crops and fiber are known as agricultural land. Crops in this land are either grown by irrigation or rain-fed. This consists of net sown area, current fallows, fallow lands other than current fallows, culturable waste land and land under miscellaneous tree crops. Agricultural lands appear in yellow in colour with varying shape and size in a contiguous and non-contiguous pattern.

It is found that drastically decrease in agricultural land noticed in gram panchayats of Matigara block. The rate of decrease are 39.51%, 36.69%, 37.07%, 15.28% and 12.36% in Atharakhai, Matigara-I, Matigara-II, Patharghata and Champasari respectively. The decrease in agricultural land in the block is due to conversion of agricultural land into urban land use category, namely commercial/ industrial/ residential areas. This has been proved by the increase in built up area by percentages. This scenario which has been observed in the block particularly in recent years is due to increase in population.

b) Changes in Forest Land

This includes the areas with evergreen trees mainly growing naturally in the reserved land. This includes all land classified either as forest under any legal enactment or administered as forest, whether state-owned or private. Forest land appears in dark green in colour with varying shape and size in a contiguous and non-contiguous pattern. Forest lands have been noticed in all parts of the study area in both the time periods.

The GPs which have been observed increase in the area under forest are Atharakhai (2.99%), Patharghata (1.45%), Champasari (3.28%). The increase in forest area coverage in these GPs is due to the implementation of afforestation works by jointly block office and subdivisional office.

The decrease in forest land coverage has been noticed in

Table 1

Summary of Land use classification area statistics for 1991

Gram Panchayats	Agricultural Land		Forest Land		Tea Garden		Built up Area		Rivers and Waterbody	
	(ha)	(%)	(ha)	(%)	(ha)	(%)	(ha)	(%)	(ha)	(%)
Atharakhai	970.3	61.47	23.12	1.46	40.17	2.54	198.51	12.57	346.69	21.96
Matigara- I	466.86	64.75	3.52	0.49	3.83	0.53	124.71	17.30	122.03	16.93
Matigara -II	339.70	52.41	34.09	5.24	17.86	2.65	224.71	34.57	33.32	5.13
Patharghata	2320.08	62.17	340.34	9.12	691.70	18.56	295.99	7.93	83.00	2.22
Champasari	2176.77	22.61	5197.54	53.98	844.78	8.82	349.18	3.63	1055.08	10.96

(Calculated by the Researcher)

Table 2

Summary of Land use classification area statistics for 2011

Gram Panchayats	Agricultural Land		Forest Land		Tea Garden		Built up Area		Rivers and Waterbody	
	(ha)	(%)	(ha)	(%)	(ha)	(%)	(ha)	(%)	(ha)	(%)
Atharakhai	346.62	21.96	70.27	4.45	14.19	0.90	768.94	48.70	378.83	23.99
Matigara- I	202.29	28.06	1.20	0.17	1.71	0.24	338.01	46.88	177.79	24.66
Matigara -II	99.74	15.34	33.46	5.15	11.00	1.69	484.71	74.56	21.17	3.26
Patharghata	1749.91	46.89	394.35	10.57	380.28	10.19	1018.05	27.28	189.24	5.07
Champasari	986.72	10.25	5513.21	57.26	363.48	3.78	1035.94	10.76	1729.09	17.96

(Calculated by the Researcher)

Matigara-I (0.32%), Matigara-II (0.09%). In Matigara-I and Matigara-II this is attributed to conversion of forest area into built up areas.

c) Changes in Tea Garden

This class of land use describes the land with tea plantation. The GPs of the Matigara block have been shown decreasing trend in area coverage of tea garden. It decreased by 1.64%, 0.29%, 0.96%, 8.37% and 5.04% in Atharakhai, Matigara-I, Matigara-II, Patharghata and Champasari respectively. During the study period the decrease areas under tea garden have been converted into built up areas like residential/ commercial/ industrial/ transportation facilities.

Table 3

Changes in Land use pattern from 1990 to 2010

Gram Panchayats	Agricultural land	Forest Land	Tea garden	Built up area	Rivers and waterbody
	Changes in %	Changes in %	Changes in %	Changes in %	Changes in %
Atharakhai	-39.51	+2.99	-1.64	+36.13	+2.03
Matigara- I	-36.69	-0.32	-0.29	+29.58	+7.73
Matigara -II	-37.07	-0.09	-0.96	+39.99	-1.87
Patharghata	-15.28	+1.45	-8.37	+19.35	+2.85
Champasari	-12.36	+3.28	-5.04	+7.13	+7

+ Land gain, - Land loss

(Calculated by the Researcher)

d) Changes in Built up Area

Built up area describes the land covered with buildings in the rural and urban area. It includes commercial, residential, industrial and transportation infrastructures. So, it is clear that built up area consists of manmade structures. Residential land uses represented by houses ranges from high density to low density. Commercial areas are those which used for particularly sale of products and services. Industrial areas are those which used for light manufacturing to heavy manufacturing units. This appears in red colour on map.

The area under built up area drastically increased in the GPs of Matigara block. The rates of increase are 36.13%, 29.58%, 39.99%, 19.35% and 7.13% in Atharakhai, Matigara-I, Matigara-II, Patharghata and Champasari. The increase in coverage of built up area is due to the nearness of the CBD of the subdivision which triggered migration of population from rural to urban area.

e) Changes in Rivers and Water body

This class of land use describes the areas covered with water either along the river bed or man-made earth dams and ponds. The area coverage under water body has been decreased in the GPs namely Matigara-II (1.87%) due to the gradual conversion of water body area into built up area or human developmental area as the population increased significantly during the past decade.

The area under water body has been increased in the GPs, viz., Atharakhai (2.03%), Matigara-I (7.73%), Patharghata (2.85%), Champasari (7.0%).

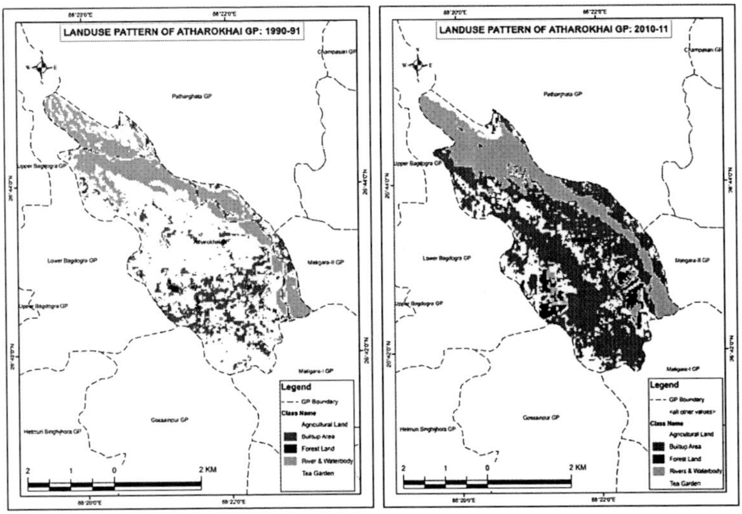

Fig. 3(a): Land Use Pattern of Atharakhai GP: 1990-91 and 2010-11

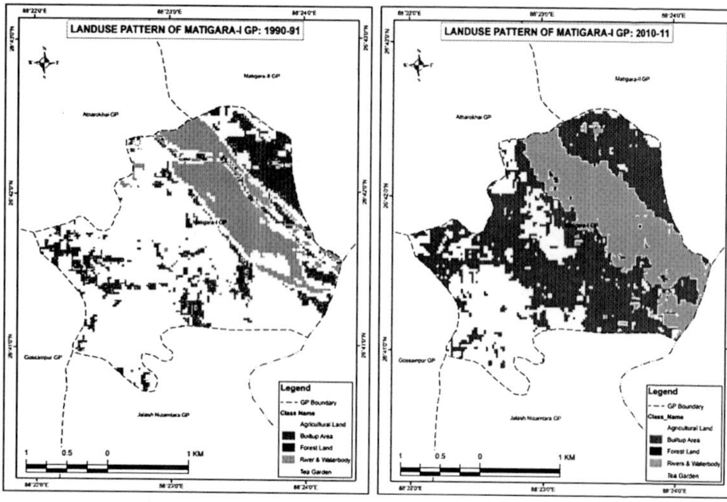

Fig. 3(b): Land Use Pattern of Matigara -I GP: 1990-91 and 2010-11

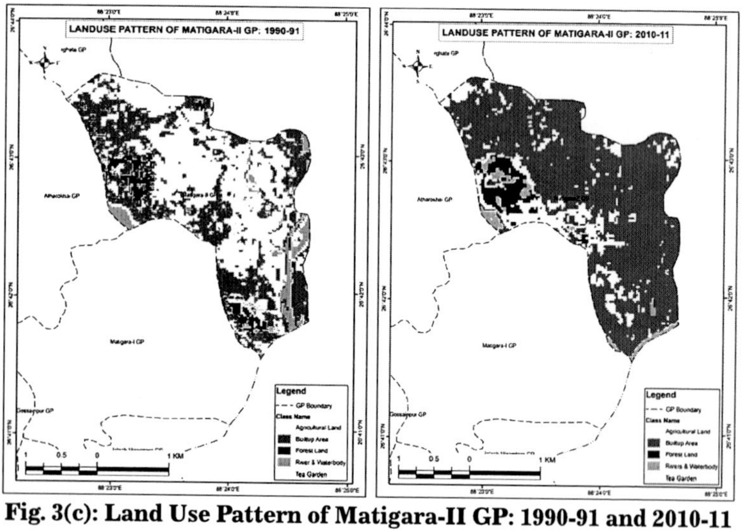

Fig. 3(c): Land Use Pattern of Matigara-II GP: 1990-91 and 2010-11

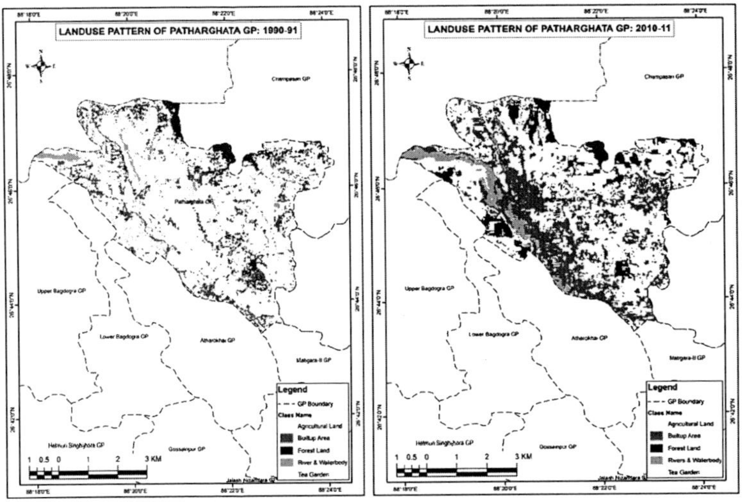

Fig. 3(d): Land Use Pattern of Patharghata GP: 1990-91 and 2010-11

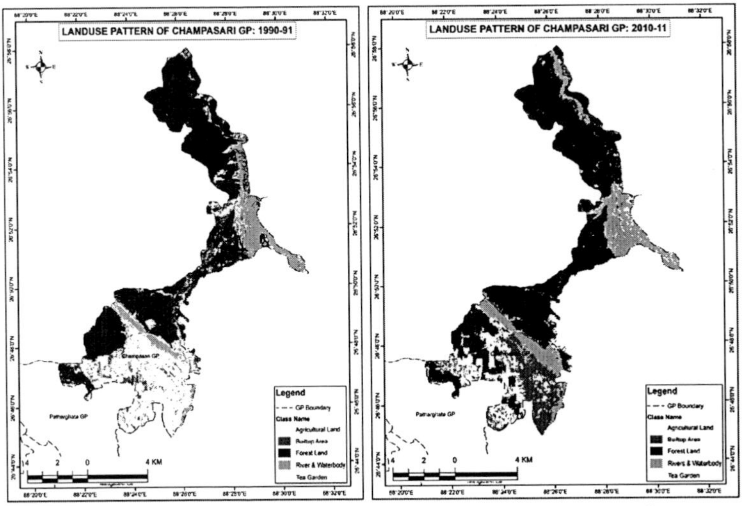

Fig. 3(e): Land Use Pattern of Champasari GP: 1990-91 and 2010-11

CONCLUSION

With the help of satellite imagery and GIS technique five category of general land use has been delineated. These are agricultural land, forest land, tea garden, built up area and river and water body. An increase in one type of land use must necessarily produce decrease in another. The significant change has been took place in case of agricultural land. In Siliguri subdivision 12.43% agricultural land decreased over the periods. All the gram panchayats have also been experienced the same. This reduction in agricultural land is for the conversion of agricultural land to other purposes like forest land, tea garden and built up area. Forest area coverage has been increased by 6.88% in the subdivision. The increase in forest area coverage is due to the implementation of afforestation works by jointly block office and subdivisional office. Area under tea garden has been decreased over the periods by 0.75%. This decline is due to the conversion of tea garden into urban areas. In Siliguri subdivision built up area is gradually increasing (6.3%) during the study period due to the significant increase in population. In most of the gram panchayats built up area has been shown increasing trend. In Siliguri subdivision there is no change in area under river and water body (5.82%) during the study.

REFERENCES

1. Aspinall, R. J. And Hill, M. J. (2008): Land use Change: Science, Policy and Management, CRC Press, Taylor and Francis Group, London, New York.
2. Boloor, A. and Nusrath, A. (2015): Spatio-Temporal Change Detection Analysis of Land-use and Land cover: A study of Mysore-Mandya corridorr region, International Journal of Advanced Research, Volume 3, Issue 11, pp. 803 - 812.
3. Cheruto, M. C., Kauti, M. K., Kisangau, P. D. and Kariuki, P. (2016): Assessment of Land Use and Land Cover Change Using GIS and Remote Sensing Techniques: A Case Study of Makueni County, Kenya, Journal of Remote

Sensing and GIS, Vol. 5, Issue 4.

4. Musa, J., Yunusa, M.B., Adamu, M. and Mohammed, A (2016, May): Change Detection Analysis of Land use and Land cover in Kafanchan, Kaduna State, IOSR Journal of Environmental Science, Toxicology and Food Technology, Vol. 10, Issue 5, Ver. II, pp. 01-10.
5. Sharma, S. C. (1990): Land use Survey in Tarai Tract: A Study of Eastern Uttar Pradesh, Concept Publishing Company, New Delhi.
6. Verburg, P. H. and Veldkemp, A. (2001): The role of spatially explicit models in land use change research: A case study for cropping patterns in China, Agriculture, Ecosystem and Environment, Vol. 85, pp.177-190.
7. Vink, A.P.A. (1975): Land Use in Advancing Agriculture, Springer-Verlag Berlin Heidelberg, NewYork.

17

Farmer's Perspective About Digital Agriculture – A Case Study in Cooch Behar District

Abdul Momin Hoque[1]

ABSTRACT

Agriculture plays important role in Indian economy. Agriculture contributes about 17% to total GDP and provides employment to over 60% of the population. The role of farmers in Indian economy is very much important. Over 70% of total population of India depends on agriculture and its allied sector. The economic growth depends on the performance of the agriculture sector. In the recent past the per capita agricultural output has seen a steady increase, the contribution of agricultural sector to the GDP has been decreasing by last few years. Decreasing in the agricultural growth is the major challenge faced by the so called Indian economy. The reasons behind the deceleration of Indian agricultural growth are many like- land fragmentation, lack of government investment in research and development, lack of irrigation facility, out- dated tenancy, lack of modern infrastructure in agriculture sector etc. To overcome all the challenges, digitization in agriculture has been introduced.

Sustainable agriculture and use of technology in the field of agriculture for socio- economic development is the main

[1]Assistant Professor, Onda Thana Mahavidyalaya
Email: abdul.momins09@gmail.com

aim to focus in this paper. The advanced knowledge sharing among small and marginal farmers in terms of digital agriculture to increase the productivity and wellbeing of the society has become crucial in present condition. Digital agriculture or e-agriculture is seen now very emerging sector focused on increasing agricultural development and rural development through improved Information and Communication Technology (ICT). Digital India was launched on 1st July 2015 by Prime Minister Sri Narendra Modi with the three main key areas- Digital Infrastructure as a Utility to Every Citizen, Governance & Services on Demand and Digital Empowerment of Citizens.

Government take initiative to make India Digitalized with the vision of Digital India programme. The m-Agriculture and m-Gram Bazar out of the seven components of m-Services, directly impact Indian agricultural sector and marketing services. A very interactive action plan are being taken to improve agriculture activities with the help of Digital India Programme. The present study is to investigate the awareness, challenges of farmers to adopt themselves to Digital India Programme in Cooch Behar District.

Key Words : Digital India, Digital Agriculture, Awareness of farmers.

Introduction

Digital India was launched by Prime Minister on 1st July 2015 with the objectives of improving digital literacy, specifically targets 9 pillars viz; High Speed Internet, Mobile connectivity, Public Internet Access, E-Governance, E-Kranti, electronic delivery services, Information for all, Electronic manufacturing and early harvest programmes. There are some other services by Govt. of India like e-Health, e-Education, e-Sign, Digital Locker. The vision of Digital India programme is the growth of Digital Infrastructure as a Utility to Every Citizen, e-governance and services and Empowerment of Citizens. Digitisation of agriculture or e-agriculture is the most emerging field focused on improving agricultural and rural development by enhancing Information and Communication Technology (ICT).

"E-agriculture is a multi-stakeholder process that involves bringing together many different ministries and departments as well as private sector players such as insurance, banking and mobile network operators. Countries have been experimenting with the use of technology for agriculture for a long time, however due to a lack of multi-stakeholder based approach in sustaining these initiatives, we see that many of these initiatives/solutions haven't moved from the pilot or experimenting phase," says Gerard Sylvester, regional knowledge and information management officer, FAO.UN International Telecommunications Union, measured the ICT Development Index (IDI) in 2015 on the level of information and communication technology access, India ranked 131 out of 167 nations. It is the reflection of very low access of the population to ICT services in India. Although India has increased its telecom density before the past. The report noted that 43.4% of the global population has access the internet whereas only 18% Indian Population has access internet services.

The e-agriculture sector can play an important role to create employment opportunities, improve the life style of farmers and reduce the risk and uncertainties of growing their crops. To meet the challenges of climate change e-agriculture can improve the condition of small holder farmers. Digital farming provides real time data from the field day to day of farming operations. With the help of the digital farming, farmers can get advices from the experts who are attached to the field, they also give their valuable advices and giving regular updates of the health of the farms through different types of applications are now available. Digital agriculture has changed the agricultural practices now a days. Remote sensing techniques has been practiced through satellite system with the resolution of 5x5 meter which can help identify the pest and diseases of crop plot. This collected data can be analysed by data analytics, with indicators like

Normalized Difference Vegetation Index (NDVI), Red Edge Index etc.

1. Objective of the study

1. To analyze the impact of demographic profile of the farmers on their level of awareness on Digital Farming.
2. To find out the influence of demographic factors of the farmers on their perception and practices under Digital Farming.
3. To assess the impact of farming experience and age of farmers' awareness on Digital farming.
4. To find the association between farmers satisfaction level on authorities approach towards the implementation of Digital Agriculture.
5. To create awareness among the farmers regarding Digital India Programme and the benefits of Digital Farming to the farmers.

2. Review of Literature

Krishna Reddy. P and R. Ankaiah (2005) in a survey stated that the Indian farming community is facing multitude problems to maximize crop productivity. One of them is that expert/scientific advice regarding crop cultivation is not reaching the farming community in a timely manner. Though India has valuable agricultural knowledge and expertise, a wide information gap exists between research and practice. AnnemieMaertens, Christopher B Barrett (2012) in a study referred that technological improvements, perhaps especially in agriculture, drive sustainable advances in labour productivity, incomes, food security and general economic growth. More recently, economists have started to explore how social networks affect farmers' learning about and uptake of new technologies. Robert Chambers (1987) discussed the transfer-of-technology (TOT) model of agriculture research in which scientists largely determine research priorities, develop technologies in controlled conditions, and hand them over to agricultural extension to transfer to farmers

3. Methodology

This section deals with the methodology adopted for the study. It includes, research approach, design for the study, sample and sampling technique, tools to assess awareness and approach of the farmers towards Digital India Program, pilot study, data collection procedure and data analysis.

3.1 Research Approach

Survey method is adopted to determine the awareness and level of satisfaction of farmers in understanding and adopting technology in farming activities.

3.2 Study area and Population

The study area is Cooch Behar District.Cooch Behar is a district under the Jalpaiguri Division of the state of West Bengal. Cooch Behar is located in the north eastern part of the state and bounded by the district of Jalpaiguri in the north, state of Assam in the east and by Bangladesh in the west as well as in the south.Cooch Behar lies between 26°57'40" to 26°32'20" North *latitude* and between 89°54'35" to 88°47'40" *Eastlongitude*. The area of the district is 3387 Sq. kms.

3.3 Sampling Frame

This is an exploratory study and a casual research. The data is collected from those farmers who are involved in Digital Farming and benefited to practice Digital Farming.

3.4 Study tool

A structured tool with four point Likert scale (Strongly agree-SA, Agree-A, Disagree-D, Strongly Disagree-SD) and is drafted to find out the awareness and level of satisfaction of farmers in learning technology to impact farming practices and also their socio demographic information.

3.5 Sampling Technique and Sample Size

A Stratified Random Sampling technique has been used to collect data from 12 blocks of Cooch Behar District. 10 sample has been collected from each block, hence the total sample became 120 farmers.

3.6 Statistical Analysis

Collected data is analysed using appropriate Statistical tools like Frequency tables, Cross tabulations, Percentages, Chi-square tests, and diagrammatic representations using SPSS version 25. Obtained results are properly concluded at respective levels of significance.

4. Result and Discussion

The following analysis brings forth the practical and factual information regarding the challenges and opportunities of the farmers in Cooch Behar District. An analysis is made to find the level of knowledge and confidence of farmers regarding Digital farming. A special focus is also made to assess the level of satisfaction of farmers on the authorities' response in supporting them to do well in farming.

4.1 Profile of the respondents

Table 1
Profile of the Farmers

Profile of the respondents			Farming Experience		
Gender	N	%	Below 10 Years	20	17
Male	85	71	11-30 years	68	57
Female	35	29	Above 30 Years	32	27
Total	120	100	Total	120	100
Age			**Income**		
Below 30 Years	36	30	Below 20000	48	40
30-50 Years	54	45	21000-50000	35	29
More than 50 years	30	25	51000-100000	22	18
Total	120	100	Above 100000	15	13
			Total	120	
Education			**Education of family**		
Primary	42	35	Only one P ersons	69	58
Secondary	56	47	Two Persons	38	32
Graduate	22	18	Three Persons	13	11
Total	120	100	Total	120	100

The table 4.1 displays the socio-demographic factors of the farmers of the study area. Among the farmers taken up for the study, 71 per cent of the farmers are male, and 29 per cent belong to female gender. 25 percent of farmers are more than 50 years of age, 45 per cent belongs to the age group of 30-50 years and 30 percent are below 30 years of age. Among the farmers, farmers with primary education are of 35 per cent, secondary education is 47 per cent and graduation are 18 per cent. When the experience is considered, it is observed that 17 per cent of the farmers have below 10 years farming experience, 57 per cent have 11-30 years farming experience and 27 per cent have above 30 years of farming experience. The income levels of the farmers are also classified and are noticed that40 per cent of the farmers have below - 20000 income level, 29 percent have income level ranging from - 21000-50000, 18 per cent farmers have the income level ranging from 51000-100000 and only 13 per cent farmers have the income level above ?-100000. It is also imperative to take into account the education of the farmers' family members. In 58 per cent of the farmers families' only one child is educated, 32 per cent of the family of the farmers have two educated persons in their families, 11 per cent of the farmers family have three and more educated members in their families.

The above figure 1 exhibits the socio-demographic profiles such as age, gender, education, level of income, education, etc. of the farmers.

4.2 Influence of gender on farmers' opinion on digital Agriculture

Gender is considered to be one of the significant factors which impact the opinions of the individuals as they share distinct social, economic, physical and emotional features. Hence, an analysis is carried out to assess the influence of gender on the level of awareness, knowledge and interests among the farmers with regard to Digital Agriculture.

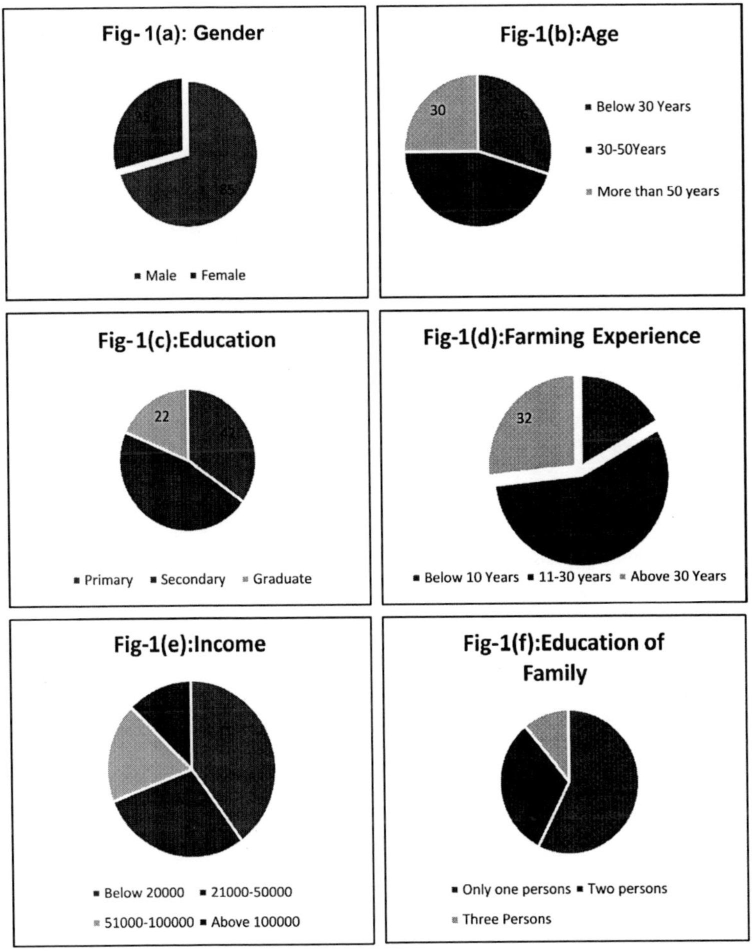

Fig. 1: Profile of Farmers

Table 2
Farmers' level of awareness on digital Farming by gender

Chi-square value	p-value	Farmers' level of awareness on Digital Farming			
1.621	0.654	Highly Aware	Moderately Aware	Unaware Highly	Total
Gender	Male	15 17.65%	28 32.94%	18 21.18%	85 100%
	Female	8 22.86%	9 25.71%	10 28.57%	35 100%
Total		23 19.17%	37 30.83%	28 23.33%	120 100%

The gender impact on the level of awareness of the farmers on Digital Farming is presented in table 2 where it clearly indicates that gender has no impact on the level of awareness of the farmers. The application of chi-square test clearly states that there is no significant impact of gender on the level of awareness of the farmers on Digital Farming. Both male and female genders are equal with their level of awareness on Digital India as it can be noticed that 33 per cent of the male farmers and 26 per cent of the female farmers are moderately aware.

Table 3
Farmers' Level of Knowledge on technology by gender

Chi-square value	p-value	Farmers' level of knowledge on technology by gender			
0.505*	0.770	Low	Medium	High	Total
Gender	Male	32 37.6%	35 41.2%	18 21.2%	85 100%
	Female	15 42.9%	12 34.3%	8 22.9%	35 100%
Total		47 39.2%	47 39.2%	26 21.7%	120 100%

*significance at 5% level

Gender does not impact the knowledge levels of the individuals. The same is assessed to find its impact with regard to technology also. It is evident from the above table that the gender has no impact on the level of knowledge of the farmers. Male farmers (41 per cent) have medium level of knowledge and female farmers (34 per cent) have medium level of knowledge on technology. The same is proved by the application of chi-square test at 5% level of significance. Refer fig. 2 for clear evidence.

Table 4
Farmers' Interest in learning about technology by gender

Chi-square value	**p-value**	**Farmers' Interest in learning abouth technology by gender**				
11.9*	0.008	Highly Interested	Interested	Somewhat Interested	Not Interested	Total
Gender	Male	42 49.4%	24 28.2%	13 15.3%	6 7.1%	85 100%
	Female	8 22.9%	10 28.6%	8 22.9%	9 25.7%	35 100%
Total		50 41.7%	34 28.3%	21 17.5%	15 12.5%	120 100%

*significance at 5% level.

The results from the above table 4 demonstrate that gender has a significant influence on farmers' interest in learning about the technology. Application of the chi-square test shows that 49 per cent of the male farmers are highly interested whereas 30 per cent of the female farmers is highly interested in learning about technology.

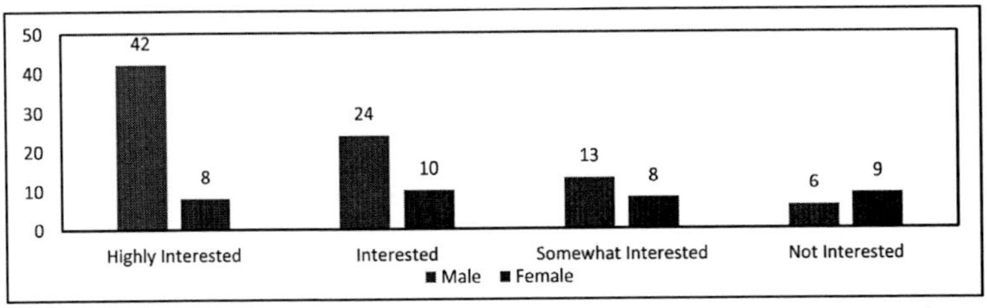

Fig. 2: Farmer's Interest in learning about technology by gender

Authorities play a key role disseminating the information about the digital India. The above table 5 displays the level of satisfaction of the farmers on the accessibility of the authorities in the time of need and support by gender. It can be identified that the female farmers (17 per cent) are satisfied than the male farmers (21 per cent). Chi-square test results also indicate the same. The fig. 3 exhibits evidently that male farmers' are highly dissatisfied than female farmers.

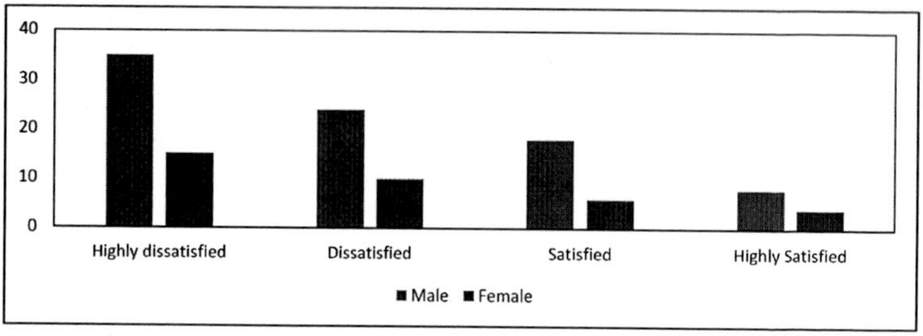

Fig. 3: Farmer's Satisfaction on the accessibility of the Authorities in need by gender

Table 5
Farmers' Satisfaction on the accessibility of the Authorities in need by gender

Chi-square value	p-value	Farmers' Satisfaction on the accessibility of the Authorities in need by gender				
0.320*	0.956	Highly dissatisfied	Dissatisfied	Satisfied	Highly Satisfied	Total
Gender	Male	35 41.2%	24 28.2%	18 21.2%	8 9.4%	85 100%
	Female	15 42.9%	10 28.6%	6 17.1%	4 11.4%	35 100%
Total		50 41.7%	34 28.3%	24 20.0%	12 10.0%	120 100%

*significance at 5% level.

The basic attitude on the usage and reliability of the farmers has more influence on the farmers' opinion. Hence an attempt is made to assess the farmers' opinion with regard to the reliability on technology and it is identified that 27 per cent of the male farmers strongly agree whereas 29 per cent of the female farmers strongly agree with regard to the reliability what they can have on the technology used under Digital Farming.

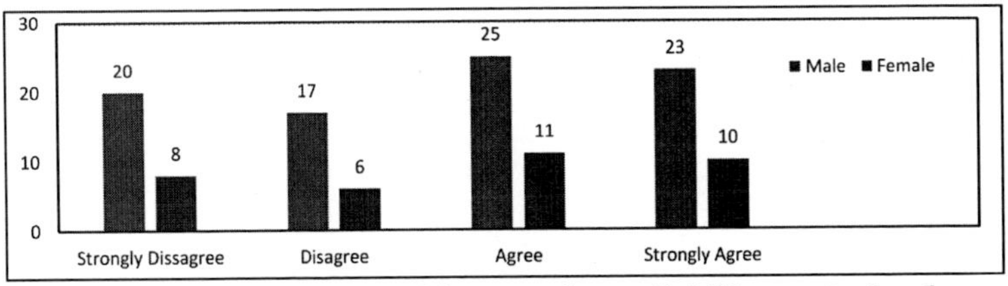

Fig. 4: Farmer's Opinion with regard to reliability on technology by gender

Table 6
Farmers' Opinion with regard to reliability on technology by gender

Chi-square value	p-value	Farmers' Opinion with regard to reliability on technology by gender				
0.165*	0.98	Strongly Disagree	Disagree	Agree	Strongly Agree	Total
Gender	Male	20	17	25	23	85
	%	23.5	20.0	29.4	27.1	100.0
	Female	8	6	11	10	35
	%	22.9	17.1	31.4	28.6	100.0
Total		28	23	36	33	120
	%	23.3	19.2	30.0	27.5	100.0

*significance at 5% level.

4.3 Influence of Age on Farmers' opinion on Digital India

Table 7
Farmers' Level of Awareness on Digital India by age

Chi-square value	p-value	Farmers' Level of Awareness on Digital India by age				
20.05*	0.002	Highly Aware	Moderately Aware	Moderately Unaware	Highly Unaware	Total
Age	Below 30 Years	14	10	8	4	36
	%	38.9	27.8	22.2	11.1	100.0

	30-50 Years	15	17	12	10	54
	%	27.8	31.5	22.2	18.5	100.0
	More Than 50 Years	2	5	8	15	30
	%	6.7	16.7	26.7	50.0	100.0
Total		31	32	28	29	120
	%	25.8	26.7	23.3	24.2	100.0

*significance at 5% level.

The above interpretation shows that there is a significant impact of age on the level of awareness on digital India.40 per cent of the farmers below the age of 30 years are highly aware of the digital farming whereas only 7 per cent of the farmers above the age of 50 years are aware of the digital India. The application of chi-square test also proves the same.

Age is one of the factors that impact the level of knowledge of the farmers. It is assumed that the level of knowledge on technology has more impact of age parameter. It is identified from the above analysis in table 8 that there is a significant impact of age on the level of knowledge of the farmers. The farmers below 30 years of age (28 per cent) have high level of knowledge on technology, farmers between 30 to 50 years of age (28 per cent) have high level of knowledge on technology and farmers who belong to the age of more than 50 years (10 per cent) have high level of knowledge. There by it can be stated that there is a significant impact of farmers' age on level of knowledge on technology. The application of chi-square presents the same.

Table 8
Farmers' Level of Knowledge on technology by age

Chi-square value	**p-value**	**Farmers' level of knowledge on technology by age**			
14.21*	0.006	Low	Medium	High	Total
Age	Below 30 Years	8	18	10	36
	%	22.2	50.0	27.8	100.0
	30-50	13	26	15	54

	Years				
	%	24.1	48.1	27.8	100.0
	More Than 50 Years	18	9	3	30
	%	60	30	10	100
Total		39	53	28	120
	%	32.5	44.2	23.3	100.0

*significance at 5% level.

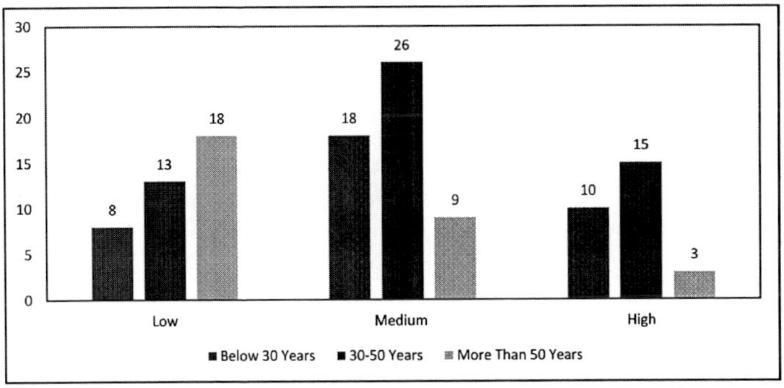

Fig. 5: Farmer's Level of Knowledge on technology by age

To learn anything there should be an inherent drive and interest in an individual. The same principle applies to the learning interest of individual towards technology.14 per cent of farmers below the age group of 30 years are not interested in learning about technology. 27 per cent of the farmers who are more than 50 years are not interested in learning about technology. This signifies that there is no correlation between farmers' age and their interest to learn about technology.

Table 9

Farmers' Interest in learning about technology by age

Chi-square value	**p-value**	**Farmers' Interest in learning about technology by age**				
11.68*	0.069	Highly Interested	Interested	Somewhat Interested	Not Interested	Total
Age	Below 30 Years	14	12	5	5	36

	%	38.9	33.3	13.9	13.9	100.0
	30-50 Years	17	22	9	6	54
	%	31.5	40.7	16.7	11.1	100.0
	More Than 50 Years	4	8	10	8	30
	%	13.3	26.7	33.3	26.7	100.0
Total		35	42	24	19	120
	%	29.2	35.0	20.0	15.8	100.0

* significance at 5% level.

Table 10
Farmers' level of confidence on technology by age

Chi-square value	p-value	Farmers' level of confidence on technology by age				
72.37*	0.00	Non Confidence	Confident Confidant	Somewhat Confident	Highly	Total
Age	Below 30 Years	6	11	12	7	36
	%	16.7	30.6	33.3	19.4	100.0
	30-50 Years	12	15	20	7	54
	%	22.2	27.8	37.0	13.0	100.0
	More Than 50 Years	15	10	5	0	30
	%	50.0	33.3	16.7	0.0	100.0
Total		33	36	37	14	120
	%	27.5	30.0	30.8	11.7	100.0

* significance at 1% level.

The table 10 above displays that there is a significant relationship between the age and the level of confidence on technology. Farmers with below 30 years of age (19 per cent) possess high confidence compared to farmers between 30-50 years (13 per cent) and above 50 years of age (0.0 per cent) with regard to their level of confidence on technology. Application of chi-square test indicates the same at the level of 1% significance. Fig. 6 apparently shows the relationship between the age of the farmer and his level of confidence on technology.

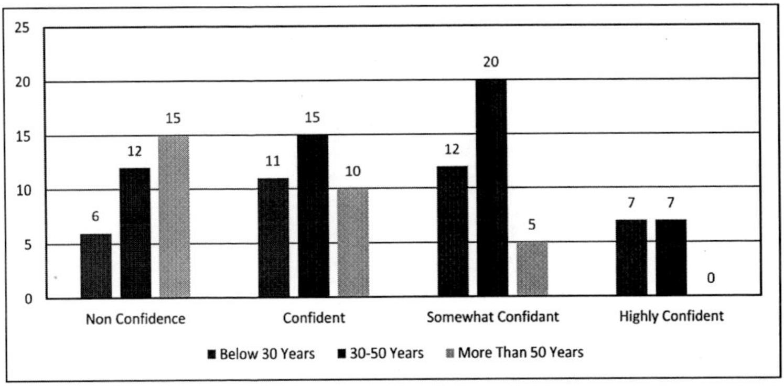

Fig. 5: Farmer's Level of confidence on technology by age

Table 11

Farmers' Opinion on that the Future is safe with technology by age

Chi-square with value	**Farmers' Opinion on that the Future is safe technology by age**				
29.69*	Strongly Agree	Agree	Disagree	Strongly Disagree	Total
Below 30 Years	9	15	6	6	36
%	25.0	41.7	16.7	16.7	100.0
30-50 Years	6	8	18	22	54
%	11.1	14.8	33.3	40.7	100.0
More Than 50 Years	0	2	13	15	30
%	0.0	6.7	43.3	50.0	100.0
Total	15	25	37	43	120
%	12.5	20.8	30.8	35.8	100.0

* significance at 1% level.

The opinion of farmers on the future safety of the technology is assessed based on the farmers' age. The results through the application of chi-square test indicate clearly that there is a significant impact of age on the opinion of farmers on the future safety of technology with regard to farming issues. 42 per cent of the farmers below the age of

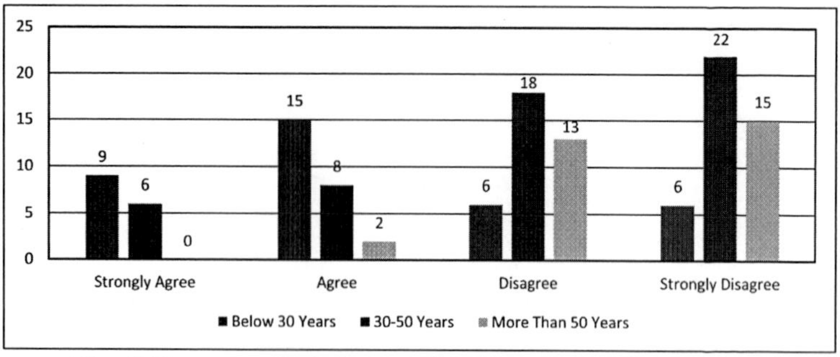

Fig. 7: Farmer's Opinion on that the Future is safe with technology by age

30 years agree on this aspect. 15 per cent of the farmers agree that future is safe with technology and 7 per cent of the farmers above the age of 50 years opined that the future is safe with technology.

4.4 Influence of Farming Experience on Farmers' opinion on Digital Farming

Table 12
Farmers' Interest in learning about technology by farming Experience.

Chi-square value	p-value	Farmers' Interest in learning about technology by farming Experience				
1.214*	0.97	Highly Interested	Interested	Somewhat Interested	Not Interested	Total
Experience	Below 10 years	5	9	5	1	20
	%	25	45	25	5	100
	11-30 years	18	24	19	7	68
	%	26.5	35.3	27.9	10.3	100.0
	Above 30 years	8	12	8	4	32
	%	25	37.5	25	12.5	100
Total		31	45	32	12	120
	%	25.8	37.5	26.7	10.0	100.0

The data indicates that there is no significant relationship between the interest of farmers in learning about technology

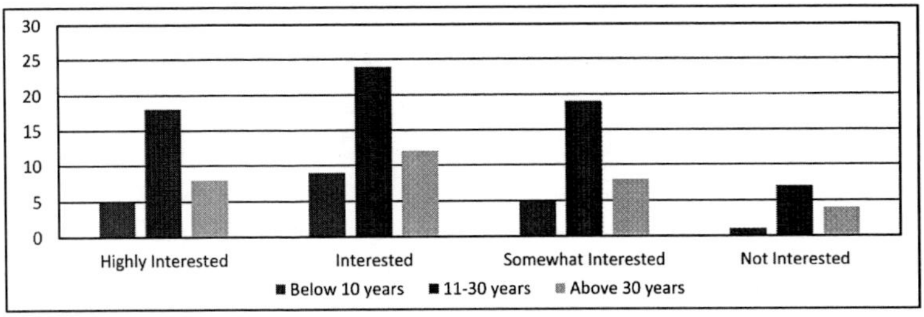

Fig. 8: Farmer's Interest in learning about technology by farming Experience

and their farming experience. The farmers below 10 years of farming experience not interested to learn about technology (5 per cent) and the farmers with above 30 years of farming experience are not interested in learning about technology (12 per cent).

Table 13
Farmers' Opinion on that the Future is safe with technology by farming Experience

Chi-square value	p-value	Farmers' Opinion on that the Future is safe with technology by farming Experience				
6.377*	0.382	Strongly Agree	Agree	Disagree Strongly	Disagree	Total
Experience	Below 10 years	6	12	2	0	20
	%	30.0	60.0	10.0	0.0	100
	11-30 years	22	35	7	4	68
	%	32.4	51.5	10.3	5.9	100
	Above 30 years	7	15	5	5	3
	%	21.9	46.9	15.6	15.6	100
Total	35	62	14	9	120	
	%	29.2	51.7	11.7	7.5	100

* significance at 5% level.

The farmers' opinion on the future safety with technology is correlated with that of the farming experience of the farmers. It is found out that the farmers with below 10 years of farming experience 6 per cent strongly agree that future is safe with usage of technology where as farmers with 11-30 years of farming experience, only 32 per cent of them strongly agree on this aspect. About 22 per cent of the farmers who are above 30 years strongly agree on the safety of technology in future. The statistical analysis indicates that there is no significant impact of farming experience on the opinion of framers on future safety of technology. Application of chi-square test confirms the same at 5% level of significance.

4.5 Influence of Education of family on Farmers' opinion on Digital India

Generally, it is assumed that education of the family members contributes to their level of awareness. The table demonstrates the association between the family educational status and the level of awareness on Digital Farming. It is found out that families with three or more persons educated are highly aware (57 per cent) of Digital Agriculture whereas the families with one person educated are highly aware at 15 per cent of Digital Farming. It can be said that the more the educated people in the family there is a chance to have improved level of awareness on Digital Farming. The application of chi-square test indicates the same results. The results are significant at the level of 5%.

Table 14
Farmers' Level of Awareness on Digital India by family educational status

Chi-square value	p-value	Farmers' Level of Awareness on Digital India by Family Educational Status				
8.05	0.234	Highly Aware	Moderately Aware	Moderately Unaware	Highly Unaware	Total
Education	Only 1 Person	12	25	18	14	69
	%	17.4	36.2	26.1	20.3	100
	2 Persons	12	15	8	3	38
	%	31.6	39.5	21.1	7.9	100
	3 and more Persons	4	7	1	1	13
	%	30.8	53.8	7.7	7.7	100

Total	28	47	27	18	120	
	%	23.3	39.2	22.5	15.0	100

* significance at 5% level.

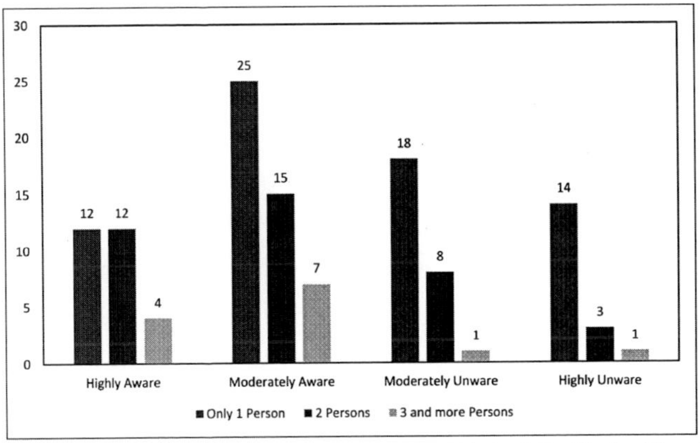

Fig. 9: Farmer's Level of Awareness on Digital India by Family Educational Status

Table 15

Farmers' Level of Knowledge on technology by family educational status

Chi-square value	**p-value**	**Farmers' level of knowledge on technology by Family Educational Status**			
5.366	0.251	Low	Medium	High	Total
Education	Only 1 Person	12	35	22	69
	%	17.4	50.7	31.9	100.0
	2 Persons	8	14	16	38
	%	21.1	36.8	42.1	100.0
	3 and more Persons	1	4	8	13
	%	7.7	30.8	61.5	100.0
Total	21	53	46	120	
%	17.5	44.2	38.3	100.0	

* significance at 5% level.

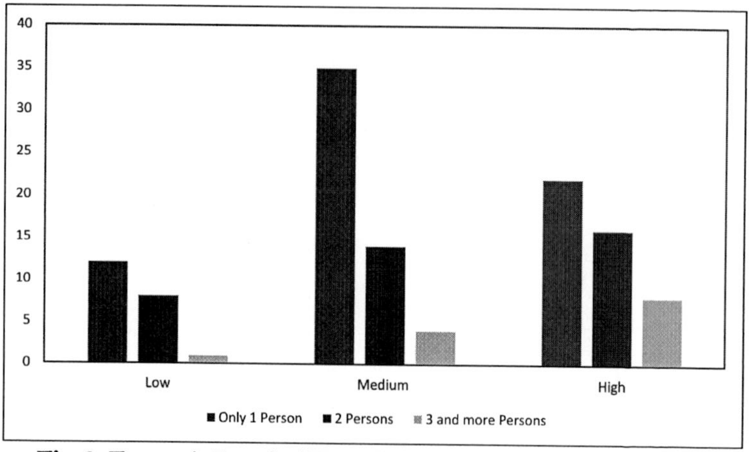

Fig. 9: Farmer's Level of Knowledge on technology by Family Educational Status

It is found out that families with three or more persons educated have 61 per cent high level of knowledge on technology while the families with one person educated have 32 per cent high level of knowledge on technology. It can be said that the more the educated people in the family there is a chance to have enhanced level of knowledge on technology among the family members. The application of chi-square test indicates the same results. The results are significant at the level of 5%.

5. Major Findings and Conclusions

The study undertaken on the awareness and satisfaction of farmers on Digital Farming has put forward thought provoking aspects.

1. There is clear evidence that there is no significant impact of gender on the level of knowledge of technology. But the high level of awareness of the farmers is remarkably low at 19 percent.
2. There is no significant impact of gender on the level of knowledge on technology.
3. It's interesting to note that female farmers have high interest to learn about technology than male farmers.
4. The analysis shows that there is no significant association

between the age and level of awareness on digital India. Male farmers are more confident compared to female farmers in this context. This may be due to the socialization skills of the male farmers.

5. The basic attitude of the farmers on the usage and reliability of the technology has been more influenced by gender.
6. Age is one of the factors that impact the level of knowledge of the farmers and it can be stated that there is a significant impact of farmers' age on level of knowledge on technology but no impact has been found on their level of awareness on Digital Farming.
7. It is also evidently clear from the analysis that the more the educated members the more the knowledge of technology prevailed in framers families.

REFERENCES

1. AnnemieMaertens, Christopher B Barrett, Measuring Social Networks Effects on Agricultural Technology Adoption, American Journal of Agricultural Economics. 2012; 95(2):353-359
2. Krishna Reddy P, Ankaiah P. A Framework of IT-Based Agriculture Information Dissemination System to Improve Crop Productivity, Current Science. 2005; 88(12):1905-1913.
3. Meera Shaik N, Jhamtani Anita, Rao DUM. Information and Communication Technology in Agricultural Development: A Comparative Analysis of Three Projectsfrom India, Indiana University, 2004. http:// dlc.dlib.indiana.edu/dlc/handle/10535/4915?show= full.
4. Rao NH. A Framework for Implementing Information and Communication Technologies in Agricultural Development in India, Technology Forecasting and Social Change. 2007; 74(4):491-518.
5. Robert Chambers. Agricultural Research for Resource - Poor Farmers Part 1: Transfer of Technology and Farming Systems Research, Agricultural Administration and Extension. 1987; 27(1):35-52.

18

Impact of Irrigation on Production Variability in North Bengal – A Special Reference to Koch Bihar District, West Bengal

Prasanta Das[1] & Dr. Bappa Sarkar[2]

ABSTRACT

Irrigation is the process of applying water to the crops artificially to fulfil their water requirements. The major types of irrigation are as follows- I) Shallow Tube Well (STW), II) River Lift Irrigation (RLI), III) Deep Tube Well (DTW), IV) Dug Well, V) Canal Irrigation and VII) Tank Irrigation. To obtain the primary data at the household level, 12 village have been selected from the 12 blocks of the district. Collected data have been presented with different cartographic technique and a statistical method was used. Stratified simple random sampling has been chosen for data collection. Total 360 farmers were interviews for the fulfilment of my study. From the field survey, it was found that RLI and DTW required a lower amount of water (in respect of no. of day apply) than another irrigation system. In RLI & DTW irrigation higher amount of water has been applying within the span of time.

Introduction

The artificial application of water to soil for the purpose of continuously supplying the moisture essential for plant

[1]Student, Presidency University, Kolkata
[2]Assistant Professor of Geography, Dinhata College
Email: bappa.geo001@gmail.com

growth is known as irrigation. It accomplished in different ways by flooding, furrows, spreading, by applying water underneath the land surfaces by sub-irrigation. "Irrigation means the application of water by human agency to assists the growth of crop and grass" (Singh, 2004). "The artificial application of water to land for growing crops is known by the term irrigation, artificial watering affects the entire organisation of the farm increasing production. However, the transformation partly or fully depends on the nature and mode of irrigation (well, canal, lift and tank) which depends largely on the physiographic and climatic condition of a region" (Anderson, 1936). As a consequence, the success of agriculture is influenced by the irrigation facilities. There are several types of irrigation practice. The major types of irrigation are as follows- I) Shallow Tube Well (STW), II) River Lift Irrigation (RLI), III) Deep Tube Well (DTW), IV) Dug Well, V) Canal Irrigation and VII) Tank Irrigation. In Koch Bihar District the irrigation is practiced mainly in the winter season.

Koch Bihar District has basically an agrarian economy facilitated by several types of the irrigation system. Five types of irrigation found in the Koch Bihar District namely i) STW (Shallow Tube Well), ii) DTW (Deep Tube Well), iii) RLI (River Lift), iv) Dug Well and v) Canal irrigation. Among the various sources of irrigation shallow tube well is the most popular irrigation scheme among the farmers of this district. Groundwater in the district occurs under both water table and confined condition in aquifer ranging in depth from 2 meters below groundwater level (mbgl) to 3.03 mbgl (Sarkar *et.al.* , 2014). Dug wells and medium to heavy duty irrigation tube wells are in use to withdraw the groundwater. The total groundwater recharge in the district Koch Bihar is 2,31,666 ham (hectometre) obtained by mainly dug wells (3,106 hectares), shallow tube wells (69,461 hectares), deep tube wells 3,968hectares), river lift irrigation (15,292 hectares), tank (5885 hectares). The total geographical area is 3387 sq km (3,38,700 ha) and the net cultivable area is 2,60,768 hectare (ha), the Net irrigated area is 1,65,723 ha (63.55%), Gross cropped area (irrigated 2,01,732 ha and non-irrigated 3,33,112 ha), the Net sown area is 2,58,737 ha (District Statistical Hand Book, 2011). The success of agricultural practice depends on irrigation availability. Irrigation has leads to transforming the crop cultivation and better production. Production of crops, cropping pattern and net benefit of the farmer depends on the availability of irrigation method and their distribution. Irrigation plays an important role in the development of Rabi crop cultivation in Koch Bihar District. Increase in the double-cropped or multi-cropped area is depends on the irrigated area.

Table 1 shows the changing pattern of different crops from 1991-92 to 2011-12 in Koch Bihar District. Among the different crops area, Aus is cultivated only 1733 ha in 2011-12. There has been an abrupt negative change (- 96.76 per cent) in the area under Aus crop and their place is taken by Amon and late Maize in the district. The area under amon crop in 2011-12 is 222220 ha but it declines 3.64 per cent due to the improvement of summer vegetable and some constraints in amon cultivation. But Boro cultivation is rapidly popular in the study area. It has increased 196.41 per cent from 1991-92 to 2011-12 due to the improvement of irrigation, introduction of HYV, secure their food consumption as well as extra profit. Wheat and pulses declined 41.18 per cent and 48.78 per cent respectively. The area of oilseeds increases 27.49 per cent and the most interesting emerging issue is maize which is popular in 2011-12, about 968-hectare areas are cultivated in 2011-12 .

Table 1
Changing Scenario of Different Crops area (Ha) of Koch Bihar District

Types of Rabi Crops	The area in Ha, 1991-92	The area in Ha, 2011-12	Change (1991-92 to 2011-12)	Change in %
Aus	53420	1733	-51687	-96.76
Amon	230620	222220	-8400	-3.64
Boro	17320	51338	34018	196.41

Jute	201560	75091	-126469	-62.75
Potato	8650	29979	21329	246.58
Wheat	17970	10570	-7400	-41.18
Pulses	3440	1762	-1678	-48.78
Oil Seed	8210	10467	2257	27.49
Maize	0	968	968	-

Source: District Statistical Hand Book, 1991-92 to 2011-12

Methodology

The present study has been carried out within various irrigated farmers in the Koch Bihar district which constitutes 12 blocks and 1188 mouzas covering an area of 3387 km^2 out of which 1284.12 km^2 (37.9%) area are irrigated area. Samples were taken from the sampled mouza according to the irrigation system used by the farmers. To obtain the primary data at the household level, 12 village have been selected from the 12 blocks of the district. Collected data have been presented with different cartographic technique and a statistical method was used. Stratified simple random sampling has been chosen for data collection. Total 360 farmers were interviews for the fulfilment of my study.

The standard deviation concept was introduced by Karl Pearson in 1823. It is the square root of the mean of the squared deviation from the arithmetic mean. The standard deviation measures the absolute dispersion, the greater the standard deviation, for the greater will be the magnitude of the deviations of the values from their mean.

$$\sigma = \sqrt{\left(\frac{x^2}{N}\right)}$$

where, σ = Standard deviation

$x^2 = X - \underline{X}$ (Deviation of the item from the mean)

N = Number of the observation

The χ^2 square test (pronounced as chi-square test) is one of the simplest and most widely used non-parametric tests in statistical work. The χ^2 test was first used by Karl

Pearson in the year 1900. The quantity χ^2 describes the magnitude of the discrepancy between theory and observation. It is defined as:

$$\chi^2 = \sum \frac{(O-E)^2}{E}$$

Where O refers to the observed frequencies and E refers to the expected frequencies.

Production Variation in Different Irrigation Systems, Cooch Behar District

The study area is covered with alluvial soils. Most of the land is covered with loamy soil suitable for agriculture. In this district 5 types of a functional irrigation system are observed i.e. 1) STW, 2) RLI, 3) DTW, 4) Dug Well and 5) Tank Irrigation. Irrigation is mainly applied in rabi season. From the study, it is clear that the main crops of Rabi season in the study area are Boro, Maize, Potato, Chilly, Oil Seeds, Brinjal, Tobacco which produce in all irrigation system of Koch Bihar District.

Boro Rice: In Koch Bihar district, rice is cultivated thrice in a year. The monsoon rice (Amon) is cultivated late July and harvested from October to November. It grows in low lying lands. The early monsoon rice (Aus) cultivated from April and harvested during June-July. Aus rice survives under mild drought conditions. The dry season irrigated rice (Boro) is grown in extremely low lying area or highly irrigated area because it is transplanted in knee-deep water (5 ± 2 cm) from December to January. The yield of Boro rice is the highest among the three seasonal traditional rice productions. High yielding varieties of seeds have much higher demand for nutrients than the ordinary seeds. In humid and semi-humid rainfed areas where rice is grown, the small watershed system of rainwater management for rice-based cropping systems has found beneficial (Majumdar, 1985). The crop is grown during rabi and pre-Kharif season depend almost entirely on irrigation. Boro is fully dependent on irrigation availability. It is an irrigated crop. The soil of

Koch Bihar is loam to clay loam thus frequent irrigations are needed in Koch Bihar district. The best method of irrigation in rice is the check flooding method. Strong bunds are prepared around the field to help stagnation of irrigation water (Photo plate-23). Irrigation water is applied in a different stage of crops grown. During the field survey, it is observed that average irrigation in Boro required 16 to 18 days irrigation in RLI and DTW irrigation system, whereas 32 to 36 days irrigation in STW irrigation system but in the poor irrigated area it required more than 38 days.

The Chi-Square value (0.000) indicates that there are significant differences of different production of crops among different irrigation system. Production of Boro rice depends on the quality of water and it needs a higher amount of water through the cropping seasons. The water crisis has greatly influenced its production. Thus the production of Boro rice differs in the different irrigation system. The production of Boro is relatively higher in RLI irrigation system. The average production of Boro rice in RLI irrigation system is 2535 kg/acre. The yield rate in Tank irrigation is 2240 kg/acre with followed by STW irrigation (2140 kg/acre), Dug Well (2032 kg/acre) whereas in poorly irrigated system yield of Boro is much lower 1685 kg/acre. The poor irrigated area faces a severe shortage of water problems which influenced on production rate. RLI irrigation has full of enriching of different nutrients and organic matter because the source of RLI irrigation is a natural lake, ox-bow lake, pond, and river.

Table 2
Production Boro Paddy in Different Irrigation System, Koch Bihar District

Types of Irrigation	Production Kg/Acre			Irrigation
	Mean	SD	Chi-Square	Number (Days)
STW	2140.00	265.06	*0.000	32-36
RLI	2535.00	114.77		16-18
DTW	1770.00	145.85		16-18
Dug Well	2032.00	95.50		30-32
Tank	2240.00	311.56		28-30

Poor Irrigation	1685.00	188.41		38-40

Source: Field Survey 2018-19 SD= Standard Deviation, *Significant at 5% significant Level

Maize Cultivation

Maize is cultivated in late winter. Some farmers choose an early variety of maize but most of the farmers cultivate a late variety of maize. Boro and maize grow parallel in winter seasons. During the last 6 to 8 years local farmers prefer maize as a cash crop. Maize requires nominal amounts of water and fertilizer. The Maize is sensitive to low as well as to the higher amount of soil water condition at teaselling and silking stages. Maize is irrigated by furrow irrigation method and furrow spacing is usually 1 to 1.5 feet. Usually, 2 to 3 irrigations are applied but it varies in the different irrigation system (Photo plate-5.2). Irrigation is required in RLI and DTW is 1 to 2 times but in STW, Dug, and Tank irrigation it required 2 to 3 times because the amount of water is much higher in RLI and DTW than other irrigation. From the field survey, it is clear that the average yield of maize in STW irrigation system is 3271.43 kg/acre whereas the yield rate of RLI irrigation area is 4560 kg/acre. But in DTW irrigation system it is 3435 kg/acre. Dug Well produced 3330 kg/acre of maize and it was 3288 kg/acre in a Tank irrigation system. But in poor irrigated area yield rate is lower than other irrigation systems i, e. 2580 kg/acre. The Chi-Square value (0.045) indicates that there are significant differences of different production of crops among different irrigation system in the District.

Table 3
Production Maize in Different Irrigation System, Koch Bihar District

Types of	Production Kg/Acre			Irrigation
Irrigation	Mean	SD	Chi- Square	Number (Days)
STW	3271.43	465.02	*0.045	2-3
RLI	4560.00	964.99		1-2
DTW	3435.00	226.50		1-2
Dug Well	3330.00	204.94		2-3
Tank	3288.00	314.20		1-3

Poor Irrigation	2580.00	395.78		2-4

Source: Field Survey, 2018-19, SD= Standard Deviation, *Significant at 5% significant Level

Potato: Potato is a shallow rooted crop requires frequent irrigations of shallower depths. On an average 3 to 4 days irrigations are applied in clay soil and 5 to 6 days irrigation for sandy loamy soil area. During the growing phase, potato requires 2 times irrigations, 3 times during tuberisation phase and 2 times during maturation. Potato is irrigated by furrow method in the study area. For production potato crops the field has never been flooded.

The RLI irrigation area, the yield rate of Potato in Koch Bihar district is 13083.33 kg/acre. This is highest among the other irrigation method of Koch Bihar district. In order to production, DTW irrigation is next to RLI. The average yield in DTW is 1133 kg/acre. Dug Well secured the third position among the different irrigation in terms of yield rate of potato, it was11048 kg/acre. The yield is 10803.33 kg/acre in STW irrigation. The yield rate is 10550 kg/acre Tank irrigation system, whereas the average yield of potato in Poor irrigated area is 8450 kg/acre. The Chi- Square value (0.005) indicates that there are significant differences of different production of crops among different irrigation system.

Table 4
Production of Potato in Different Irrigation System, Koch Bihar District

Types of Irrigation	Production Kg/Acre			Irrigation Number (Days)
	Mean	SD	Chi- Square	
STW	10803.33	1332.72	*0.005	2-3
RLI	13083.33	1289.00		1-2
DTW	11330.00	720.83		1-2
Dug Well	11048.00	647.70		2-3
Tank	10550.00	1577.97		1-3
Poor Irrigation	8450.00	1564.16		2-3

Source: Field Survey, 2018-19,SD= Standard Deviation, Significant at

5% significant Level

Chilly: The crop is irrigated usually by the bed and furrow method. The number of irrigations required for this crop is 4 to 5 in the study area. Based on the field survey it is noticed that the application of water varies in different soil quality.

As per field survey, the average yield of Chilly of Koch Bihar District is 17725.28 kg/acre and its composition from different irrigation system as follows table 5. The yields per acre are as high as 23886.67 kg/acre (in RLI system), 18016.67 kg/acre (in DTW irrigation), 17200 kg/acre (in Tank irrigation), 16800 kg/acre (in Dug Well), 16360 kg/acre (in STW irrigation) and 14088.33 kg/acre (in poorly irrigated area). The Chi- Square value (0.004) indicates that there are significant differences of different production of crops among different irrigation system.

Table 5
Production of Chilly in Different Irrigation System, Koch Bihar District

Types of Irrigation	Production Kg/Acre Mean	SD	Chi- Square	Irrigation Number (Days)
STW	16360.00	4625.65	*0.004	4-5
RLI	23886.67	1312.41		3-4
DTW	18016.67	3513.44		3-4
Dug Well	16800.00	3698.65		4-5
Tank	17200.00	1346.60		3-4
Poor Irrigation	14088.33	1917.77		4-5

Source: Field Survey, 2018-19, SD= Standard Deviation, *Significant at 5 % Significant Level

5.1.3.5. Oil Seeds

Agriculture of Koch Bihar has made considerable progress in rice cultivation; however, performance has not been so good in case of other crops particularly oilseeds and pulses. Rabi pulses require well-drained, deep soil free from excessive soluble salts having sandy loamy to sandy clay loam soil texture. The ideal soil pH for growing these crops is 6.0-8.5 and pulses are highly sensitive to salinity and acidity. In Koch Bihar District oil Seeds is practiced on the basis of domestic needs and depends on irrigation potential. Most of the oilseeds are grown in low fertility and problematic soils struggling with salinity and alkalinity. Mustard is the main oilseed in the study area. Oilseeds are irrigated by border strip method in the study area. The crop is given the first irrigation at the beginning of flowering and second at the seed formation stage.

Koch Bihar District is still facing severe challenges in oils seeds and pulses production. Poor productivity and low gross production compel the district to frequent imports for meeting the domestic demand of oilseeds and pulses. Among the different irrigation system of Koch Bihar district, RLI possesses the highest yield of oilseeds followed by Tank, STW, DTW, poor irrigated area and Dug Well irrigation system. The Chi- Square value (0.005) indicates that there are significant differences of different production of crops among different irrigation system.

Table 6
Production Maize in Different Irrigation System, Koch Bihar District

Types of Irrigation	Production Kg/Acre Mean	SD	Chi- Square	Irrigation Number (Days)
STW	740.00	123.58	*0.005	1-2
RLI	920.00	147.71		1-2
DTW	706.00	205.60		1-2
Dug Well	548.92	355.91		1-2
Tank	840.00	402.43		1-2
Poor Irrigation	650.00	95.16		1-2

Source: Field Survey, 2018-19, SD= Standard Deviation, *Significant at 5 % Significant Level

Tobacco: Tobacco is grown under irrigation conditions. Dinhata, Sitai, and Sitalkuchi are famous for tobacco cultivation in Koch Bihar district. Proper irrigation facilitates production of tobacco crops. From the survey, it is revealed that the water requirement and consumption were 2 to 3 time of the season. Tobacco has been practiced in different irrigation systems such as STW, RLI, DTW, Dug Well, and Tank and also in the poor irrigated area. Application of water in tobacco crop depends upon the types of tobacco and the region where it is practiced. The requirement of irrigation is more frequent in a dry area for tobacco cultivation. Tobacco cannot tolerate water logging at any stage of growth and also withstand drought. Therefore, a unique method of irrigation is noticed in tobacco cultivation. Here altogether 3-4 times watering is required starting one week after transplanting at the rate of 200-250 ml each plant and 400 ml after two weeks. When crops are matured water is applied to the whole area within a short span of time.

Tobacco is normally not grown as a mixed crop. In Koch Bihar District, it is a common practice with the tobacco farmers to raise tobacco as a rotation crop year after in the same field. As per field survey, the average yield of tobacco Koch Bihar district is 623.33 kg/acre and its composition from different irrigation system as follows table 8 The yields per acre are as high as 730 kg/acre (in RLI system), 660 kg/acre (in DTW irrigation), 690 kg/acre (in Tank irrigation), 540 kg/acre (in Dug Well), 610 kg/acre (in STW irrigation) and 510 kg/acre (poorly irrigation area). The Chi- Square value (0.000) indicates that there are significant differences of different production of crops among different irrigation system.

Table 7
Production of Tobacco in Different Irrigation System, Koch Bihar District

Types of	Production Kg/Acre			Irrigation
Irrigation	Mean	SD	Chi- Square	Number (Days)
STW	14,830.00	785.53	*0.000	2-3
RLI	15,890.00	1,214.47		2-3
DTW	14,973.33	792.57		2-3
Dug Well	14,600.00	1,082.22		2-3

Tank	15,000.00	1,042.05	2-3
Poor Irrigation	12,713.33	746.94	2-3

Source: Field Survey, 2018-19,SD= Standard Deviation, *Significant at 5% Significant Level

Vegetables (Brinjal): Brinjal or eggplant is an important crop of Koch Bihar district among all other vegetables. Brinjal has practiced in all the blocks and in all types of irrigation of Koch Bihar district. In the study area, it is one of the most common, popular and principal vegetable crop grown throughout the district except lower area. Brinjal is cultivated both the seasons i.e. summer and winter. But a long and cold growing season is desirable for successful brinjal farming. The brinjal plants can be grown in all types of soil varying from light sandy to heavy clay. It prefers well-drained soil rich in organic matter with Ph 6.5 to 7.5. The soil should be thoroughly prepared by ploughing 3-5 times before the seedlings.

Brinjal has a deep root system and can draw soil water from deeper layers. Properly irrigation is quite essential for good growth and the development of fruits. Irrigation water is applied at a different time in the different irrigation system. RLI and DTW irrigation system are applied every 15 to 17 days during winter. But STW, Dug Well, Tank irrigated area apply every 10 to 12 days whereas in poorly irrigated area water is applied in every 20 days in the study area by furrows method.

The RLI irrigation area, the yield rate of Brinjal in Koch Bihar District is 15890 kg/acre with which is highest among the other irrigation method of Koch Bihar District. With regards to production, Tank irrigation is next to RLI. The average yield in Tank irrigation is 15000 kg/acre. STW secure the third position among the different irrigation in terms of yield rate of brinjal, it was 14830 kg/acre. The yield is 14973.33 kg/acre in DTW irrigation. The yield rate is 14600 kg/acre in Tank irrigation system. Whereas the average yield of potato in the poorly irrigated area is 12713.33 kg/acre. The Chi- Square value (0.000) indicates that there are significant differences of different production of crops among different irrigation system.

Table 8

Production Bringal in Different Irrigation System, Koch Bihar District

Types of Irrigation	Production Kg/Acre			Irrigation Number (Days)
	Mean	SD	Chi- Square	
STW	610.00	95.16	*0.000	6-8
RLI	730.00	80.23		4-5
DTW	660.00	108.54		4-5
Dug Well	540.00	69.28		6-8
Tank	690.00	60.00		6-8
Poor Irrigation	510.00	90.45		6-8

Source: Field Survey, 2018-19, SD= Standard Deviation, * Significant at 5 % significant Level

From the field survey, it was found that RLI and DTW required a lower amount of water (in respect of no. of day apply) than another irrigation system. In RLI &DTW irrigation higher amount of water has been applying within the span of time. But due to different constraint STW, Dug Well, Tank poorly irrigated irrigation have a lower withdrawal of water which leads to increase the number of days.

Table 9

Average Production (kg/acre) of Different Crops

Types of Irri-gation	Boro	Maize	Potato	Chilly	Oil Seeds	Brinjal	Toba-cco
STW	2,140.00	3,271.43	10,803.33	16,360.00	740.00	14,830.00	610.00
RLI	2,535.00	4,560.00	13,083.33	23,886.67	920.00	15,890.00	730.00
DTW	1,770.00	3,435.00	11,330.00	18,016.67	706.00	14,973.33	660.00
Dug Well	2,032.00	3,330.00	11,048.00	16,800.00	548.92	14,600.00	540.00
Tank	2,240.00	3,288.00	10,550.00	17,200.00	840.00	15,000.00	690.00
Poor	1,685.00	2,580.00	8,450.00	14,088.33	650.00	12,713.33	510.00

Irriga-
tion

Source: Field Survey, 2018-19

CONCLUSION

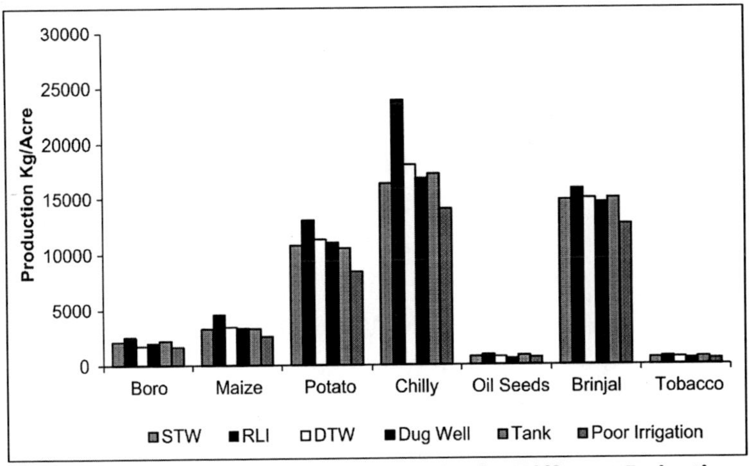

Fig. 1: Production of Different Crops in the Different Irrigation System and Poorly Irrigated Area

Irrigation is the key factor for improvement of cultivation. In Koch Bihar District the relation between irrigated area and cropping area is found to be weak. Irrigation cost varied from one system to the other which adversely affect the production and the economy of the farmer as well. Due to the higher cost of irrigation, farmers tend to change their cropping pattern. There are significant differences in irrigation system among caste composition, household size and housing condition. Koch Bihar Distrcit is agririan area. It is a lowlaying plain area where numbers of river , wetland, beel, and pond area available. But still the district face several probelm in irrigation. Only 47.71 per cent area are irrigated (2011-12). Irrigation play a importanc role on crooping parctice but the irrigation is not only the signifiacant role on changing of the cropping pattern in the district. It need to be further intesive reseach. The surface water as well as ground water of the region seems to have potential to heaven for irrigation.

REFERENCES

1. Banerjee, U. (1964). "A short note on the forests of Darjeeling district, West Bengal". Forest Centenary Commemoration. Government of W. B., Calcutta, 91-95.
2. Bell, M and Roberts, N. (1991). "The political ecology of dambo soils and water resources in Zimbawe". Unpublished report, Longhborugh University and University of Zimbabwe, 77-81.
3. Census of India (2001-2011): West Bengal Census Office, Calcutta, Series 23, Part XIII, A and XIII-B.
4. Central Ground Water Board, 2011.
5. Central Ground Water Commission, 2011.
6. Chowdhury, H, N. (1903). "The Koch Bihar state and its land revenue settlement" Koch Bihar state press, 56-59.
7. Chowdhury, H.N. (1903). "The Cooch Behar State and its Land Revenue Settlement", Cooch Behar State Press, 1-294: Edited by Dr.NripendraNath Pal, (2010), Published by N. L. -Publishers, Siliguri. 3-4
8. Dam.M, 2016. "River and Wetland of Koch Bihar" Ganga Publication, Kolkata,1-179.
9. District Statistical Hand Book (2001-2011), Bureau of Applied Economics and Statistics (2001 to 2013), Government of West Bengal.
10. District Statistical Hand Book (2011). Bureau of Applied Economics and Statistics. Government of West Bengal
11. District Statistical Hand Book (2011). Bureau of Applied Economics and Statistics. Government of West Bengal.
12. Israelsen, W., & Hansen, V. (1962). "Irrigation principles and practices" (3rd ed.). New York, London. 212-241.
13. Majumdar. D, K. (1985). "Concept of micro-watershed system water management and cropping for higher crop production in rainfed areas", Proc. Symp. Cropping Sys., Indian Soc. Agron, New Delhi, 66.
14. Mazumder, D.D. (1977). West Bengal District Gazetteers: Koch Bihar, Government of West Bengal. 9-12.

15. Minor Irrigation Census, 2011
16. Minor Irrigation Census, Government of India, Ministry of water resource, 1993-94.
17. Minor Irrigation Census, Government of India, Ministry of water resource, 2001-02.
18. Minor Irrigation Census, Government of India, Ministry of water resource, 2011-12.
19. Monthly Weather Report (2001-2011), Indian Meteorological Department, http://www.imd.gov.in
20. Ogilvie, A., & Geddes, S. (1938). "The technique of regional geography with special reference to India", Journal of the Madras Geographical Society, 121-123.
21. Olesen, J., & Bindi, M. (2002). Consequences of climate change for European agricultural productivity, land use and policy. European Journal of Agronomics, 16, 239-262.
22. Sarkar, B., & Roy, R. (2017). "Impact of Deep Tube Well irrigation on cropping intensity- A case study of Koch Bihar District, West Bengal. Indian Science Cruiser, 31(4), 21-27.
23. Schroeder, B., & Panitz, J. (2007). "Accelerating the adoption of best practice nutrient management: Burdekin district', Brisbane: BSES Limited. 88-92.
24. Singh. J (1974). "Spatio-temporal developments in land efficiency in Haryana", Geographical Review of India, Vol. 29, No. 4, 314-326.
25. State Water Investigation Directorate, 2011
26. West Bengal State Water Investigation Directorate (SWID), 2006.
27. Wires, (1990) "The effects of education on farmer productivity in rural Ethiopia", Working paper series 99-7, a centre for the study of African economics, University of Oxford, UK, 104-15.

19

Analysis of Land Use and Land Cover Change in North Bengal Plain: A Study in Cooch Behar District between 2001 to 2021

***Manoj Debnath*[1], *Sheuli Ray*[2] & *Jolly Saha*[3]**

ABSTRACT

The present study tries to analysis the land use and land cover changes occurred in Cooch Behar district between 2001 to 2021 period. The LULC assessment is very much essential for sustainable environmental management, land use planning and monitoring, conservation and resource management. For the purpose of the present study, multispectral high resolution satellite image such as Enhanced Thematic Mapper-ETM+ (2001) and Landsat 8 Operational Land Image-OLI (2021) with spatial resolution 30 m are used for LULC change detection for the present study. The main aim of this study is to find out the spatio-temporal change of LULC in Cooch Behar in last two decades using Landsat image. The change detection results are fond

[1]Department of Geography, School of Human and Environmental Sciences, North Eastern Hill University, Shillong-793022, Meghalaya, India.
Corresponding author email: manojdebnathtfg@gmail.com
[2]Department of Geography, Mahatma Gandhi College (Sidho Kanho Birsha University), Purulia, West Bengal, India.
Email: sheuliraynehu@gmail.com
[3]Department of Geography, Thakur Panchanan Mahila Mahavidyalaya (Cooch Behar Panchanan Barma University), Cooch Behar, West Bengal.
Email: Jollysaha21.3.81@gmail.com

that a significant proportion agricultural land is converted into fallow land in last two decades in Cooch Behar. Similarly, overall proportion of forest cover area is decreasing in Cooch Behar district which need to especial attention for policymakers.

Key Words : Land Use and Land Cover (LULC) Change; NDVI; NDWI; NDBI; Cooch Behar

Introduction

Although the term land use and land cover (LULC) are often used interchangeably, their actual meaning is quite distinct. Land cover refers to features of land surface which may be natural, Semi-natural. Other hand, land-use refers to activities on land or classification of land according to how it is being used, such as residential, industrial, commercial, agricultural, recreational etc. (Burley 1961; Lo, 1986; Bhatta, 2011). Recently LULC change gives more concentration on forest, water and land management (Chamling and Bera, 2020). The change detection of LULC has massive concern for policy making on various human-physical environment (David et al. 2016; Shaw and Banba 2017). LULC change monitoring has been used from NASA's Landsat moderate and high resolution satellite image for global coverage (Lu and Weng, 2004; Gao and Zhang, 2009). Here, Cooch Behar district in North Bengal plain region is considered for present study. This region has been experienced drastic land use and land cover change over the last two decades (2001-2021). A significant proportion of land has been converted from agricultural land to fallow land. Similarly, vegetation cover also reduced significantly over the last two decades. Given this reality and the fact that this is the region which experienced massive land use and land cover changes in recent past which need to special attention for further planning and development. The main aim of this study is to find out the spatio-temporal change of land use and land cover (LULC) in Cooch Behar district in last two decades using Landsat image.

Data and Methods

Remotely sense data has been used for the analysis of spatio-temporal change of LULC in Cooch Behar in last two decades (2001-2021). Multispectral high resolution satellite image such as Enhanced Thematic Mapper-ETM+ (2001) and Landsat 8 Operational Land Image-OLI (2021) with spatial resolution 30 m are used for LULC change detection for the present study. These satellite images are obtained from United State Geological Survey (USGS) Earth Explorer archive.

Assessment of vegetation health is done with the help of Normalized Difference Vegetation Index (NDVI) in Arc GIS. The output images are done by following formula [Eq. 1], i.e.

1. Normalized Differential Vegetation Index (NDVI): (NIRDN-RDN)/ (NIRDN+RDN)......................(1)
2. Where, DNNIR is the Brightness values of pixel in NIR band and DNR is the Brightness values of pixel in Red band.
3. Normalized Difference Water Index (NDWI) introduced by McFeeters (1996) used to identify the water bodies with the help of satellite image for present study [Eq. 2].
4. Normalized Difference Water Index (NDWI): (GREEN-NIR) / (GREEN+NIR).................(2)
5. Normalized Difference Built-up Index (NDWI) calculated by following formula for the present study [Eq. 3].
6. Normalized Difference Built-up Index (NDBI): (SWIR - NIR) / (SWIR + NIR).................(3)

Supervised image classification has been used to analysis the land use land cover distribution for the present study. Maximum Likelihood Classification (MLC) method is used for land use land cover classification.

Results and Discussions

Analysis of land use and land cover change in Cooch Behar district between 2001 to 2021 period done by applying maximum likelihood classifier (MLC) method (Fig. 1). The results are witness of several significant change of LULC area in the study area. The LULC change detection analyses consider more attention on change of water body, vegetation cover and built-up area (Table 1). The result shows that among the total geographical area 63.95 per cent geographical area is under agricultural land followed by fallow land (20.39%), built-up area (8.72%), water body (3.80%) and vegetation cover area (3.15%) respectively.

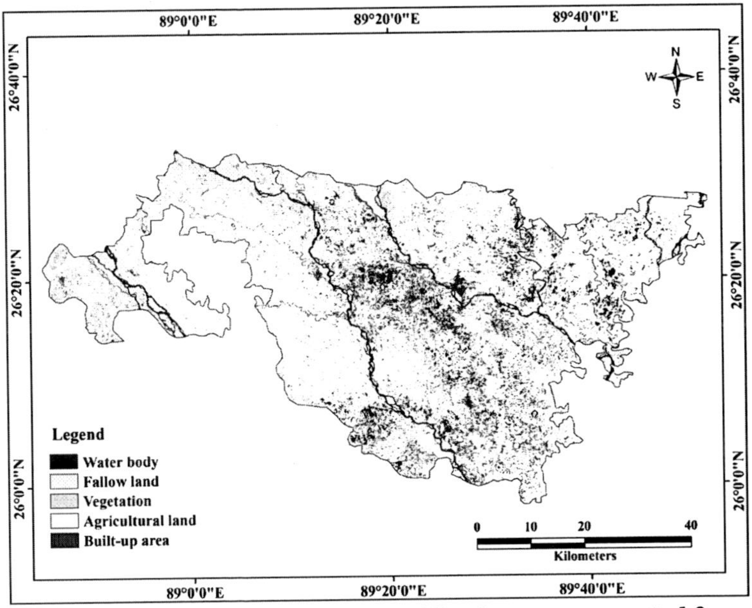

Fig. 1: Land use and land cover classification map computed from satellite images, Landsat OLI (2021)

The result shows that in last two decades Cooch Behar district experienced massive change of different land use and land cover area. During these decades, agricultural land and vegetation cover area have been reduced by 587.92 sq. km and 36.14 sq. km. respectively. While, water body, built-up area and fallow land are increased by 21.63, 165.48 and 436.86 sq. km. respectively. The rate of change is found highest at fallow land conversion followed by built-up area in the study area. The change detection result found that a significant agricultural land is converted into fallow land (465.15 sq.km.)

in the study area which need to especial attention (Fig. 2).

Table 1
Land use and land cover (LULC) change in the study area (2001-2021)

LULC Class	2001	2021	Change (2001-2021)
Water body	105.45	127.18	21.63
Fallow land	245.64	682.49	436.86
Vegetation	141.53	105.39	-36.14
Agricultural land	2728.40	2140.46	-587.93
Built-up area	126.29	291.78	165.48

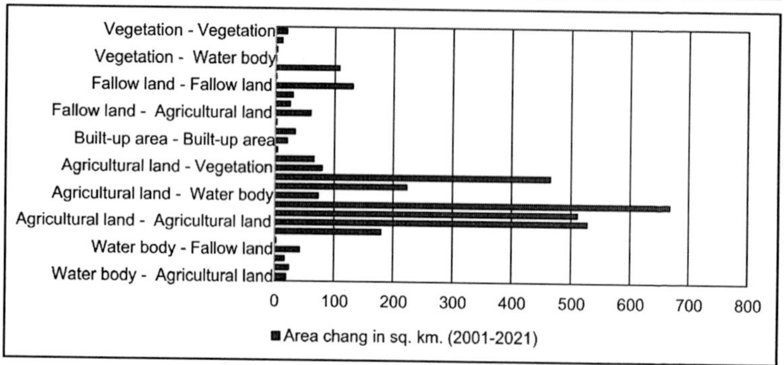

Fig. 2: Land use and land cover (LULC) change in the study area (2001-2021)

Vegetation health is an assessment of monitoring, diagnosis and predicting long- and short-term land environmental conditions and climate-dependent socioeconomic activities. Vegetation health is an important parameter of chlorophyll concentration in leaf, crop yield, climate change, drought effect etc. There are plenty of ways to assess vegetation health through remote sensing. Vegetation health index derived from NDVI (Normalized Deference vegetation Index) is one typical example vegetation health measure. NDVI is an important parameter to show distress and healthy vegetation, crop condition and soil moisture condition and drought. The remote sensing data provides that about 4.23 per cent geographical area of Cooch

Behar district was covered by forest in 2001 (Fig. 3). Though, the proportion of forest cover (3.15% in 2021) area is decreasing significantly in Cooch Behar. The change detection analysis provides the information regarding the change of vegetation cover area. During last two decades (2001-2021) about 25 per cent forest cover area converted into built-up area, fallow land and agricultural land. Highest forest cover area is converted into agricultural land (107.84 sq. km) during the last two decades. Similarly, about 2.90 sq. km. area has been converted as built-up area. Meanwhile, about 79.50 sq. km. agricultural land has been converted into forest cover area. Though, overall proportion of forest cover area is decreasing in Cooch Behar district which need to especial attention for policymakers.

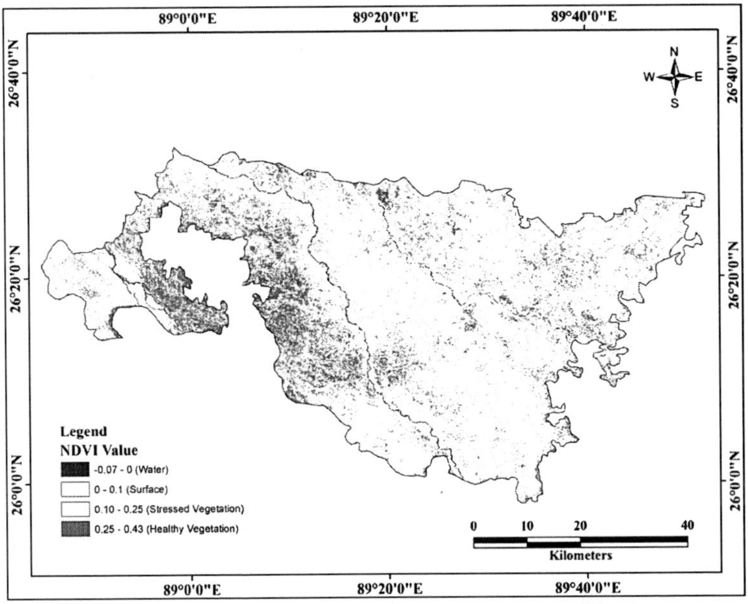

Fig. 3: Vegetation cover map computed from satellite images, Landsat OLI (2021)

Normalized Difference Water Index (NDWI), introduced by McFeeters (1996) used for present study. The study found that about 21.63 sq. km. geographical area is increasing as water body during the last two decades in Cooch Behar district (Fig. 4). Though, change detection analysis gives some interesting findings. The highest proportion of water body has been converted to fallow land (41.92 Sq. km.) followed by agricultural land (20 sq. km.), built-up area (16.37 sq.km.), vegetation (2.93 sq. km.) respectively during last two decades (2001-2021). Meanwhile, a significant proportion of geographical area also converted into water body in due course. Highest geographical area converted in from agricultural land to water body (72.86 sq. km.) in Cooch Behar in last two decades.

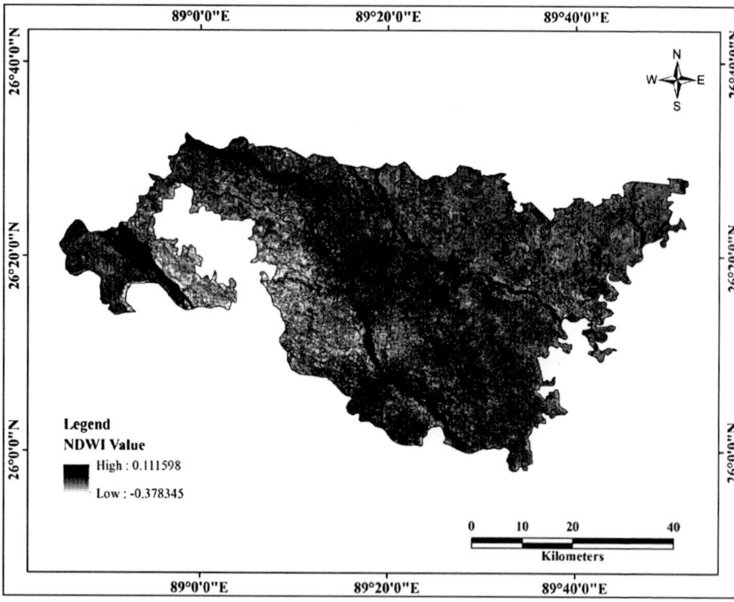

Fig. 4: Water index cover map computed from satellite images, Landsat OLI (2021)

Normalized Difference Built-up Index (NDWI) calculated for identification of human settlement and human activity on the earth surface. The remote sensing data provides that about 165.48 sq. km (Fig. 5) geographical area is increasing as built-up area during the last two decades in Cooch Behar district. Growth rate of increasing built-up area is 131.03 per cent during the last two decades. The greater proportion of built-up area converted from agricultural land (223.16 sq. km.)

followed by fallow land (29.12 sq. km.). Though, due course 65.48 sq. km. built-up area has been converted into agricultural land.

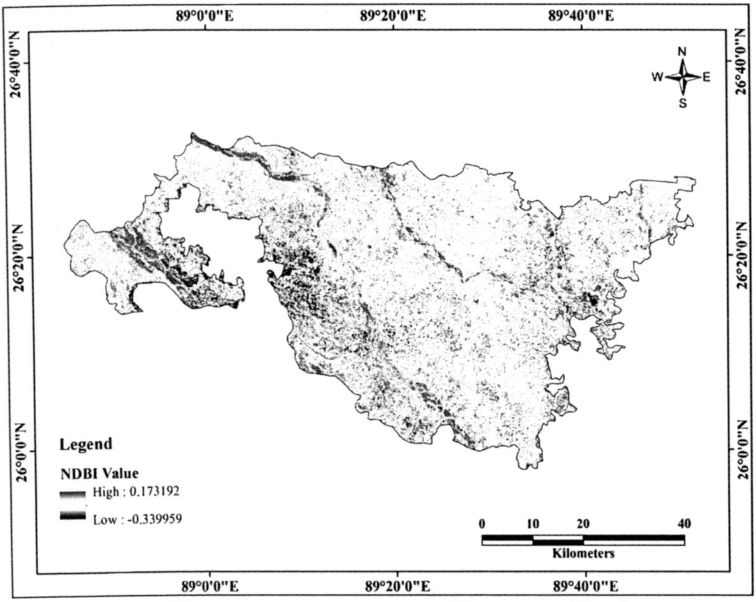

Fig. 5: Built-up area map computed from satellite images, Landsat OLI (2021)

CONCLUSION

Cooch Behar district from North Bengal plain region is considered for the present study to analysis the land use land cove change in last two decades. Remotely scene data has been used for the analysis of spatio-temporal change of LULC in Cooch Behar. The study reveals that in last two decades Cooch Behar district experienced massive change of different land use and land cover area. During these decades, agricultural land and vegetation cover area have been reduced by 587.92 sq. km and 36.14 sq. km. respectively. Moreover, the rate of change is found highest at fallow land conversion followed by built-up area in the study area. During last two decades (2001-2021) about 25 per cent forest cover area is converted into built-up area, fallow land and agricultural land.The study also found that the geographical area is increasing as built-up area during the last two decades in Cooch Behar district.

REFERENCES

1. Bhatta, B. (2011). *Remote Sensing and GIS,* Oxford Higher Education, New Delhi.
2. Burley, T.M. (1961). Land use or land utilization, *Prof Geogr* 13(6):18-20. https://doi.org/10.1111/j. 0033-0124.1961.136_18.x.
3. Chamling, M., and Bera, B. (2020). Spatio-temporal Patterns of Land Use/Land Cover Change in the Bhutan-Bengal Foothill Region between 1987 and 2019: Study towards Geospatial Applications and Policy Making, *Earth Systems and Environment, 4*: 117-130. https://doi.org/ 10.1007/s41748-020-00150-0.
4. David, K., Yetta, G., Agung, F., Sharon, H., and Alison, C. (2016). Land use planning for disaster risk reduction and climate change adaptation: operationalizing policy and legislation at local levels. *International Journal of Disaster Resilience Built Environ* 7(2):158-172.
5. Gao, Y., and Zhang, W. (2009). LULC classification and topographic correction of Landsat-7 ETM+ imagery in the Yangjia River Watershed: the influence of DEM resolution. *Sensors 9*(3): 1980-1995. https://doi.org/10.3390/ s9030 1980.
6. Lo, C.P. (1986). *Applied remote sensing.* Pp. 60-60. https :/ /doi.org/10.1080/10106 04860 93540 71.
7. Lu, D., and Weng, Q. (2004). Spectral mixture analysis of the urban landscape in Indianapolis with Landsat ETM+ imagery. Photogram *Eng Remote Sens 70*(9): 1053-1062. https://doi.org/10.14358 /PERS.70.9.1053.
8. McFeeters, S. K. (1996). The use of the Normalized Difference Water Index (NDWI) in the delineation of open water features. *International journal of remote sensing, 17*(7), 1425-1432. https://doi.org/10.1080/01431169608948714
9. Shaw, R., and Banba, M. (2017). Land use management in disaster risk reduction: an overview. In: Land use management in disaster risk reduction. Springer, Tokyo, pp 3-12. https://doi.org/10.1007/978-4-431-56442 -3_1.